The
Link Between
Childhood Trauma
and Mental Illness

To our clients, past and present.

To all survivors of childhood trauma, and
to the dedicated mental health professionals
who walk with them, one step or many,
on their journey toward healing and recovery.

The

Link Between Childhood Trauma and Mental Illness

Effective Interventions for
Mental Health Professionals

Barbara Everett / Ruth Gallop

Sage Publications, Inc.
International Educational and Professional Publisher
Thousand Oaks ▪ London ▪ New Delhi

For information:

Sage Publications, Inc.
2455 Teller Road
Thousand Oaks, California 91320
E-mail: order@sagepub.com

Sage Publications Ltd.
6 Bonhill Street
London EC2A 4PU
United Kingdom

Sage Publications India Pvt. Ltd.
M-32 Market
Greater Kailash I
New Delhi 110 048 India

Printed in the United States of America

Library of Congress Cataloging-in-Publication Data

Everett, Barbara.
  The link between childhood trauma and mental illness: Effective interventions for mental health professionals / by Barbara Everett and Ruth Gallop.
    p. cm.
Includes index.
  ISBN 0-7619-1698-9 (alk. paper) — ISBN 0-7619-1699-7 (pbk. : alk. paper)
  1. Adult child abuse victims. I. Gallop, Ruth. II. Title.
  RC569.5.C55 E94 2000
  616.85′82239—dc21   00-009214

This book is printed on acid-free paper.

01 02 03 04 05 06 07 7 6 5 4 3 2 1

Acquisition Editor:	Nancy Hale
Production Editor:	Sanford Robinson
Editorial Assistant:	Candice Crosetti
Typesetter:	Danielle Dillahunt
Indexer:	Jean Casalegno
Cover Designer:	Michelle Lee

Contents

Introduction

Many people seeking help from the mental health system have histories of childhood trauma, defined in this work as sexual and physical abuse. In fact, up to two thirds of women hospitalized in psychiatric settings report a history of child abuse. Although many authors write on the topic of specialized therapy for abuse survivors, little is available for other mental health professionals, such as psychiatric nurses, case managers, rehabilitation counselors, crisis and housing workers, occupational and physical therapists, family physicians, and social workers. These important practitioners are often the first to hear about abuse, and they are likely to be caring for clients experiencing the severest consequences. They see firsthand the devastating results of child abuse, and they have a crucial role to play in helping clients heal and recover. They also have learning needs that differ from those of trauma treatment professionals. This book is designed for them.

Our goals are twofold:

1. To provide mental health professionals who are *not* childhood trauma specialists with particular forms of knowledge and skills relevant to their direct service role and practice context. These professionals need to know when it is appropriate to ask clients about an abusive past, how

to listen to disclosures with sensitivity, and how to integrate this information into their helping strategies.

2. To introduce a conceptual bridge between biomedical and psychosocial understandings of mental disorder—a multidimensional approach that allows professionals to think in holistic terms and to link clients' abusive pasts with their present-day symptoms and behaviors.

Although each chapter can be read independently, the book is designed as a progression, with each part building upon the previous one. The first section is focused on providing the knowledge necessary to think critically about the many issues and debates that affect how mental health professionals in a variety of roles and settings provide services to survivors of childhood trauma. In Chapter 1, we briefly review the systemic and individual barriers that inhibit the acknowledgment of child abuse as an important factor in clients' backgrounds and constrain the inclusion of this information in our helping strategies. Next, we present a unique multidimensional model of understanding that unites, in a holistic relationship, factors such as the specific nature of the abuse, social and cultural values, genetics and biology, interpersonal relationships, and a sense of self and worldview. Chapters 3 and 4 review the research knowledge about the prevalence of childhood trauma and its potential impact in adult psychiatric and nonpsychiatric populations. Chapter 5 discusses not only the possible ways traumatic memory is stored and recalled, but also the controversial issues of recovered memory and false memory syndrome. Finally, as a lead-in to the book's second section on practice issues, Chapter 6 introduces the topic of asking about child abuse. For many mental health professionals, asking clients about their abusive pasts is anxiety producing. We believe the guidelines in this chapter will facilitate comfort for both the professional and the client.

Part 2 of the book is focused on client-professional relationships and active practice strategies. In Chapter 7, we consider the nature of power in the helping relationship by discussing both "power over" and "power with." Given the centrality of abuse survivors' experiences of both powerlessness and the misuse of power, understanding how power works in the mental health system as a whole, as well as in client-professional relationships, is critical. Chapters 8, 9, and 10 highlight issues such as the full recovery process; credible treatment models; the creation of basic relational, emotional, and physical safety; and ways to listen to clients' stories so that, as professionals, we can make sense of what we are hearing.

In the book's last chapters, we address special topics by utilizing the expertise of three guest authors. Dr. Lee Ann Hoff, an authority in crisis theory and practice, considers the abuse survivor who is overwhelmed by crisis events. She provides both a theoretical basis for action and practical guidelines for offering care and intervention. A chapter is also especially devoted to men's concerns, because research and clinical literature have been focused predominantly on women. Although we have tried to ensure that the book's previous sections are applicable to men as well as women, John McManiman provides his own insights into the needs of men. Dr. Kathy Lawrence works with the families of survivors of civil war and torture, and she writes about the special issues facing clients from diverse ethnoracial and ethnocultural backgrounds. Finally, we address personal and professional self-care, because working with survivors of childhood trauma has special dangers, such as secondary trauma and vicarious traumatization, both of which go well beyond burnout.

As joint authors, we represent a partnership between theory and practice that has functioned as a unifying force in our own thinking. Throughout the writing of this text, we have endeavored to present a balanced review of current models, practice strategies, and controversies. It is our hope that our work will deepen professional understanding of the link between childhood trauma and mental disorder and improve the capacity of mental health professionals to provide real, meaningful help.

NOTE

1. Emotional abuse is also a component of childhood trauma, but there is little research defining its consequences. Thus, the principal focus of this text will be sexual and physical abuse.

PART 1

THEORY AND KNOWLEDGE

CHAPTER 1

Why We Often Miss a History of Childhood Trauma

Our culture's view of childhood is built upon images of sweet-smelling babies, chubby hands dragging teddies, pony rides, science projects, piano lessons, prom dresses, and graduation ceremonies. Sadly, for many children, the list would be more accurate if it included broken bones, chipped teeth, black eyes, burns, unexplained vaginal or anal infections, night terrors, empty stomachs, and lonely hearts. Children are the world's most precious resource, and the idea that society may be doing a poor job of keeping them safe is challenging enough; to imagine that trusted adults specifically charged with their care are committing atrocities such as beating, raping, torturing, or starving them remains somehow inconceivable, despite increased media attention and regular exposés.

As mental health professionals, we work in a world where a history of child abuse is the sad reality for many of our adult clients. But we, too, are products of our society, and as a consequence, we can be forgiven if we struggle to maintain our illusions. Eventually, however, we have to confront the facts if we are going to provide meaningful help. In this chapter, we discuss the many individual and systemic barriers that can interfere with our capacity to understand and respond to our clients' experiences.

Before beginning this discussion, it is vital that we remind ourselves that the denial of abuse can also mean the denial of recovery. We ask, "If you are well now, then it couldn't have been that bad, could it?" Despite beginning life amidst horror and living in a culture that prefers to turn its back on abuse, survivors of childhood trauma can and do heal. Hope is often the only light that guides their journey and optimism the most valued asset of those who assist them. Children can endure abuse at the hands of those they would have loved and not only retain their humanity but grow into competent, caring adults who value other humans even as they themselves were not valued.

O'Connell Higgins (1994) defined *resilience* as "a firm refusal to join the ranks of the sour and dispirited" (p. 319). However, resilience is much more than making it through. It is a process of "self-righting" in which hurt children become adults who have learned to grow and develop instead of wither and die. They are capable of acknowledging both their suffering and their losses while at the same time cultivating a capacity for love. These are people who have been denied the chance to become the adults they would have been had the abuse never occurred, but they do not re-create hatred and violence in their own lives.

The field of mental health might be more properly called the field of mental illness, because researchers and clinicians tend to focus almost exclusively on what has gone wrong, rather than on what has gone right. Mental health professionals encounter their clients when they are at their lowest ebb, and research findings typically offer a static snapshot of this unhappy moment. Wellness is something that happens outside hospital walls and beyond the clinic door. As we proceed through our discussion of the many barriers that impede our understanding of survivors of childhood trauma, it is important to recall two realities: Small children can be subjected to the basest acts of cruelty, *and* they can defeat these violent impulses by becoming adults who are capable of both giving and receiving love.

SYSTEMIC BARRIERS

Systemic barriers refer to largely invisible but nonetheless powerful social beliefs and values that either suppress our ability to recognize child abuse or encourage us to ignore it.

The Family as Sacred. Children, who are the most vulnerable members of society, remain largely unprotected, walled off from public scrutiny by the agreed-upon sanctity of the family. Family values are held up as a universal but rarely explained ideal, and the wholesome nuclear family remains one of our most cherished myths. That many marriages end in divorce, that some parents live in poverty, and that some neighborhoods are violent are realities that hover on the edge of social consciousness. Ultimately, these facts do nothing to erode the central belief that, generally, children are reared in plenty and in safety. Indeed, most parents are not abusive, but many are alone, unsupported, and ill equipped for the never-ending demands of child care. Others are poor, struggle with their own illnesses or substance abuse problems, or live in violent relationships. And a few, a very few, it must be stressed, are viciously and sadistically abusive, targeting their own defenseless children as objects of hatred. These are facts that are hard to reconcile with our need to see the family as the benign building block for all society.

Authority should not be questioned. People in positions of authority are viewed as trustworthy, not necessarily because they have personally earned that trust but because of the valued attributions we assign the roles they occupy. Priests, ministers, teachers, doctors, scoutmasters, coaches, and others are respectable by definition, and sanctions exist for those who question their authority or fail to follow their orders. Power inequities without the benefit of the checks and balances of accountability mean that abuse *can* occur even though most people conduct themselves with integrity. We admire powerful people and trust that they will treat our children with wisdom and kindness. The fact that some do not is hard to believe.

Violence is normal. We are surrounded by violence. It is in our homes, schools, and neighborhoods. It is reported in the newspaper and on the nightly news, and it is glorified on television and in films. Violence, in these terms, is the typical, straightforward kind: robbery, rape, assault, and murder. However, violence can also be defined in broader social terms, as in the discriminatory blocking of opportunity or the denial of basic needs and rights (Gil, 1996). Sanctioned overt violence and more insidious forms such as racism, classism, sexism, and homophobia are the sorts of realities that combine to suppress both the disclosure and the acknowledgment of child abuse. Miller (1984) argued that traumatic experience, in one form or another, is the rule rather than the exception. All of us have been hurt in some fashion, but paradoxically, having experienced victimization does not make people more empathetic. Instead, as a form of defense, we may resist being reminded of our own pain by refusing to acknowledge others' suffering (van der Kolk & McFarlane, 1996).

The victim is at fault. Powerlessness and vulnerability are not valued qualities, and nowhere are people more powerless than when they are victimized. We are invested in retaining the belief that the world is just and fair. To hear stories of abuse or abandonment, let alone torture, of children is to peer into evil. Most draw back from this brink and work hard to reassure themselves that people are essentially good and that bad things happen only to those who deserve it (McFarlane & van der Kolk, 1996). To maintain these beliefs, we must see victims as having brought their abuse upon themselves, although we are often unclear as to exactly what actions they took to do so. Sometimes, we conclude that being powerless and vulnerable is, in itself, "asking" to be victimized. Herman (1992) added that all perpetrators require is that bystanders remain silent and do nothing. Victims demand action. Doing something to confront abuse is to risk possible danger, because it reminds us all too vividly of our own vulnerability.

We are not our brother's (or our sister's) keeper. Western culture in particular values individual freedom and, by extension, individual responsibility. People are expected to keep their problems to themselves. When they encounter difficulties, they are to pull themselves up by their bootstraps. "Get over it!" is the current version of this sentiment. Although charity is an old and honored tradition of giving to those who are less fortunate, close examination reveals that it is offered at the whim of the do-nor and typically requires proof of worthiness. Openly asking for help is considered shameful, and neediness is seen as a character flaw.

Adults who have experienced childhood trauma do not have equal opportunity, and they don't "get over it" all alone. Their pain is difficult to witness, and their struggle for survival is a challenge to the myths that society automatically rewards individual initiative and that all adversity can be overcome with the right attitude and a solid work ethic. Although it is often said that it takes a village to raise a child, the value placed on individual responsibility can interrupt the community's watchfulness, leaving children to fend for themselves. Citizens ask, "If it really happened, why didn't they just tell someone?"—all the while forgetting that no one particularly wanted to hear.

Gender Stereotypes. Themes of power as they relate to gender leave us with uncomfortable stereotypes that exclusively categorize men as abusers and women as perennial victims (see Chapter 13 for a fuller discussion). The corollary belief is that women never perpetrate violence and abuse and that men cannot be victimized. Statistics broadly support these stereotypes, in that men are more likely to be the perpetrators of child abuse and wife assault, and little girls are victimized in higher numbers than little boys. Feminist scholars, researchers, and clinicians have attacked the forces of patriarchy, arguing that men's violence against women and children is largely ignored because we live in a society that privileges the male sex. Nonetheless, women's suffering continues to be pathologized and reinterpreted as a matter for psychiatric diagnosis and treatment rather than a predictable response to repeated victimization at the hands of men. Alternatively, adult men with histories of childhood trauma, some of whom were victimized by women, struggle with the widely held but erroneous belief that they are inevitably violent and will eventually abuse others. Suffering has no gender and is simply a human reaction to the aftermath of trauma. Stereotypes interfere with our capacity to empathize equally with both male and female survivors of abuse and to treat them as unique individuals.

Taboo Subjects. Child abuse and mental illness are both taboo subjects, and society would prefer to avert its gaze. When both occur in combination, as they so often do, they engender the deepest of fears. Herman (1992) argued that the study of human emotional life took a wrong turn late in the 19th century, when Freud first published his famous paper *The Aetiology of Hysteria* (Freud, 1961). In this work, he boldly stated that at the base of each diagnosis of hysteria lay experiences of childhood incest and rape. Encountering open threats of professional ostracism, he recanted and instead developed intricate theories of infant and child sexual fantasies. His patients, he reasoned, only *thought* that these things had happened to them, when in fact they were expressing their own infantile sexual desires directed at the parent. Freud's preeminence in the world of psychiatry and psychology meant that his failure became the failure of the entire mental health world. Consequently, professional after professional was trained not just to ignore clients' stories of incest and abuse, but to redefine them as symptoms of disease. Despite ample argument to the contrary, this legacy remains with us today.

The Nature Versus Nurture Debate. The history of mental illness is a record of the ebb and flow of two categories of views regarding causation, nature versus nurture, a debate that can be traced back as far as ancient Roman times (Pilgrim & Rogers, 1993). Nature theorists hold that mental illness is bodily affliction, the result of physical or biochemical abnormalities or disease processes. Depending on the era, cures are obtained through a variety of methods, but all are focused on some sort of alteration to the corporal body. Presently, biological psychiatry is aimed at exploring the genetics of mental illness and amending chemical imbalances in the brain. Preferred treatments include a wide variety of psychotropic medications and electroconvulsive therapy. Mental health services that work within the nature ideology are typically seen as following the "medical model."

Alternatively, nurture theorists blame society and the family for creating mental disorder. Violence, abuse, poverty, neglect, abandonment, starvation, and war are seen as root causes of the sorts of emotional and behavioral problems that psychiatry then wrongly labels as disease. Early psychodynamic and psychoanalytic theory explained mental illness in terms of parenting experiences. Mothers were seen as the cause of everything from schizophrenia to homosexuality. Treatment involves changing patients' environments, not the patients themselves, and a cure results from providing a psychodynamic understanding of the failures of early childhood—"good counsel," as it was simply known in ancient times, or psychotherapy in its modern iteration (Pilgrim & Rogers, 1993).

Although there have been advances in reconciling the nature versus nurture debate, many mental health settings, particularly those serving the seriously mentally ill, remain divided, and both paradigms have their share of passionate devotees, each attempting to answer a fundamental question: Who is ultimately responsible for all this misery? Depending on the answer, the burden (financial, emotional, and moral) is either shared by all citizens or borne by the individual. Although it is true that one side of the debate is less likely, and the other more likely, to acknowledge people's histories of childhood trauma, the most damaging problem arises when unresolvable conflicts between the two theories leave professionals arguing over whom to blame rather than focusing on how to help. When professionals war with one another, we deny clients the benefits of a holistic perspective. For example, a strictly biochemical focus can harm clients by ignoring the very real impact that childhood trauma has had on their lives, whereas a strictly social causality view can prevent clients from receiving helpful psychiatric medications.

Finding the Words. It is impossible to acknowledge that which cannot be named. Early in this century, psychiatric theories that focused exclusively on the inborn character defect theory of mental illness received a substantial setback when it was discovered that well-educated young soldiers from upstanding families broke down in battle at least as frequently as their lower-class comrades (Pilgrim & Rogers, 1993). Evidence of mental illness in these men led psychiatrists and others to relabel their symptoms as battle fatigue or shell shock, but when the wars ended, so too did professional interest. Vietnam was a different matter. The nightly television broadcasts of the horrors of war made the suffering of thousands of young men impossible to ignore. Although it is legitimate to argue that returning veterans did not receive either the welcome or the care they deserved, their plight resulted in a new psychiatric diagnosis that appears to have some cultural staying power. The creation of a diagnosis for posttraumatic stress disorder (PTSD) was intended to capture and legitimate the aftermath of war, but it was not long before similarities began to be recognized between the symptoms of veterans and those of, for example, rape or robbery victims. Certainly, the women's movement can be credited with forcing professionals to face this connection, as early feminists broke the silence by exposing rape, family violence, and child abuse. The creation of this new psychiatric diagnosis offered professionals a

way to name the aftereffects of all kinds of violence and, as a consequence, to begin to develop more effective treatments that addressed the
source of clients' suffering.

PTSD was an excellent beginning point in the process of developing an
accurate diagnostic category, but since its inception, recognition has
grown that the violence and terror encountered in childhood create a
more extensive and complex set of symptoms than violence experienced
in adulthood. Unlike adults, children do not have the cognitive defenses
in place to assist in mitigating the impact of trauma. Abuse also robs them
of the capacity to meet their developmental goals, and as they grow up,
they are left struggling with a child's emotional and behavioral patterns
trapped inside an adult persona. Complex posttraumatic stress disorder
is a proposed new psychiatric diagnostic category that is intended to capture the intricacies and the severity of the adult trauma survivor's symptoms. However, it has yet to be included in the *Diagnostic and Statistical
Manual of Mental Disorders* (American Psychiatric Association, 1994).
As a result, it has not had a great deal of effect on the current practice of
the many mental health professionals who continue to take sides in the
nature-nurture debate.

The Role of the Mental Health System. The mental health system is the
primary collision point for the many conflicting forces that define our social response to child abuse and mental disorder. As a microcosm of societal values, it has a long history punctuated by incidents of abuse and violence. The subject of mental illness is deeply emotional, and for over 200
years governments have alternated between two impulses: Should the
mentally ill be protected and cared for, or should they be punished? Records of psychiatry's formal discourse and scholarly debates show an intent to develop caring and curative treatments, but patient accounts, regardless of the century in which they were written, tell tales of cruelty and
abuse (Everett, 1994).

When we consider that the present-day mental health system is defined
by legislation that allows for compulsory detainment, forced medication,
and legal restraint, it is not surprising that violence continues to be an issue. Serious problems in the quality of service provision are well documented and include yelling, pushing, hitting, and, in extreme cases, physical and sexual assault (Roeher Institute, 1995). Abuse can also be
perceived in collective staff attitudes that promote overt or covert coer-

cion (Morrison, 1990). Former patients, now calling themselves consumers and psychiatric survivors, have published exposés of their experiences (Capponi, 1992; Shimrat, 1989; Supeene, 1990), and they are startlingly similar to historical accounts (Everett, 1994). This time, however, their views are confirmed by academic research (College of Nurses of Ontario, 1993; Firsten, 1991; Roeher Institute, 1995). It has also been shown that, in addition to abuses suffered in psychiatric hospitals, women with previous histories of child sexual abuse are the most likely clients to become victims of sexual exploitation by therapists (Avery & Disch, 1998). As in other instances in which people in authority abuse their power, accounts of mistreatment often contain a cry of betrayal. Supeene (1990) wrote, "They'd promised to help me" (p. 71), but instead, "abuse and oppression is what psychiatry meant by help, care and therapy" (p. 231).

The many societal barriers that block our understanding of childhood trauma and the warring forces within the mental health system itself combine, first, to suppress the development of an agreed-upon multifactoral model of the aftermath of trauma that bridges the gap between genetics, biology, and physiology (nature) and environmental influences (nurture) (see Chapter 2). Second, these barriers prevent the dissemination of known effective treatments, as discussed in Chapter 9. It is our contention that mental health professionals can no longer afford to ignore the fact that many of our clients have histories of child abuse and, further, that we have a responsibility to acquire the skills and knowledge necessary to respond effectively to their needs. However, having stated this position, we would like to address another set of obstacles that are more personal than social. These are the individual factors of which we, as professionals, must become aware so that we can confront the internal barriers that may interfere with our learning.

INDIVIDUAL BARRIERS WITHIN MENTAL HEALTH PROFESSIONALS

Individual barriers are those unique qualities that are intimately bound up with who we are as people and as professionals, as well as the feelings and beliefs that lie buried deep inside each of us, all of which under certain circumstances may constitute blocks to our capacity to hear and respond to survivors' experiences.

Who We Are. One school of thought holds that professional training turns us into observers of the human condition, distant and apart from the pain and misery we witness. We become "experts," and in so doing, we don metaphorical robes of objectivity and impartiality. When we turn our professional interest toward our clients' problems, we may attempt to maintain the fiction that our personhood is not part of the interactional equation and that what we do is "to" or "for" clients—never "with" them. Yet, all relationships are mutual and dialectic, meaning that clients affect us even as we are affecting them. Gender, ethnicity, race, and sexual orientation are examples of components of identity that shape our interactions with clients. Whether or not we are married, do or do not have children, are new to our professional careers or are seasoned veterans—all of these are factors that may affect how we respond to survivors. In addition, religious or political beliefs define attitudes regarding parenting, child rearing, and sexuality. Although, upon reflection, we may decide that none of these personal factors constitutes a barrier, as professionals, we have a responsibility to examine our "selves" closely in order to expose individual attributes, judgmental attitudes, or hidden beliefs that might interfere with our ability to provide effective help.

We'd rather not know. Some of us have no desire to confront the evil deeds that people inflict upon one another, because to do so would shatter the faith we have both in humanity and in the essential goodness of the world. This stance is legitimate. Childhood innocence should be considered sacred, and the thought that the most vulnerable among us are not kept safe is repellent. Not everyone is drawn to work with survivors of childhood trauma. There are many roles within the mental health field that are valuable but are not directly involved in assisting this client group in their healing and recovery journey. However, we need to be cautious that we are not so invested in maintaining our own innocence that we inadvertently silence survivors yet again by telegraphing the message that we simply do not want to hear what they have to say. Willful blindness harms, because it recapitulates the inaction survivors experienced as children when no one stepped in to protect them.

We've experienced childhood trauma ourselves. The prevalence of child abuse in the general population is such that there can be no doubt that some mental health professionals were abused as children. For example, a recent survey of 323 psychiatric nurses revealed that 17% had themselves been abused (Gallop, McKeever, Toner, Lancee, & Lueck, 1995). However, these experiences need not constitute a barrier if the professionals in question are able to meet their own emotional and relational needs and are engaged in, or have completed, a personal journey of recovery. In fact, Gallop and colleagues (1995) found that many of those who reported abuse in their own pasts felt comfortable working with survivors. Trouble arises when we have not confronted our own histories and seek to defend ourselves against further hurt by ignoring or actively silencing clients. Some professionals may also play out their own desires for revenge by urging clients to confront or charge their abusers or by insisting that clients adopt the same political views—all without regard for the client's needs and wishes. When any professionals, whether abuse survivors or not, use their role to satisfy unhealthy and unconscious needs, they have abandoned their clients.

Discomfort With Strong Emotion. In Western culture, the overt expression of emotion is discouraged. Although the subtext of this prohibition is the hope that mature adults have learned how to manage their emotional lives responsibly, civility remains defined as an ability to quell anger and hide tears. Losing control is considered shameful, and strong emotion is discouraged unless sanctioned through the auspices of, for example, organized sports, drunkenness, or televised talk shows. Mental health professionals may well subscribe to these beliefs, and if so, survivors will challenge us because they are enraged and deeply despairing. Early experiences of terror and betrayal have left them with an inability to achieve mastery over their emotional lives. Without a full understanding of why they behave the way they do, we can draw away in discomfort at the abandoned way in which many express themselves. One protective strategy professionals may employ is deciding never to mention child abuse, fearing that even gentle questioning may "set them off" or "make things worse." When, where, and how clients are questioned is a complex matter (see Chapter 6), but if we are not inquiring into their pasts because we fear witnessing strong emotion, then our anxiety constitutes a barrier that impedes learning about, first, our clients' abuse histories and, second, their healing and recovery.

A Lack of Knowledge and Skills. A legitimate concern many profession-als have is that they just do not know what to do. For example, Gallop, McCay, Austin, Bayer, and Peternelj-Taylor (1998) found that psychiat-ric nurses specifically identified a lack of knowledge as a barrier that pre-vented them from effectively responding to the needs of survivors of child abuse. Because we live in a culture that prefers not to recognize abuse as a widespread social problem, and because psychiatry is presently focused on genetic and biochemical factors in mental disorder, it is not surprising that relevant information and practical training in this area has been scarce. Although it is true that it takes substantial, focused, and lengthy training to produce qualified childhood trauma therapists, all mental health professionals can acquire elementary skills that will render them more confident in their work. In fact, the need for basic-level, profession-ally targeted information is the impetus behind this book.

BARRIERS WITHIN SURVIVORS

Survivors, too, are products of our culture. They believe in the sanctity of the family, are loath to question authority, see violence as normal, and view themselves as being at fault for their own victimization. These internalized belief systems can prevent them from revealing what happened to them, even as their potential listeners are signaling their reluctance to hear.

Children don't automatically tell. Abuse is often accompanied by overt threats that outline in terrifying detail exactly what the perpetrator will do to the child if he or she were to tell about it. Sometimes these threats are accompanied by a demonstration of what is to come—if the child de-fies the abuser. Even when not openly threatened, abused children can be purposefully isolated, kept away from sympathetic adults who just might believe what the children have to say. In other instances, the abuser may be one of the very few adults who has shown some level of caring, leaving the child in a terrible quandary. Telling means losing what little "love" the child has ever received. Sometimes, perpetrators work hard to estab-lish themselves as upstanding citizens, people who have enough stature in the community that very few adults, let alone children, could counter their reputations. Indeed, abused children are often told that if they tell, no one will believe them anyway—and this statement is all too often accurate. What children say is not considered credible. Often adult survivors will recall incidents in which, having told as a child, they did not receive comfort and safety but instead were punished for lying. Others believe the abuse is "their own fault" and keep silent because of shame and guilt. Still others may have told a well-meaning adult who immediately confronted the perpetrator, exposing them to retaliation. Some told, were believed, and were subsequently ostracized from the family or even from the community. These forces combine to suppress the disclosure rates (Herman, 1992) and leave survivors extremely ill at ease when, at long last, they are invited to tell their story.

No Words. Researchers have discovered that the side of the brain that processes emotion becomes hyperactive when research participants are presented with traumatic subject matter, whereas Broca's area—the speech portion of the brain—slows its activity (van der Kolk & Fisler, 1994). People who have experienced trauma in adulthood will verify that they struggle to find words "large" enough and "deep" enough to describe what has happened. Slowly, with a mature capacity to build verbal meaning, they can eventually make themselves and others understand. However, children abused early in life either have no vocabulary at all or have such basic verbal skills that they have no specific words to communicate their terror and pain. As adults, they may recall these early abusive incidents only as a series of sensory impressions, smells, tastes, touches, shortness of breath, pains in certain portions of the body, or impressions of light and dark or hot and cold. Despite the fact that they have developed mature vocabularies, the secrets of their abusive childhood can remain locked in wordless memory. In order for them to describe what has happened, they must first return to their store of infant and toddler sensations and then find the appropriate words to describe the events that created them. This is a troubling and complex task that often leaves survivors questioning their own memories, asking, "Did it really happen? Have I made it up?" In the context of a culture that prefers not to hear stories of child abuse and that, if challenged, can exhibit a blame-the-victim attitude, some survivors cease the effort of exploring their pasts, preferring to remain silent rather than expose themselves to further hurt and rejection.

No Memory of the Abuse. Some survivors report that they only recently recalled their abusive pasts and that they simply "forgot" what happened to them, sometimes for decades. The process of how memories are stored and then later recalled is the subject both of extensive and often contradictory research and of media attention and civil action (see Chapter 5 for a fuller discussion). However, survivors who report what are being called "recovered memories" and the many trauma therapists who treat them are of the opinion that forgetting the abuse is a protective strategy arising from the child's being completely cognitively, emotionally, and physiologically overwhelmed. To forget is to wall off unbearable pain so that abused children can survive and continue to function. Of course, forgetting constitutes one of the most complete barriers there is to understanding, because the past simply disappears. In some senses, the survivor's need to deny the abuse merges with the perpetrator's goal of evading detection, and they agree: The abuse never happened.

CONCLUSION

Despite the numerous barriers that stand between survivors of childhood trauma and recovery, many people are eventually able to find some measure of relief from the aftermath of abuse. The mental health system is the place to which most turn when they begin to experience troubling symptoms. But mental health professionals are also products of society, and they can offer services and treatments that deny or ignore clients' experiences. For example, the majority of us work within a medical-model framework—the nature side of the nature-nurture debate. This model focuses on genetic, biochemical, and physiological factors in the etiology of mental disorder. Other professionals take the nurture side and view child abuse as an environmental or social issue. When our knowledge and skills are derived from a single perspective, we only have the capacity to address one set of consequences. From the viewpoint of the survivor, reality is not based in nature *or* nurture, but in nature *and* nurture. Survivors experience biochemical and physiological consequences as well as emotional, psychological, and cognitive dysfunction. Without a holistic outlook that allows for the peaceful coexistence of *both* a nature and a nurture view, mental health professionals are in danger of ignoring fully half of the problem we are trying so hard to treat. The impact of childhood abuse is all-encompassing, and it demands a conceptual model that is multidimensional.

REFERENCES

American Psychiatric Association. (1994). *Diagnostic and statistical manual of mental disorders* (4th ed.). Washington, DC: Author.

Avery, N., & Disch, E. (1998, October). *Effects on clients of sexual abuse by clergy, mental health practitioners and medical practitioners.* Paper presented at the Fourth International Conference on Sexual Misconduct by Psychotherapists, Other Health Professionals and Clergy, Boston.

Capponi, P. (1992). *Upstairs at the crazy house.* Toronto, Canada: Viking.

College of Nurses of Ontario. (1993). *Abuse of clients by RNs and RNAs.* Toronto, Canada: Author.

Everett, B. (1994). Something is happening: The contemporary consumer and psychiatric survivor movement in historical context. *Journal of Mind and Behaviour, 15*(1/2), 55-70.

Firsten, T. (1991). Violence in the lives of women on psychiatric wards. *Canadian Women's Studies, 11*(4), 45-48.

Freud, S. (1961). The aetiology of hysteria. In J. Strachey (Ed. and Trans.), *The standard edition of the complete psychological works of Sigmund Freud* (Vol. 3, pp. 191-221). London: Hogarth Press.

Gallop, R., McCay, E., Austin, W., Bayer, M., & Peternelj-Taylor, C. (1998). The educational needs of Canadian psychiatric nurses who work with clients who have a history of childhood sexual abuse. *Canadian Nurse, 94*(7), 30-34.

Gallop, R., McKeever, P., Toner, B., Lancee, W., & Lueck, M. (1995). The impact of childhood sexual abuse on the psychological well-being and practice of nursing. *Archives of Psychiatric Nursing, 9,* 137-145.

Gil, D. (1996). Preventing violence in a structurally violent society: Mission impossible. *American Journal of Orthopsychiatry, 66,* 77-84.

Herman, J. (1992). *Trauma and recovery.* New York: Basic Books.

McFarlane, A., & van der Kolk, B. (1996). Trauma and the challenge to society. In B. van der Kolk, A. McFarlane, & L. Weisaeth (Eds.), *Traumatic stress: The effects of overwhelming experiences on mind, body and society* (pp. 224-246). New York: Guilford.

Miller, A. (1984). *Thou shalt not be aware: Society's betrayal of the child.* New York: Meridian.

Morrison, E. (1990). The tradition of toughness: A study of nonprofessional nursing care in psychiatric settings. *Image: Journal of Nursing Scholarship, 22,* 32-38.

O'Connell Higgins, G. (1994). *Resilient adults: Overcoming a cruel past.* San Francisco: Jossey-Bass.

Pilgrim, D., & Rogers, A. (1993). *A sociology of mental health and illness.* Philadelphia: Open University Press.

Roeher Institute. (1995). *Harm's way: The many faces of violence and abuse against persons with disabilities*. Toronto, Canada: Author.

Shimrat, I. (1989). *Analyzing psychiatry*. (Transcript available from CBC Radio, P.O. Box 500, Station A, Toronto, Ontario, Canada M5W 1E6)

Supeene, S. (1990). *As for the sky, falling: A critical look at psychiatry and suffering*. Toronto, Canada: Second Story Press.

van der Kolk, B., & Fisler, R. (1994). Childhood abuse & neglect and loss of self-regulation. *Bulletin of the Menninger Clinic, 58*(2).

van der Kolk, B., & McFarlane, A. (1996). The black hole of trauma. In B. van der Kolk, A. McFarlane, & L. Weisaeth (Eds.), *Traumatic stress: The effects of overwhelming experiences on mind, body and society* (pp. 3-23). New York: Guilford.

CHAPTER 2

A Multidimensional Model of Understanding

The complexity of childhood trauma cannot be explained simply. People are products of their genetic, biological, relational, social, and cultural environments. These many factors affect both the impact of the original trauma and the expression of its aftermath. Aspects of the abuse itself are also critical. Did it start early in the child's life? Was it violent and ongoing? Who was the perpetrator, and what was his or her relationship to the child? As mental health professionals, we need a way to include these many factors in our thinking if we are to provide effective help for clients with these sorts of histories.

Although it may make intuitive sense, the link between child abuse and subsequent mental disorder is not always easily understood or explained. What is clear is that although trauma affects every child, only some develop symptoms so severe that they are forced to turn to the mental health system for help. In order to explain why some adult survivors do more poorly than others, we propose a multifaceted and dynamic model of childhood abuse. This model takes into account the nature of the abuse and age of onset, as well as the unique biological dimensions of individuals as expressed within the context of their social environment. The model also demonstrates which relational circumstances may magnify the impact of the abuse and which circumstances may decrease the likelihood of severe consequences.

THE NEED FOR A NEW MODEL

In an ideal world, psychiatric treatment and mental health services would conform to the needs of the client. For this to happen, however, mental health professionals would have to take a holistic view that honors the uniqueness of each individual and his or her background. Presently, however, it is much more common to attempt to fit the client into the treatment model than it is to fit the treatment to the client. In North America, the dominant paradigm for psychiatry is the medical model. The *Diagnostic and Statistical Manual of Mental Disorders* (American Psychiatric Association, 1994), now in its fourth edition, was designed to provide systematic and reliable guidance for the categorization and identification of mental disorders. Diagnosis is based, with few exceptions, on behavioral signs and symptoms. The fact that clients may be poor or unemployed, live in substandard housing, or have abuse histories does not figure into the diagnostic process. In addition, biomedical knowledge is considered objective and culturally neutral—a view that many reject as not only inaccurate but ethnocentric (Austin, Gallop, McCay, Peternelj-Taylor, & Bayer, 1999). Many clinicians are also adherents of a highly specialized theoretical or biological model within specific disease categories and will align their treatments accordingly. For example, some may be proponents of the chemical imbalance view of depression and may therefore prescribe psychiatric medication for all clients who report this constellation of symptoms, never further investigating the client's personal history or present living circumstances. Valuable help such as trauma therapy for a history of child abuse and psychosocial interventions such as referrals for decent housing, social assistance, and work preparation may be ignored. This one-size-fits-all approach denies clients a full understanding of their difficulties and reduces complex lives and complicated problems to the level of a single solution.

In reaction to the power and pervasiveness of the medical model, alternative theories, often grounded in principles of social and environmental causality, have developed. These models define mental disorder as a natural response to noxious environmental triggers, such as child abuse, community and family violence, gender discrimination, racism, or socioeconomic disadvantage. Advocates of this position argue that depression is exclusively the result of social and environmental factors and offer as evidence, for example, the fact that twice as many women as men are depressed, presumably because society silences women and renders them powerless. Within this view, clinicians concentrate on therapy and psychosocial interventions to the exclusion of medication, because "pills can't cure poverty and violence."

As a way of addressing the complexity of human growth under traumatizing conditions, researchers in the field of developmental psychopathology, such as Cicchetti and Lynch (1993), suggest an ecological-transactional model that argues that factors such as larger cultural values, the local community environment, family context, and individual characteristics interact to mutually influence functioning and adaptation. Specifically, they examined the influence of community violence (social environment), child maltreatment (physical abuse in family context), and child functioning. They found that growing up in a violent community is a risk factor for child maltreatment, developmental difficulties, and for later symptomatology (Lynch & Cicchetti, 1998). This model, though multifactorial, does not emphasize or integrate important genetic or biological issues into its concepts.

Neither the medical model nor the various social models capture the complete picture for the mental health client. Therapists who deny the role of biology or genetics in the creation of mental disorder are just as narrow in their view as psychiatrists who refuse to ask questions about a client's history of trauma. In many senses, the causality debate at the bottom of this nature versus nurture, medical versus nonmedical split is irrelevant to mental health professionals who are charged with the responsibility of helping clients reduce their symptoms and alter dysfunctional behavioral patterns. Professionals need a way to link abuse histories to subsequent mental disorder for the purpose of providing real, meaningful help, not for discovering cause. Adequate mental health care requires a full understanding of the genetic and biological underpinnings of mental disorder, as well as of the social and environmental imperatives in clients' lives.

As a final note, it is never in the best interest of the client for medical and nonmedical professionals to be in an adversarial position. These sorts of antipathies re-create the inconsistent and acrimonious backgrounds from which survivors of childhood trauma are attempting to free themselves. Both sides of this pervasive nature versus nurture debate must recognize the need for an integrated, whole-person approach.

DIMENSIONS OF THE MODEL

The multidimensional model we propose includes six components. Factors external to the client's personal world of influence are twofold: the nature of the trauma itself and the social and cultural values that permeate human interaction. Internal factors include four individual characteristics: genetics, biology, interpersonal relationships, and sense of self and worldview. Each of these aspects has degrees of influence in the impact of abuse and the subsequent expression of mental disorder, and they all interact with one another.

Dimensions External to the Individual

The nature of the trauma and the social and cultural context in which it occurs are factors that mediate impact, but they are outside the child's personal sphere of influence.

The Nature of the Traumatic Experience. There are both quantitative and qualitative differences in the nature of child abuse. Trauma that begins early in life interrupts developmental tasks and subjects young children to overwhelming emotional and physiological stimuli before they are able to understand what is happening and before they have the verbal capacity to communicate their pain. Their distress is heightened in proportion to the amount of violence used and to the invasive nature of the assaults (sexual, physical, or psychological; Elliott & Briere, 1995; Finkelhor, 1979; Herman, Russell, & Trocki, 1986; Russell, 1986).

Should the abuse continue over long periods of time, children grow up under conditions that are literally warlike, including the dimensions of captivity, terror, and torture (Herman, 1992a). In addition to the normal strains of childhood, they carry the heavy, unchildlike burdens of broken bones, physical illness, rage, despair, shame, guilt, and humiliation—all borne in silence and isolation.

Sadism is a further component of abuse that, when present, increases the pain and turmoil. Sadistic abuse, which combines deliberate cruelty with perversion, separates children even further from human connection and mainstream society. In these terms, children are not only the object of abuse but are also forced to abuse others or to participate in scenarios in which pets are killed or younger children are raped or tortured. Formative experiences this far outside the bounds of the social norm mean that isolation is complete—for who could ever understand the things that have happened to them, or what they have seen and done?

A final aspect of the abusive event relates to the perpetrator of these crimes. Children who are abused by their own parent (Finkelhor, 1979; Herman et al., 1986; Russell, 1986) or by a nonrelative in a position of trust (Browne & Finkelhor, 1986) suffer the further insult of a fundamental betrayal. These are the people who are supposed to love and protect the child, but instead they become sources of harm. Familial perpetrators are rarely consistently abusive and can intersperse terrorizing violence with weeping apologies and protestations of love. Children learn that their world is completely unpredictable, and because there is no discernible pattern to the abuse (at least to young minds), they are constantly caught off guard, never knowing what they can do to avoid further assaults. Intergenerational abuse or a climate of community violence can mean that children are serially abused by multiple perpetrators or that they are abused in groups. In these instances, children learn that all adults are to be feared and that nowhere is safe.

Additional environmental factors add to the impact of the trauma. Children who are moved from home to home; who do not have even one adult figure to whom they can turn for protection and comfort; who live in violent neighborhoods (Lynch & Cicchetti, 1998); who are subjected to racism; or who are abandoned, neglected, or starved are likely to suffer the complete impact of a traumatic childhood. In these situations, children have been failed on every level, and survival, when it occurs, is truly a miracle.

The converse of exacerbating dimensions are circumstances that protect against extensive impact. These are instances when the abuse occurs when the child is older, happens on a one-time or limited basis, does not involve violence or penetration, or is not perpetrated by someone in a caregiving role. In addition, when the child's story is believed and action is taken by trusted adults to see that he or she is comforted and kept safe in the future, the likelihood of a lasting impact is lessened. Finally, if abused children have a positive relationship with at least one parental figure, they tend to fare better (Kroll, 1993; Romans, Martin, Anderson, Herbison, & Mullen, 1995).

Social and Cultural Context. Humans are born into, and develop within, ever expanding and overlapping social and cultural circles. This context provides our values, habits, practices, customs, and beliefs. Often, we are not consciously aware of the influence of these beliefs because they pervade our existence and are known to us as "just the way things are." Social and cultural values influence our individual thinking, the reactions of those around us, and the responses of society at large.

When these fixed beliefs are forced to the surface and challenged, considerable controversy and upheaval can occur. For example, Western culture has traditionally accorded men substantial power—whether or not individual men perceive themselves as being powerful. Women have historically lived in circumstances remote from public centers of power, with their opinions counting for little. In addition, our primary view of power is that it is an aid to dominance. Dominance allows those whom society views as stronger to use force to achieve their ends—often with impunity (Wartenberg, 1990). Indeed, Gil (1996) argued that the mechanisms of dominance have created a society that is structurally violent, meaning that violence is both embedded in our common practices and sanctioned by our large social institutions. The widespread existence of family violence supports this perspective. The state has historically declined to interfere in what has been defined as a private matter, allowing wife assault and child abuse to continue. The rise of the feminist movement in the 1970s challenged these "truths" in ways that made many men (and some women) uncomfortable. Feminists provided opportunities for women to speak out publicly, rendering interpersonal violence jarringly visible for the first time in history. With the help of this trend, men, too, have begun to recount their experiences of childhood sexual and physical abuse.

Presently, child abuse in all its insidious forms has become a media standard, with all manner of adults in authority positions being exposed as child abusers and pedophiles. Once-revered social institutions such as churches, schools, and organized sports have come under attack for turning a blind eye to what has often proved to be the blatant and systemic abuse of vulnerable children or, in the case of the military, young female and sometimes male recruits. Nevertheless, despite increased awareness and substantial changes in the police, court, child welfare, and mental health systems, numerous barriers to disclosure and effective action remain (as pointed out in Chapter 1). These barriers constitute the lingering power of social and cultural values that privilege a certain segment of society over another: men over women, adults over children, whites over nonwhites, able-bodied over disabled, and haves over have-nots.

When abused children grow up in a social and cultural context that ignores or dismisses their experiences as "just the way things are," they may not be protected from harm or rescued from violent situations. Thus, in addition to having no listening ear within the family, they live in communities that ignore obvious signs of abuse or join in their victimization. Added burdens such as racism, sexism, homophobia, discrimination, poverty, and the denial of opportunity create encompassing cultural forces that combine to increase both the impact of abuse and the likelihood that it will be reproduced intergenerationally, as the child becomes an adult who knows no other option than to harm or be harmed.

Dimensions Particular to the Individual

Factors near at hand or within children themselves also have the potential to mediate the impact of traumatic experience.

Genetics. One of the basic building blocks of each human is his or her genetic makeup. The idea that infants are *tabula rasa,* or blank slates, upon which personalities are imposed solely by environmental influences has not been supported in research. In fact, some work suggests that as much as 50% of personality may be genetically determined (Stone, 1993). The concepts of resilience and vulnerability arise out of this research—with the caveat that environmental influences also figure into their expression (Luthar & Zigler, 1991). Resilience is the notion that some individuals can withstand greater levels of psychological or physiological assault than others can, whereas vulnerability refers to the opposite effect. As theoretical constructs, both these ideas have the potential to explain why the same set of circumstances may affect children differently.

Temperament is another personality trait with genetic roots. As any new parent will attest, babies appear to be born with specific temperaments. They can be placid, cuddly, cheerful, weepy, alert, dozy, fussy, difficult to hold, or easily comforted. These characteristics in turn influence parents' behavior and may shape their nurturing responses. The "easy" baby enables parents to feel successful, making it more likely that positive, mutually reinforcing activities will occur. On the contrary, a child with a fussy temperament may generate more negative events and reactive parental responses. Furthermore, children who respond well to mildly negative environmental influences, for example, those who sleep well even in noisy conditions or those who can be easily comforted when upset, may be born with aspects of temperament that moderate the impact of stress (Block & Block, 1980). Parents, too, have their own temperaments, which can react with the child's. A parent who is depressed can qualitatively change the psychological development of the child, independent of the child's own temperament characteristics. Thus, nature (inherited genetic features) and nurture (the responses in the environment) become intertwined.

Biology. Very early in the understanding of mental disorder and trauma, Janet (1889, cited in Freud, 1961) observed, and Freud (1961) later confirmed, that patients reacted to current and apparently neutral stimuli with intense responses reminiscent of their original traumatic experiences, although this linkage was rarely apparent to the person who was suffering the distress. Present-day survivors of childhood trauma exhibit similar reactions. For example, benign stimuli, such as a certain texture of clothing, a time of year, a particular smell, or a kind of touch, can become internalized trigger points that arouse intense emotions. These feelings are especially disconcerting because they are unexpected and their source is obscure. Moreover, many survivors do not associate the initial trigger with their own intense reactions and describe themselves as out of control or "going crazy."

Kolb (1987) suggested that physical and sexual trauma may result in permanent neural changes that have consequences for learning, habituation, and stimulus discrimination; recent research has confirmed these ideas (van der Kolk, 1994). Research has also shown that survivors of Vietnam combat and of child abuse, who both have had to deal with prolonged stress, have changes in hippocampal function and volume (Bremner, 1999). This critical region of the brain is important for memory and learning. Excessive exposure to stress appears to result in memory deficits and hippocampal atrophy, possibly interfering with the ability to connect individual elements of memory (Bremner, Krystal, Charney, & Southwick, 1996; Sapolsky, 1996). This physiological impact is one possible explanation for the fragmentary nature of trauma recall (Bremner, 1999). The actual physiology of stress and memory is described in more detail in Chapter 5.

Childhood trauma can lead to a variety of overwhelming emotions, such as anger, sadness, guilt, and shame. In order to avoid these intense feelings, children can take refuge in dissociation (a process of splitting consciousness), denial, amnesia, or numbing. Although these responses are at first an adaptive way to survive the traumatic experience, they can become overgeneralized and maladaptive with time. The symptoms that result interfere with attention and concentration and, in extreme instances, create a feeling that time has been "lost"; such symptoms can also prevent protective action when danger threatens (see Chapter 4 for a fuller discussion).

Many studies report that people who experience severe abuse are unable to integrate the memory of these events into a coherent whole. When, in adulthood, fragments of dislocated memory become intrusive triggers, they are accompanied by concomitant physiological changes in the body, just as if the trauma were happening all over again (van der Kolk, 1994). Under traumatic conditions, the body's physiology responds by creating biological patterns in the brain that keep the child on guard or hypervigilant. But the body becomes accustomed to the constantly high levels of this "fight or flight" biological response, which results in a steady state of hyperarousal. These adaptive symptoms, too, become overgeneralized with time and return unbidden when the adult encounters relatively innocent stimuli. As might well be imagined, adult survivors who are always aroused and vigilant have difficulty controlling their emotions and their actions. These alterations in affect and impulse regulation are typically expressed as behavioral problems as survivors, for example, lash out in anger, burst into uncontrolled weeping, or slide into deep despair in response to what others see as relatively minor events (Herman, 1992b). Conversely, survivors may numb or "space out" when threatened or assaulted so that they do not respond protectively when real danger looms. Psychobiological symptoms are not independent of interpersonal disruptions. Each is a manifestation of the other. Extreme reactions seriously interfere with the capacity to establish and maintain relationships. Survivors are also in danger of becoming targets for further violence as others react strongly either to their vulnerability or to their attacking behavior.

Relationships With Others. Children who are surrounded by caring and responsible adults learn that people, by and large, are trustworthy. They develop an internalized sense of safety that allows them to accurately modulate interpersonal closeness. They also have an innate sense for danger, because it violates the security they have come to expect. Adult caregivers act as havens where sad tales are told and broken hearts mended. As children grow older, they gradually learn to solve their own problems and dry their own tears. Their emerging sexuality is allowed to develop in privacy and at its own pace. The "self" becomes defined as apart from others, but as a part of the community and the world. Trauma experienced under these conditions is shocking, as always, but there is every chance that the child can be helped to recover with a minimum of lasting damage.

Conversely, children who experience severe and persistent abuse have never known life without danger. Abuse that occurs early in life and that is of an interpersonal nature interferes with subsequent psychological and psychobiological maturation in far more profound ways than previously acknowledged (Herman, 1992a; Terr, 1991). Abused children have no opportunity to formulate a sense of self independent of the perpetrator or outside of perpetual chaos. Their relationships are contaminated with unpredictability, violence, and cruelty.

Never having experienced a sense of intimacy, these children grow up fearing any sort of closeness. They know that people cannot be trusted and will harm them if given an opportunity. This form of dysfunction can occur in different ways and with differing intensities depending on the nature and extent of the abuse or neglect. For example, survivors may be overly intrusive in relationships or, conversely, avoidant. Sex becomes coupled with violence and pain. Puberty is terrifying, and the true nature of their sexual orientation may be confused or misunderstood. The im-

pact of their abuse is all-encompassing and affects all aspects of their behavior and every relationship they attempt to enter. Even under extreme
circumstances, one caring relationship or one protective adult can make a
difference, because the child has somewhere to turn, however intermit-
tent or limited the contact. It is even possible that abused children value
this scarce human resource far beyond what would normally have been
the case, because the love and connection provided is so rare that it stands
out against a backdrop of continuous violence. If they have encountered
one kind human being, they can retain a hope, based on experience, that
sometime in the future they may encounter another one. Children who
have no one, ever, to hear their pain or to dry their tears become adults
who believe that humans are universally dangerous and must either be
defended against or attacked in retaliation.

The Sense of Self and Worldview. Object relations theory is rooted in the
belief that we develop a sense of self during childhood. This body of literature focuses on understanding how early experiences in relationships
with others are central to the development of personality and to the ability to form satisfying relationships as adults. Object relations theorists
speak of internalized representations of events (objects) that evolve into a
child's sense of personhood and, eventually, into his or her worldview
(Mahler, 1972).

Initially, the only way children can know themselves is through the responses of those near to them. If parents are primarily positive and non-
critical, children develop a sense of worth that constitutes the internal
"glue" that enables them to deal with frustration, disappointment, and
loneliness, as well as the successes in life. These children learn how to
modulate their emotions and to soothe themselves when upset. As they
mature, self-soothing techniques become abstracted. They may eat the
favorite foods of childhood, have a long bath, watch a movie, paint, play
sports, or seek out the company of reliable others. Although the capacity
to comfort oneself may seem a small thing, it is absolutely central to a
sense of mastery and to the perception that the world is, primarily, a safe
place to be. Abused children do not have the opportunity to internalize
representations of caring and comfort, which results in what is called a
lack of object constancy (the capacity to call upon soothing internal representations or memories). Hence, they lack the ability to comfort themselves in times of stress and aloneness.

The world in which childhood trauma occurs, particularly when the abuse is by a family member, is by definition unsafe and uncaring. According to Herman (1992b), the abused child is challenged with the impossible task of finding a way to develop a sense of basic trust and safety with caretakers who are untrustworthy and unsafe. Abused children experience a fundamental sense of betrayal because they are powerless to halt or control the impingement on their bodies or their "selves." Abuse, if it is continuous and prolonged, becomes the defining experience that prevents attachment. Try as the child might, he or she cannot obtain the closeness so necessary to security. However, the abusive caregiver is not likely to abandon the child outright because of the exploitative nature of the relationship—the child has come to serve the perpetrator's needs. Instead of promoting independence, autonomy, and an integrated sense of self, abusive caretakers reward dependent and clinging behaviors while at the same time punishing independence. In these circumstances, children cannot develop a positive, internalized sense of self. Instead, they learn that meeting even their most basic needs depends on unpredictable and punitive others who reward only occasionally and then inconsistently and paradoxically. Their sense of self becomes completely dependent on the validation of others. To know or define themselves requires a constant state of hypervigilance as they monitor the actions and emotions of others, looking always for cues of approval, rejection, acceptance, or withdrawal. If others are pleased or kind, then for a fleeting moment, abused children will see themselves as "good" and worthy. If others are angry, then they are "bad" and will surely be punished. Worst of all, when abused children grow into adults, they cannot tolerate being alone, because it is at these moments that their sense of self is at its lowest ebb. With no one present to pursue or defend against, they are literally nothing.

All these experiences combine to create a firmly held worldview that guides individual choice and action. Children acquire their ideas about how the world operates during their early years. Optimal experiences mean that they are able to attach positive feelings to being in the world and to develop a sense of belonging. They can "attach" in the literal sense of the word, because they are able to form intimate relationships with others and modulate interpersonal closeness in a manner that maintains their security.

Adult survivors view the world as dangerous and unpredictable. Nowhere is safe, and there is no sense of belonging. They are alienated and alone, constantly on the lookout for the next attack. Because the desire for comfort and solace is ever present, they find alternative and unhealthy ways of relieving internal tension. Substance abuse, eating disorders, self-harm, dissociation, and suicide attempts are just a few examples; these are also examples of behaviors that bring survivors into contact with the mental health system. Revictimization dynamics (discussed more fully in Chapter 4) are defined as the unconscious need to reencounter trauma-tizing circumstances and are thought to be another type of anxiety-reducing strategy, one that is particularly complex and hard to understand (Miller, 1994). The resulting chaos in the survivor's life confirms over and over again that which is already known to be true: The world is an evil place, and human beings can never be trusted.

A MULTIDIMENSIONAL MODEL

Factors such as the nature and the extent of the trauma, social and cultural values, genetic and biological makeup, interpersonal relationships, and sense of self and worldview are dimensions that ultimately define the impact of child abuse, but their effects are ever shifting as they interact with, or potentiate, one another. The model as illustrated in Figure 2.1 is but a two-dimensional representation of these many factors and their relationships, and, as such, it suffers from the inherent limitations of a static drawing. Nonetheless, the choice of concentric circles serves to convey the message that linkages are not necessarily linear. They can both build upon and interact with each other.

    The circle of *social and cultural context* represents the all-encompassing background into which each individual is born. Although it is against these values and beliefs that the drama of abuse is played out, the encircling influence of Western society and culture serves, generally, to support and sustain the expression of violence in all its forms. The *genetic makeup* of the individual is represented by a small but central circle, because it is the elementary foundation upon which each human being is built. It influences how children respond, and are responded to, in the world. Upon this genetic inheritance is layered the many facets of life, only one of which may be traumatic experience. When abuse occurs, it has *biological consequences* that influence the processing of information in the brain. Developing brains subjected to overwhelming terror are

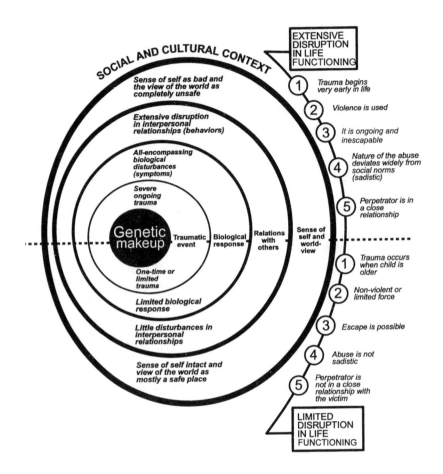

Figure 2.1. Multidimensional Trauma Model.

chemically, and perhaps physically, altered in ways thought to be immutable. Mediated through violence and subsequent biological disruptions are the child's self-perception and his or her relationships with others. Children come to know humans through how they are treated, and an early life of violence and chaos teaches lessons that are never forgotten.

One of these lessons is that bad children are treated badly. Abused children internalize this formative message and create a defiled *sense of self* that cannot help but hold the *worldview* that life is fundamentally inhospitable and unsafe.

When these factors are combined, the resulting multidimensional model bridges the traditional gap between the medical model and the social and environmental causality theories because it includes both perspectives in one paradigm. It provides for a link between a history of trauma and subsequent mental disorder without entering into a causality debate. By making a distinction between symptoms and behaviors, the model differentiates between biochemical disturbances and dysfunctional individual actions and interactions without privileging one over the other. This separation is somewhat artificial, in that symptoms and behaviors have a dialectical relationship, interacting and building upon each other to create what is arguably a whole greater than the sum of its parts. Nevertheless, from a practice perspective, it is a useful distinction to make, because it lays the groundwork for the development of different helping strategies for each. Mental health professionals need to respond to their clients as whole people, as survivors of traumatic events whose troubling behaviors need therapeutic and psychosocial interventions, and as physiological beings who have genuine physical and biological disturbances that require appropriate medical assistance to reduce the symptoms of mental disorder.

CONCLUSION

The multidimensional model presented in this chapter is designed, first, to provide a conceptual link between experiences of childhood trauma and subsequent mental disorder and, second, to bridge the traditional gap between medical and nonmedical mental health treatment paradigms. It is intended as a holistic representation of the complex factors that affect the impact of abuse on the individual—as expressed through observable behaviors and symptoms. However, it is important to acknowledge that this, too, is a model and, as a result, it suffers from the standard limitations attached to any attempt to distill complex human behavior onto a single page. Its usefulness lies in its ability to form the basis of meaningful and effective helping strategies.

REFERENCES

American Psychiatric Association. (1994). *Diagnostic and statistical manual of mental disorders* (4th ed.). Washington, DC: Author.

Austin, W., Gallop, R., McCay, E., Peternelj-Taylor, C., & Bayer, M. (1999). Culturally competent care for psychiatric clients who have a history of sexual abuse. *Clinical Nursing Research, 8*(1), 5-23.

Block, J. H., & Block, J. (1980). The role of ego-control and ego-resiliency in the organization of behavior. In W. Collins (Ed.), *The Minnesota symposia on child psychology: Vol. 13. Development of cognition, affect, and social relations* (pp. 39-101). Hillsdale, NJ: Lawrence Erlbaum.

Bremner, J. D. (1999). Does stress damage the brain? *Biological Psychiatry, 45,* 797-805.

Bremner, J. D., Krystal, J., Charney, D., & Southwick, S. (1996). Neural mechanisms in dissociative amnesia for childhood abuse: Relevance to the current controversy surrounding the "false memory syndrome." *American Journal of Psychiatry, 153,* 1671-1682.

Browne, A., & Finkelhor, D. (1986). Impact of child sexual abuse: A review of the research. *Psychological Bulletin, 99*(1), 66-77.

Cicchetti, D., & Lynch, M. (1993). Toward an ecological/transactional model of community violence and child maltreatment: Consequences for child development. *Psychiatry, 56,* 96-118.

Elliott, D., & Briere, J. (1995). Posttraumatic stress associated with delayed recall of sexual abuse: A general population study. *Journal of Traumatic Stress, 8,* 629-647.

Finkelhor, D. (1979). *Sexually victimized children.* New York: Free Press.

Freud, S. (1961). The aetiology of hysteria. In J. Strachey (Ed. and Trans.), *The standard edition of the complete psychological works of Sigmund Freud* (Vol. 3, pp. 191-221). London: Hogarth Press.

Gil, D. (1996). Preventing violence in a structurally violent society: Mission impossible. *American Journal of Orthopsychiatry, 66,* 77-84.

Herman, J. (1992a). Complex PTSD: A syndrome in survivors of prolonged and repeated trauma. *Journal of Traumatic Stress, 5,* 377-391.

Herman, J. (1992b). *Trauma and recovery.* New York: Basic Books.

Herman, J., Russell, D., & Trocki, K. (1986). Long-term effects of incestuous abuse in childhood. *American Journal of Psychiatry, 143,* 1293-1296.

Kolb, L. C. (1987). A neuropsychological hypothesis explaining posttraumatic stress disorders. *American Journal of Psychiatry, 144,* 989-995.

Kroll, J. (1993). *PTSD/Borderlines in therapy: Finding the balance.* New York: Norton.

Luthar, S., & Zigler, E. (1991). Vulnerability and competence: A review of research on resilience in childhood. *American Journal of Orthopsychiatry, 61,* 6-22.

Lynch, M., & Cicchetti, D. (1998). An ecological-transactional analysis of children and contexts: The longitudinal interplay among child maltreatment, community violence, and children's symptomatology. *Development and Psychopathology, 10,* 235-257.

Mahler, M. (1972). On the first three subphases of the separation-individuation process. *International Journal of Psycho-Analysis, 53,* 333-338.

Miller, D. (1994). *Women who hurt themselves.* New York: Basic Books.

Romans, S. E., Martin, J. L., Anderson, J. C., Herbison, G. P., & Mullen, P. E. (1995). Sexual abuse in childhood and deliberate self-harm. *American Journal of Psychiatry, 152,* 1336-1342.

Russell, D. E. H. (1986). *The secret trauma: Incest in the lives of girls and women.* New York: Basic Books.

Sapolsky, R. (1996). Why stress is bad for your brain. *Science, 273,* 749-750.

Stone, M. (1993). *Abnormalities of personality.* New York: Norton.

Terr, L. (1991). Childhood traumas: An outline and overview. *American Journal of Psychiatry, 148,* 10-20.

van der Kolk, B. A. (1994). The body keeps the score: Memory and the evolving psychobiology of posttraumatic stress. *Harvard Review of Psychiatry, 1,* 253-265.

Wartenberg, T. (1990). *The forms of power: From domination to transformation.* Philadelphia: Temple University Press.

CHAPTER 3

The Research
Story

The research literature on childhood trauma is vast, and this chapter is not intended as a complete review—such a task would require a separate book. However, we will provide an overview, and wherever possible, studies represent the most recent work published in any given area. We have chosen research employing the most rigorous and sound methodology (e.g., controlled studies using well-established instruments versus uncontrolled studies with untested measures), and we have also included pioneer or seminal research, or the only research available in a particular domain. The studies presented are primarily North American, although key work from other countries, such as Australia, New Zealand, and Britain, is included. We will not report research on the short-term or initial effects seen in children who have experienced abuse, because this literature has been reviewed elsewhere (Beitchman, Zucker, Hood, daCosta, & Akman, 1991; Browne & Finkelhor, 1986; Kendall-Tackett, Williams, & Finkelhor, 1993), and this topic is outside the focus of our work, which is concerned primarily with adult clients with psychiatric diagnoses.

The chapter begins with a discussion of the prevalence rates of childhood trauma both in general (community) and in psychiatric (clinical) populations, including research that looks at prevalence within specific mental disorders. Most of the literature has concentrated on childhood sexual abuse (CSA) and to a lesser extent on childhood physical abuse (CPA), with very little attention paid to neglect or emotional abuse. The focus of this chapter will be CSA, although we do report briefly on CPA when sufficient research is available. Finally, we examine research on system issues and the attitudes of clinical staff toward clients with histories of child abuse, looking for indicators of how we might improve our service to this population.

As a special note, *emotional abuse,* also termed *psychological abuse,* has been defined as rejecting, degrading, devaluing, neglecting, or engaging in terrorizing behaviors (Briere, 1992, p. 10). Although clinicians and clients are certain, based on anecdotal evidence, that psychological abuse is harmful, currently, little empirical research has been conducted to evaluate either the prevalence or the long-term effects of this type of childhood abuse.[1]

ISSUES IN ABUSE RESEARCH

Before beginning, it is important to acknowledge that there are some limitations inherent in abuse research that affect how it is read and what conclusions are drawn. First, there are problems with defining abuse in a consistent manner. Some investigators, particularly in research reports written before 1990, use broad definitions of CSA that do not necessarily involve touching. For example, an experience of seeing genitals exposed might be listed as sexual abuse, along with violent penetration. Recent research generally employs more restrictive definitions, with investigators defining CSA specifically and as always including some form of sexual exploitation. See Finkelhor (1994) for examples of definitions. CPA is defined as occurring before the age of 17 and involves an adult who is in charge of the child purposefully hitting, punching, cutting, or pushing the child (as some examples), causing bruises, scratches, bleeding, broken bones, or broken teeth (Briere, 1992). However, even today, the precise definition of abuse may not be clearly spelled out, and the subject's age at the time of the abuse may vary, making comparisons between studies difficult.

Aside from variations among definitions, a second problem with abuse research is that most studies are based on recall. People report retrospectively, thinking back over time and relying on memory. Not only can memory be unreliable, but the current climate of debate regarding "recovered memories" means that research results may be challenged. A third problem is the capacity of research to assess accurately and clearly the impact of child abuse. The relationship between childhood trauma and subsequent mental disorder is not straightforward. In fact, there may not be a relationship that can be categorically proven. We are not sure why some people develop severe symptoms after abuse and some do not. Most studies are cross-sectional, meaning that the findings reflect a single moment in time. The bottom line is that research methodology simply does not allow us to say with absolute certainty that child abuse *causes* a specific disorder.

As a fourth point, it is important to remember that the majority of research has focused on people who have already been diagnosed with mental disorders and, in particular, with disorders of personality (e.g., borderline personality disorder [BPD]). It is here that the consequences of abuse are assumed to be most easily observed. And this makes sense. Frequently, childhood trauma occurs at an age when the personality is in the early stages of development. Internal structures that will later influence interpersonal relationships and a sense of self are in the process of being laid down. However, most people who experience abuse do not, in fact, develop BPD—so the riddle remains. Does child abuse create mental disorder? Is it one among many contributing factors? Or is it a coincidence that child abuse and BPD are often observed in the same person? No matter how we feel about it from a commonsense perspective, understanding the pathway from childhood trauma to mental disorder is a complex matter and one that has so far defied causal inferences. Nonetheless, the growing literature provides strong support for the argument that abuse is a serious social problem and that it has serious consequences.

PREVALENCE RATES: COMMUNITY SAMPLES

Researchers have undertaken a number of large-scale studies investigating child physical and sexual abuse among the general population (see Table 3.1).

TABLE 3.1 Prevalence of Childhood Abuse in Community Samples
Expressed as Percentages

| Study | Sample | *Percentage Who Experienced* | | |
		CSA	CPA	CSA and CPA
MacMillan et al., 1997	4,518 women	12.8	21.0	6.7
	5,434 men	4.3	31.2	2.4
Boudewyn & Huser Liem, 1995	314 women	9.9	—	—
Mullen et al., 1992	1,376 women	2.2	—	—
Bushnell et al., 1992	314 women	9.9	—	—
Stein et al., 1988	3,132	6.8 (women)	—	—
		3.8 (men)	—	—

NOTE: CPA = childhood physical abuse; CSA = childhood sexual abuse.

Prevalence rates for child abuse vary in women, ranging from 3.6% to 62% (Boudewyn & Huser Liem, 1995; Bushnell, Wells, & Oakley-Browne, 1992; Greenwald, Leitenberg, Cado, & Tarran, 1990; MacMillan et al., 1997; Mullen, Martin, Anderson, Romans, & Herbison, 1993; Stein, Golding, Siegel, Burnam, & Sorenson, 1988; Wyatt & Peters, 1986). A number of these studies also investigated the rate of child abuse among men and in general reported lower rates than for women, with results ranging from 3.8% to 16% (Bagley, 1989; Boudewyn & Huser Liem, 1995; Stein et al., 1988; MacMillan et al., 1997). In a multinational study, Finkelhor (1994) reviewed community prevalence research from 21 countries. He found that international prevalence rates for CSA mirror those in North America, clustering around 20% for women and 9% for men. When physical abuse is examined in community samples (both women and men), prevalence rates ranged from 10% to 20% (Gelles & Straus, 1987; Graziano & Namaste, 1990; MacMillan et al., 1997). It is probable that the variation in rates seen in these studies reflects many of the limitations of the research approach itself rather than a true difference in prevalence (Gorey & Leslie, 1997; Mullen et al., 1993; Peters, Wyatt, & Finkelhor, 1986; Wyatt & Peters, 1986). Other variations may relate to the age of the victim at the time of the assault; the age of the perpetrator; age differences between the victim and perpetrator; the sexual act (contact versus noncontact); and whether the assault was accompanied by physical violence, force, aggression, or consent (when consent is a legal possibility). Not surprisingly, when narrower definitions of abuse are employed, lower prevalence rates are reported. It has also been found that the use of activity-specific questions (e.g., "When you were a child, do you recall being touched by an adult in ways that made your uncomfortable?") relates to higher prevalence and disclosure rates than broad screening questions, such as "Have you ever been sexually or physically abused?" (Peters et al., 1986). When similar methodologies and definitions are used, similar prevalence rates are found (Finkelhor, 1994). For example, two studies conducted nearly 10 years apart reported CSA rates among women as 17.6% (Bagley, 1989) and 12.8% (MacMillan et al., 1997). However, when the definitions used were narrowed to match each other, the rates were nearly identical, 13% and 11.1%, respectively (MacMillan et al., 1997).

PREVALENCE RATES: CLINICAL POPULATIONS

In the following sections, we discuss prevalence rates first for clinical populations (people who have a psychiatric diagnosis) and then by specific disorder (rates found within a diagnostic category). It should be noted, however, that categorizing this literature under prevalence is problematic because we are unable to make causal inferences. However, the sheer quantity of literature reporting an association between abuse and subsequent disorder demonstrates that childhood trauma affects individuals in such a way as to influence symptom expression, disorder vulnerability, or both.

There have been extensive investigations of the prevalence rates of childhood abuse in psychiatric populations (see Table 3.2). As before, issues of methodological differences and unmatched definitions result in a wide variation in rates.

Sexual Abuse. For women, the rates of CSA range from 13% to 70% (Beck & van der Kolk, 1987; Briere, Woo, McRae, Foltz, & Sitzman,

TABLE 3.2 Prevalence of Child Abuse in Clinical Samples Expressed as Percentages

		Percentage Who Experienced		
Study	Sample	CSA	CPA	CSA and CPA
Briere et al., 1997	93 female OP	53	42	—
Lipschitz et al., 1996	86 female OP	55	36	—
	34 male OP	18	29	—
Palmer et al., 1992	115 female IP/OP	49.6	—	—
Surrey et al., 1990	140 female OP	12	26	25
Goff et al., 1990	61 IP	25	38	—
Jacobson & Herald, 1990	50 female IP	54	44	—
	50 male IP	26	54	—
Jacobson, 1989	26 female OP	42	35	—
	5 male OP	20	60	—
Craine et al., 1988	105 female IP	51	—	—

NOTE: CPA = childhood physical abuse; CSA = childhood sexual abuse; IP = inpatients; OP = outpatients.

1997; Briere & Zaidi, 1989; Bryer, Nelson, Miller, & Krol, 1987; Carmen, Rieker, & Mills, 1984; Craine, Henson, Colliver, & MacLean, 1988; Goff, Brotman, Kindlon, Waites, & Amico, 1991; Jacobson, 1989; Jacobson & Herald, 1990; Lipschitz et al., 1996; Lobel, 1992; Palmer, Chaloner, & Oppenheimer, 1992; Surrey, Swett, Michaels, & Levin, 1990). For men, the rates for sexual abuse are generally lower, ranging from 0% to 26% (Carmen et al., 1984; Jacobson, 1989; Jacobson & Herald, 1990; Lipschitz et al., 1996). As a general overview, all rates cluster around 42% for females and 12% for males.

Physical Abuse. CPA prevalence rates for women range from 31% to 74%, clustering around 42% (Briere et al., 1997; Bryer et al., 1987; Chu & Dill, 1990; Coons, Cole, Pellow, & Milstein, 1990; Craine et al., 1988; Jacobson, 1989; Lipschitz et al., 1996; Mancini, van Ameringen, & MacMillan, 1995; Surrey et al., 1990). For men, the rates of physical abuse range from 29% to 78%, clustering around 49% (Jacobson, 1989; Lipschitz et al., 1996; Mancini et al., 1995).

PREVALENCE RATES FOR
SPECIFIC DISORDERS

Depression. Depression is the most common symptom reported by survivors of CSA (Briere, 1992; Browne & Finkelhor, 1986). According to Herman (1992), "the disruptions in attachments in chronic abuse reinforce the isolation and withdrawal of depression. The debased self-image of chronic abuse fuels the guilty ruminations of depression, and the loss of faith suffered in chronic abuse merges with the hopelessness of depression" (p. 218). Among community samples, the relationship between depression and CSA has been explored from two different perspectives. The first approach has been to compare rates of depression between sexual abuse survivors and a control group. For example, one large community study found the risk of clinical depression among sexually abused women to be 21.9%, as compared to only a 5.5% risk for those without a CSA history (Stein et al., 1988). Other studies report depression rates of from 53% to 56% for sexually abused women (Mullen et al., 1993; Stein et al., 1988) and of 34% for sexually abused men (Stein et al., 1988). All findings were statistically significant when compared to control groups. The second method examines the rates of CSA among people with a history of depression. This route also verified a significant correlation between depression and CSA (Boudewyn & Huser Liem, 1995; Bushnell et al., 1992; Greenwald et al., 1990; Mullen et al., 1993; Stein et al., 1988). The association held even after controlling for demographic factors and other stressors, including family dysfunction, loss, divorce, illness, and physical and emotional abuse. The higher prevalence of both clinical depression and depressive symptoms among survivors has also been reported among clinical samples, with 89% of female incest victims experiencing depression versus 57% of comparison psychiatric subjects (those without a history of incest) and versus only 10% of the general population (Pribor & Dinwiddie, 1992). These findings have been supported by other work (Briere et al., 1997; Bryer et al., 1987; Mancini et al., 1995; Saxe et al., 1993; Surrey et al., 1990).

Research has also demonstrated that women are twice as likely as men to receive a diagnosis of a major affective disorder—such as depression (Kessler & McGonagle, 1994), but then, women are more likely than men to have a history of abuse. Female child abuse survivors are overrepresented in populations that come to the attention of the mental health system. They also tend to have a poor response to antidepressant therapy, introducing the possibility that their abuse histories have gone unrecognized in treatment plans.

Substance Abuse. A correlation has been established between childhood abuse and alcohol abuse in later life. Community studies have shown that survivors of CSA are more likely to have substance abuse problems, as compared with a control group (Bushnell et al., 1992; Mullen et al., 1993; Stein et al., 1988; Winfield, George, Swartz, & Blazer, 1990). Bushnell and colleagues (1992) found rates of substance abuse to be 18% among a community sample of CSA survivors, and Stein and colleagues (1988) found that 55.4% of men with a history of CSA had a lifetime prevalence rate of substance abuse disorders two times higher than that of a nonabused control group (26.7%). For women, the rate was fourfold higher in the abused sample.

Similar findings have been reported in studies of clinical populations (Briere & Runtz, 1988; Briere & Zaidi, 1989; Goff et al., 1991; Margo & McLees, 1991; Pribor & Dinwiddie, 1992; Shearer, 1994). Craine and associates (1988) found that 69% of sexually abused women also had a history of chemical dependency, versus 31% of a control group, and Briere and Zaidi (1989) found drug abuse rates of 57% among abuse survivors, versus a 27% rate for controls.

Eating Disorders. In a recent review of the literature, Wonderlich, Brewerton, Jocic, Dansky, and Abbott (1997) concluded that there is significant evidence that CSA is related to a heightened incidence of other forms of psychiatric problems among people with eating disorders. These authors suggest that there is modest support for a higher prevalence of bulimia nervosa, rather than anorexia nervosa, among those who have a history of CSA. They hypothesize that "binge eating and purging may serve to facilitate avoidance of, or escape from continued memories of the abuse, fears of recurrence, and negative attributions about the self and others after CSA" (p. 1113). Briere (1992) also suggests that bulimia is related to the avoidance of abuse-related feelings and memories and that it is a behavioral strategy used to mediate despair.

Large community studies also offer growing evidence that CSA is related to eating disorders. Several studies found a higher prevalence of eating disorders, both anorexia nervosa and bulimia nervosa, among those with histories of sexual abuse (Greenwald et al., 1990; Mullen et al., 1993). For example, Mullen and colleagues (1993) found that subjects who had been sexually abused had a three times higher chance of developing an eating disorder than did nonabused control subjects. Conversely, 12% of those with sexual abuse history also had an eating disorder. Other community studies examined bulimia nervosa, and here, too, researchers found a higher prevalence among those with CSA histories as compared to a control group (Bushnell et al., 1992). Bushnell and colleagues (1992) found that 19% of subjects with eating disorders had a history of CSA.

Overall, the prevalence of CSA among those with eating disorders ranges from 20% to 85% (Bulik, Sullivan, & Rorty, 1989; Hall, Tice, Beresford, Wooley, & Klassen, 1989; McClelland, Mynors-Wallis, Fahy, & Treasure, 1991; Oppenheimer, Howells, Palmer, & Chaloner, 1985; Palmer, Oppenheimer, Dignon, Chaloner, & Howells, 1990). Research has also demonstrated that eating disorder clients with histories of CSA are more likely to have major depression (Bulik et al., 1989; Hall et al., 1989) and personality disorders (McClelland et al., 1991). Clinical studies of female psychiatric patients have shown that women with a CSA history are 43% more likely to have a concomitant eating disorder than are those who do not have this kind of history (Lobel, 1992; Shearer, 1994).

Dissociative Identity Disorder. Dissociation refers to a compartmentalization of experience. There is "a failure to integrate various aspects of identity, memory, or consciousness" (*Diagnostic and Statistical Manual of Mental Disorders* [*DSM-IV*], American Psychiatric Association, 1994, p. 484). Elements of experience are not integrated into a unitary whole but are stored in memory as isolated fragments consisting of sensory perceptions or affective states. Theorists hypothesize that dissociation may help a child cope during the traumatic event by building a defense against overwhelming emotion (Allen, 1993; Briere, 1992). Therefore, it is not surprising that many studies have found very high rates of dissociative symptomatology in those with histories of CSA and, conversely, high rates of CSA among those diagnosed with dissociative identity disorder

(DID), formerly called multiple personality disorder. The *DSM-IV* (1994) defines DID as:

> (a) the presence of two or more distinct personalities or personality states (each with its own relatively enduring pattern of perceiving, relating to, and thinking about the environment and self); (b) at least two of these identities or personality states recurrently take control of the person's behavior; (c) inability to recall important personal information that is too extensive to be explained by ordinary forgetfulness; and (d) the disturbance is not due to the direct physiological effects of a substance (e.g., blackouts or chaotic behavior during alcohol intoxication) or a general medical condition (e.g., complex partial seizures). (p. 487)[2]

DID is considered a posttraumatic condition that results from the most serious forms of childhood abuse. Experiences of physical abuse are also common among this group of patients, with prevalence rates ranging from 74% to 87% (Ross et al., 1991; Saxe et al., 1993). When physical and sexual abuse are studied together, research reports rates of childhood trauma ranging from 75% to 90% among both female and male DID patients (Putnam, Guroff, Silberman, Barban, & Post, 1986; Ross et al., 1991; Saxe et al., 1993).

Dissociative symptomatology, as opposed to the extremes of DID, has also been documented in clinical samples of women and men with histories of child abuse (Brodsky, Cloitre, & Dulit, 1995; Goff et al., 1991). In a clinical outpatient study of both men and women, Goff and colleagues (1991) found that patients with CSA histories had higher dissociation scores than both the physically abused patients and the nonabused controls. Other research supports this finding (Brodsky et al., 1995; Chu & Dill, 1990). As might be expected, how early the abuse begins, how severe it is, and how close the relationship is between the perpetrator and the victim represent factors that are positively correlated with higher levels of dissociation in the adult survivor (Brodsky et al., 1995; Chu & Dill, 1990).

Borderline Personality Disorder. The high prevalence rates of child abuse among BPD patients is not surprising given that abuse affects personality development. The *DSM-IV* (1994) describes BPD as "a pervasive pattern of instability of self-image, interpersonal relationships, self-image, and affects, beginning in early adulthood and present in a variety of contexts"

(p. 650). Persons with a diagnosis of BPD and those with a history of abuse often share three central cognitive views: (a) they are powerless and vulnerable, (b) they are inherently bad and unacceptable to both themselves and others, and (c) others are dangerous and malignant figures (Arntz, 1994). Rates of CSA among BPD patients cluster around 71% for women, ranging from 45% to 86% (Brodsky et al., 1995; Bryer et al., 1987; Nigg et al., 1991; Paris, Zweig-Frank, & Guzder, 1994; Shearer, 1994; Silk, Lee, Hill, & Lohr, 1995; Weaver & Clum, 1993; Zanarini et al., 1997). In a study in which CSA was reported separately for BPD men, the prevalence rate was 41.7% (Silk et al., 1995).

Some studies have explored the higher rates of child abuse among BPD patients in comparison with patients with other psychiatric diagnoses, including other forms of personality disorder. These authors report significantly higher rates of CSA among BPD patients than among comparison groups (on average 40% higher), as well as 20% higher rates of CPA (Herman, Perry, & van der Kolk, 1989; Nigg et al., 1991; Paris et al., 1994; Weaver & Clum, 1993).

Given these findings, it is not surprising that a substantial amount of research has been devoted to investigating the relationship between childhood trauma and BPD. Herman and colleagues (1989) compared BPD subjects to a clinical control group and found that the BPD clients experienced more types of abuse, which occurred earlier in childhood and lasted longer than abuse experienced by controls. More recent studies have documented the same findings (Paris et al., 1994; Silk et al., 1995; Weaver & Clum, 1993). Weaver and Clum (1993) also found that this relationship held even after separating out such factors as physical abuse, depression scores, family environment, and diagnostic differences.

These results have led a number of researchers and clinicians to suggest that the symptoms and behaviors that borderline clients exhibit result from reactions to experiences of abuse early in life (Briere, 1992). However, we offer a cautionary note. These findings, as suggestive as they are, must be viewed in context—only a small percentage of people with a history of child abuse develop mental disorders, and of these, only a few develop BPD.

In an attempt to shed light on this puzzle, Paris et al. (1994) specifically examined the role of risk factors such as childhood trauma in borderline patients. These investigators found that CSA marginally discriminated between the BPD and the non-BPD groups. An additional finding that emerged was that the BPD group was more likely to experience multiple perpetrators and abuse involving penetration, suggesting that these specific factors may increase the risk for BPD.

Posttraumatic Stress Disorder. Posttraumatic stress is defined as the after-the-fact reactions that occur when people live through terrifying events, such as rape, robbery, hostage taking, war, and natural disasters. Briere (1992) describes posttraumatic stress disorder (PTSD) as "certain enduring psychological symptoms that reliably occur in reaction to a highly distressing, psychically disruptive event" (p. 20). Individuals with PTSD experience intrusive, recurrent symptoms such as flashbacks; nightmares; hallucinations; disturbing images, thoughts, or perceptions; irritability; and detachment (*DSM-IV,* 1994).

This diagnosis was developed to describe obvious clinical disorders that developed in persons who had no history of psychiatric problems prior to the traumatizing event or events, but it is now acknowledged that the diagnosis may not be adequate for those who experience trauma at a young age. Nonetheless, PTSD gave researchers and clinicians a starting point, and in the last two decades, they have explored the prevalence and the association of PTSD with child abuse. For example, one study of female state hospital inpatients found that 66% of those with CSA histories also met the diagnostic criteria for PTSD, although none had actually received this diagnosis (Craine et al., 1988). Similar rates were reported by Rowan, Foy, Rodriguez, and Ryan (1994), and Pribor and Dinwiddie (1992) found a prevalence rate of 50% for PTSD among incest survivors over their lifetimes versus an 8.7% rate in a clinical comparison group.

In the next chapter, we will discuss a new diagnosis, complex PTSD, suggested by Judith Herman (1992) and designed to cover the bewildering array of behaviors and symptoms expressed by survivors of childhood trauma.

MENTAL HEALTH PROFESSIONALS' RESPONSE TO CHILDHOOD TRAUMA

Survivors who enter the mental health system typically have a complex presentation composed of a broad constellation of symptoms and behaviors. Without the benefit of a new diagnosis (e.g., complex PTSD, as discussed in Chapter 4), mental health professionals have had trouble finding a relevant diagnostic category. As a consequence, survivors have often acquired multiple diagnoses that may include schizophrenia, bipolar affective disorder, schizoaffective disorder, depression, BPD, and DID. It is also not uncommon for one person to have received two or more quite oppositional diagnoses (such as schizophrenia and bipolar affective disorder). They may also be on a "cocktail" of medications, indicating clinicians' dedicated efforts to find something, anything, that brings some measure of relief. In addition, survivors typically have a history of multiple admissions to psychiatric hospitals, complicating physical problems, and a chaotic set of involvements with a host of social services.

It has been suggested that these clients have the most severe clinical problems (Read, 1998), and there is evidence to support this claim. For example, an extensively tested self-report scale designed to measure nine symptom categories was employed to assess patients with histories of childhood trauma. These patients scored significantly higher on the global severity index than did nonabused comparison patients (Bryer et al., 1987; Margo & McLees, 1991; Surrey et al., 1990). Other measures of illness severity also yielded higher scores when abused patients were compared to nonabused subjects, and these results held true in both clinical and community samples. Women with histories of CSA were admitted more often and stayed longer in psychiatric hospitals (Carmen et al., 1984; Read, 1998; Shearer, Peters, Quaytman, & Ogden, 1990). Also, their symptoms appeared at an earlier age (Goff et al., 1991), and they were first hospitalized at an earlier age (Margo & McLees, 1991). In addition, survivors of child abuse were more likely to receive psychotropic medication (Briere & Runtz, 1988; Bryer et al., 1987) and had, on average, more lifetime psychiatric diagnoses than did control subjects (Pribor & Dinwiddie, 1992; Saxe et al., 1993). Greater severity of illness has also been documented in general population studies that found that women survivors of CSA were more likely than control subjects to have received some form of psychiatric treatment (22% vs. 10%), with the incidence of inpatient treatment being between 5 and 16 times higher among the abused subjects (Mullen et al., 1993). In another community study including both men and women, 63.6% of those with a history of CSA had received a psychiatric diagnosis at some point during their lifetime, as opposed to only 29% of the nonabused comparison group (Stein et al., 1988).

Despite increasing awareness of the severe consequences of childhood trauma, clients with abuse histories present an enormous challenge for mental health professionals, particularly in institutional and hospital settings. There is great danger in these more restrictive environments of reinforcing the powerlessness and silencing that many survivors of child abuse have experienced. However, in contrast to earlier work (Cochrane, 1987; Damrosch, Gallo, Kulak, & Whitaker, 1987), recent studies of nurses' attitudes have found that they reject a victim-blaming perspective (Boutcher & Gallop, 1996; Kelly, 1990). In a much larger survey (N = 2,500), these results were confirmed (Gallop, McCay, Austin, Bayer, & Peternelj-Taylor, 1998a, 1998b). These authors found that nurses were sensitive to the concerns of survivors of child abuse and had nonjudgmental attitudes; however, the nurses did not feel that they had the knowledge and skills to intervene appropriately. Despite this shift in attitude, the limited literature that has examined clients' experiences suggests that survivors themselves still experience hospitalization as disempowering (Doob, 1992; Firsten, 1991; Urbancic, 1992). For example, in recent work (Gallop, McCay, Guha, & Khan, 1999), women with histories of abuse who had been physically restrained during psychiatric hospitalization were interviewed. *All* women reported that they felt unheard and powerless and that they had reexperienced the feelings associated with the original trauma during the restraint episode.

The idea that psychiatric hospitalization can be revictimizing is not new. As early as 1984, Carmen and colleagues found that, while in the hospital, abuse victims, in particular women, were more likely to cope with angry feelings by engaging in self-harming behaviors. Authors such as Fromuth and Burkhart (1992) question whether there can be a benign psychiatric hospitalization for survivors, arguing that, like the original abuse, psychiatric hospitalization carries with it themes of stigmatization, betrayal, and powerlessness. Cohen (1994) employed Herman's (1992) model of captivity, in which fear is produced by unpredictable violence and the capricious application of rules. These authors argue that psychiatric hospitalization, with its locked units, isolation from familiar people, use of restraint, and indigenous violence, can produce a form of captivity trauma. In a moving article, Jennings (1994) used the 17 years' worth of mental health records of her sexually abused daughter to document the mental health system's failure. Not only was the abuse ignored during hospitalization, but according to Jennings, many of the common practices that occurred led to a form of institutional retraumatization of her daughter.

Harris (1994) states that hospitalization for victims of childhood trauma must be carefully planned, voluntary when possible, and under the control of the client. She also suggests that alternatives should be explored and efforts made to reframe the hospital as a place of safety. Gallop, Engels, DiNunzio, and Napravnik (1999) interviewed female inpatients with histories of CSA to learn how these women would change clinical environments so they would feel safer, more in control, and empowered. Their suggestions provide guidelines for clinicians. However, insofar as new information and improved attitudes are not translated into practice, there remains a considerable distance to go before mental health professionals can acquire the capacities to deal more effectively with abuse survivors.

CONCLUSION

The substantive literature reported in this chapter provides ample evidence that a history of childhood trauma can have significant implications for provision of support and care. Clients with these backgrounds deserve effective and meaningful help when they come into contact with the mental health system. Professionals must understand both the prevalence of child abuse and its potential impact. Although abuse is not a necessary or sufficient explanation for the incidence of psychiatric disorders, for those clients with this experience, the aftermath is long-term and devastating. What we do know is that childhood trauma may precipitate some disorders and exacerbate others. For the mental health system not to acknowledge and use this information in treatment and care plans is yet another form of abuse. In the next chapter, we take an in-depth look at the major consequences associated with a history of childhood trauma among psychiatric clients.

NOTES

1. Ali and colleagues (2000) found that a history of emotional abuse in women was significantly associated with a diagnosis of irritable bowel disease.

2. Reprinted with permission from *Diagnostic and Statistical Manual of Mental Disorders*, Fourth Edition, Copyright © 1994 American Psychiatric Association.

REFERENCES

Ali, A., Toner, B. B., Stuckless, N., Gallop, R., Diamant, N. E., Gould, M. I., & Vidins, E. I. (2000). Emotional abuse, self-blame and self-silencing in women with irritable bowel syndrome. *Psychosomatic Medicine, 62*(1), 76-82.

Allen, J. G. (1993). Dissociative processes: Theoretical underpinnings of a working model for clinician and patient. *Bulletin of the Menninger Clinic, 57,* 287-308.

American Psychiatric Association. (1994). *Diagnostic and statistical manual of mental disorders* (4th ed.). Washington, DC: Author.

Arntz, A. (1994). Treatment of borderline personality disorder: A challenge for cognitive-behavioural therapy. *Behavioural Research and Therapy, 32,* 419-430.

Bagley, C. (1989). Prevalence and correlates of unwanted sexual acts in childhood in a national Canadian sample. *Canadian Journal of Public Health, 80,* 295-296.

Beck, J. C., & van der Kolk, B. (1987). Reports of childhood incest and current behaviour of chronically hospitalized psychotic women. *American Journal of Psychiatry, 144,* 1474-1476.

Beitchman, J. H., Zucker, K. J., Hood, J. E., daCosta, G. A., & Akman, D. (1991). A review of the short-term effects of childhood sexual abuse. *Child Abuse & Neglect, 15,* 537-556.

Boudewyn, A. C., & Huser Liem, J. H. (1995). Childhood sexual abuse as a precursor to depression and self-destructive behavior in adulthood. *Journal of Traumatic Stress, 8,* 445-459.

Boutcher, F., & Gallop, R. (1996). Psychiatric nurses' attitudes towards sexuality, sexual assault/rape and incest. *Archives of Psychiatric Nursing, 10,* 184-191.

Briere, J. N. (1992). *Child abuse trauma: Theory and treatment of the lasting effects.* Newbury Park, CA: Sage.

Briere, J., & Runtz, M. (1988). Symptomatology associated with childhood sexual victimization in a nonclinical sample. *Child Abuse and Neglect, 12,* 51-59.

Briere, J., Woo, R., McRae, B., Foltz, J., & Sitzman, R. (1997). Lifetime victimization history, demographics, and clinical status in female psychiatric emergency room patients. *Journal of Nervous and Mental Disease, 185,* 95-101.

Briere, J., & Zaidi, L. Y. (1989). Sexual abuse histories and sequelae in female psychiatric emergency room patients. *American Journal of Psychiatry, 146,* 1602-1606.

Brodsky, B. S., Cloitre, M., & Dulit, R. A. (1995). Relationship of dissociation to self-mutilation and childhood abuse in borderline personality disorder. *American Journal of Psychiatry, 152,* 1788-1792.

Browne, A., & Finkelhor, D. (1986). Impact of child sexual abuse: A review of the research. *Psychological Bulletin, 99,* 66-77.

Bryer, J. B., Nelson, B. A., Miller, J. B., & Krol, P. A. (1987). Childhood sexual and physical abuse as factors in adult psychiatric illness. *American Journal of Psychiatry, 144,* 1426-1430.

Bulik, C. M., Sullivan, P. F., & Rorty, M. (1989). Childhood sexual abuse in women with bulimia. *Journal of Clinical Psychiatry, 50,* 460-464.

Bushnell, J. A., Wells, J. E., & Oakley-Browne, M. A. (1992). Long-term effects of intrafamilial sexual abuse in childhood. *Acta Psychiatrica Scandinavica, 85,* 136-142.

Carmen, E., Rieker, P. P., & Mills, T. (1984). Victims of violence and psychiatric illness. *American Journal of Psychiatry, 141,* 378-383.

Chu, J. A., & Dill, D. L. (1990). Dissociative symptoms in relation to childhood physical and sexual abuse. *American Journal of Psychiatry, 147,* 887-892.

Cochrane, D. (1987). Emergency nurses' attitudes towards the rape victim. *American Association of Registered Nurses Newsletter, 43*(7), 14-18.

Cohen, L. (1994). Psychiatric hospitalization as an experience of trauma. *Archives of Psychiatric Nursing, 8,* 78-81.

Coons, P. M., Cole, C., Pellow, T. A., & Milstein, V. (1990). Symptoms of posttraumatic stress and dissociation in women victims of abuse. In R. P. Kluft (Ed.), *Incest related syndromes of adult psychopathology* (pp. 205-226). Washington, DC: American Psychiatric Press.

Craine, L. S., Henson, C. E., Colliver, J. A., & MacLean, D. G. (1988). Prevalence of a history of sexual abuse among female psychiatric patients in a state hospital system. *Hospital and Community Psychiatry, 39,* 300-304.

Damrosch, S., Gallo, B., Kulak, D., & Whitaker, C. (1987). Nurses' attributions about rape victims. *Research in Nursing and Health, 10,* 245-251.

Doob, D. (1992). Female sexual abuse survivors as patients: Avoiding retraumatization. *Archives of Psychiatric Nursing, 6,* 245-251.

Finkelhor, D. (1994). The international epidemiology of child sexual abuse. *Child Abuse & Neglect, 18,* 409-417.

Firsten, T. (1991). Violence in the lives of women on psych wards. *Canadian Woman Studies, 11,* 45-48.

Fromuth, M. E., & Burkhart, B. R. (1992). Recovery or recapitulation? An analysis of the impact of psychiatric hospitalization on the child sexual abuse survivor. *Women & Therapy, 12*(3), 81-95.

Gallop, R., Engels, S., DiNunzio, R., & Napravnik, S. (1999). Abused women's concerns about safety and the therapeutic environment during psychiatric hospitalization. *Canadian Journal of Nursing Research, 31*(2), 53-70.

Gallop, R., McCay, E., Austin, W., Bayer, M., & Peternelj-Taylor, C. (1998a). Caring for the sexually abused client. *Canadian Nurse, 94*(7), 30-34.

Gallop, R., McCay, E., Austin, W., Bayer, M., & Peternelj-Taylor, C. (1998b). A survey of psychiatric nurses working with psychiatric clients who have a history of childhood sexual abuse. *Journal of the American Psychiatric Nursing Association, 4,* 9-17.

Gallop, R., McCay, E., Guha, M., & Khan, P. (1999). The experience of hospitalization and restraint for women with a history of childhood sexual abuse. *Health Care for Women International, 20,* 401-416.

Gelles, R., & Straus, M. (1987). Is violence toward children increasing? A comparison of 1975 and 1985 national survey rates. *Journal of Interpersonal Violence, 2,* 212-222.

Goff, D. C., Brotman, A. W., Kindlon, D., Waites, M., & Amico, E. (1991). Self-reports of childhood abuse in chronically psychotic patients. *Psychiatry Research, 37,* 73-80.

Gorey, K. M., & Leslie, D. R. (1997). The prevalence of child sexual abuse: Integrative review adjustment for potential response and measurement biases. *Child Abuse & Neglect, 21,* 391-398.

Graziano, A., & Namaste, K. (1990). Parental use of physical force in child discipline: A survey of 679 college students. *Journal of Interpersonal Violence, 5,* 449-463.

Greenwald, E., Leitenberg, H., Cado, S., & Tarran, M. J. (1990). Childhood sexual abuse: Long-term effects on psychological and sexual functioning in a nonclinical and nonstudent sample of adult women. *Child Abuse & Neglect, 14,* 503-513.

Hall, R. C. W., Tice, L., Beresford, T. P., Wooley, B., & Klassen, A. H. (1989). Sexual abuse in patients with anorexia nervosa and bulimia. *Psychosomatics, 30*(1), 73-79.

Harris, M. (1994). Modifications in service delivery and clinical treatment for women diagnosed with severe mental illness who are also the survivors of sexual abuse trauma. *Journal of Mental Health Administration, 21,* 397-406.

Herman, J. (1992). *Trauma and recovery.* New York: Basic Books.

Herman, J. L., Perry, J. C., & van der Kolk, B. A. (1989). Childhood trauma in borderline personality disorder. *American Journal of Psychiatry, 146,* 490-495.

Jacobson, A. (1989). Physical and sexual assault histories among psychiatric outpatients. *American Journal of Psychiatry, 146,* 755-758.

Jacobson, A., & Herald, C. (1990). The relevance of childhood sexual abuse to adult psychiatric inpatient care. *Hospital and Community Psychiatry, 41,* 154-158.

Jennings, A. (1994). On being invisible in the mental health system. *Journal of Mental Health Administration, 21,* 374-387.

Kelly, S. (1990). Responsibility and management strategies in child protection workers, nurses and police officers. *Child Welfare, 69,* 43-51.

Kendall-Tackett, K. A., Williams, L. M., & Finkelhor, D. (1993). Impact of sexual abuse on children: A review and synthesis of recent empirical studies. *Psychological Bulletin, 113,* 164-180.

Kessler, R. C., & McGonagle, K. (1994). Lifetime and 12-month prevalence of DSM-III-R psychiatric disorders in the United States. *Archives of General Psychiatry, 51,* 8-19.

Lipschitz, D. S., Kaplan, M. L., Sorkenn, J. B., Faedda, G. L., Chorney, P., & Asnis, G. M. (1996). Prevalence and characteristics of physical and sexual abuse among psychiatric outpatients. *Psychiatric Services, 47,* 189-191.

Lobel, C. M. (1992). Relationship between childhood sexual abuse and borderline personality disorder in women psychiatric inpatients. *Journal of Child Sexual Abuse, 1*(1), 63-80.

MacMillan, H. L., Fleming, J. E., Trocme, N., Boyle, M. H., Wong, M., Racine, Y. A., Beardslee, W. R., & Offord, D. R. (1997). Prevalence of child physical and sexual abuse in the community: Results from the Ontario Health Supplement. *Journal of the American Medical Association, 278,* 131-135.

Mancini, C., van Ameringen, M., & MacMillan, H. (1995). Relationship of childhood sexual and physical abuse to anxiety disorders. *Journal of Nervous and Mental Disease, 183,* 309-314.

Margo, G., & McLees, E. (1991). Further evidence for the significance of a childhood abuse history in psychiatric inpatients. *Comprehensive Psychiatry, 32,* 362-366.

McClelland, L., Mynors-Wallis, L., Fahy, T., & Treasure, J. (1991). Sexual abuse, disordered personality and eating disorders. *British Journal of Psychiatry, 158*(Suppl. 10), 63-68.

Mullen, P. E., Martin, J. L., Anderson, J. C., Romans, S. E., & Herbison, G. P. (1993). Childhood sexual abuse and mental health in adult life. *British Journal of Psychiatry, 163,* 721-732.

Nigg, J. T., Silk, K. R., Westen, D., Lohr, N. E., Gold, L. J., Goodrich, S., & Ogata, S. (1991). Object representations in the early memories of sexually abused borderline patients. *American Journal of Psychiatry, 148,* 864-869.

Oppenheimer, R., Howells, K., Palmer, R. L., & Chaloner, D. A. (1985). Adverse sexual experience in childhood and clinical eating disorders: A preliminary description. *Journal of Psychiatric Research, 19,* 357-361.

Palmer, R. L., Chaloner, D. A., & Oppenheimer, R. (1992). Childhood sexual experiences with adults reported by female psychiatric patients. *British Journal of Psychiatry, 160,* 261-265.

Palmer, R. L., Oppenheimer, R., Dignon, A., Chaloner, D. A., & Howells, K. (1990). Childhood sexual experiences with adults reported by women with eating disorders: An extended series. *British Journal of Psychiatry, 156,* 699-703.

Paris, J., Zweig-Frank, H., & Guzder, J. (1994). Psychological risk factors for borderline personality disorder in female patients. *Comprehensive Psychiatry, 35,* 301-305.

Peters, S. D., Wyatt, G. E., & Finkelhor, D. (1986). Prevalence. In D. Finkelhor (Ed.), *Sourcebook on child sexual abuse* (pp. 15-59). Beverly Hills, CA: Sage.

Pribor, E. F., & Dinwiddie, S. H. (1992). Psychiatric correlates of incest in childhood. *American Journal of Psychiatry, 149,* 52-56.

Putnam, F., Guroff, J., Silberman, E., Barban, L., & Post, R. (1986). The clinical phenomenology of multiple personality disorder: A review of 100 recent cases. *Journal of Clinical Psychiatry, 47,* 285-293.

Read, J. (1998). Child abuse and severity of disturbance among adult psychiatric inpatients. *Child Abuse & Neglect, 22,* 359-368.

Ross, C. A., Miller, S. D., Bjornson, L., Reagor, P., Fraser, G. A., & Anderson, G. (1991). Abuse histories in 102 cases of multiple personality disorder. *Canadian Journal of Psychiatry, 36,* 97-101.

Rowan, A. B., Foy, D. W., Rodriguez, N., & Ryan, S. (1994). Posttraumatic stress disorder in a clinical sample of adults sexually abused as children. *Child Abuse & Neglect, 18,* 51-61.

Saxe, G. N., van der Kolk, B. A., Berkowitz, R., Chinman, G., Hall, K., Lieberg, G., & Schwartz, J. (1993). Dissociative disorders in psychiatric inpatients. *American Journal of Psychiatry, 150,* 1037-1042.

Shearer, S. L. (1994). Dissociative phenomena in women with borderline personality disorder. *American Journal of Psychiatry, 151,* 1324-1328.

Shearer, S., Peters, C., Quaytman, M., & Ogden, R. (1990). Frequency and correlates of childhood physical and sexual abuse in adult patients with borderline personality disorder. *American Journal of Psychiatry, 147,* 1008-1013.

Silk, K. R., Lee, S., Hill, E. M., & Lohr, N. E. (1995). Borderline personality disorder symptoms and severity of sexual abuse. *American Journal of Psychiatry, 152,* 1059-1064.

Stein, J. A., Golding, J. M., Siegel, J. M., Burnam, M. A., & Sorenson, S. B. (1988). Long-term psychological sequelae of child sexual abuse: The Los Angeles epidemiologic catchment area study. In G. E. Wyatt & G. J. Powell (Eds.), *Lasting effects of child sexual abuse* (pp. 135-154). Newbury Park, CA: Sage.

Surrey, J., Swett, C., Jr., Michaels, A., & Levin, S. (1990). Reported history of physical and sexual abuse and severity of symptomatology in women psychiatric outpatients. *American Journal of Orthopsychiatry, 60,* 412-417.

Urbancic, J. (1992). Empowerment support with adult female survivors of childhood incest. *Archives of Psychiatric Nursing, 6,* 282-286.

Weaver, T. L., & Clum, G. A. (1993). Early family environments and traumatic experiences associated with borderline personality disorder. *Journal of Consulting and Clinical Psychology, 61,* 1068-1075.

Winfield, I., George, L. K., Swartz, M., & Blazer, D. G. (1990). Sexual assault and psychiatric disorders among a community sample of women. *American Journal of Psychiatry, 147*, 335-341.

Wonderlich, S., Brewerton, T., Jocic, Z., Dansky, B., & Abbott, D. (1997). Relationship of childhood sexual abuse and eating disorders. *Journal of the American Academy of Child and Adolescent Psychiatry, 36*, 1107-1115.

Wyatt, G. E., & Peters, S. D. (1986). Issues in the definition of child sexual abuse in prevalence research. *Child Abuse & Neglect, 10*, 231-240.

Zanarini, M. C., Williams, A. A., Lewis, R. E., Reich, R. B., Vera, S. C., Marino, M. F., Levin, A., Yong, L., & Frankenburg, F. R. (1997). Reported pathological childhood experiences associated with the development of borderline personality disorder. *American Journal of Psychiatry, 154*, 1101-1106.

CHAPTER 4

Recognizing
the Signs and
Symptoms

Over the years, psychiatry has been vigorously criticized for its neglect of the whole social being of
the patient (e.g., Breggin, 1991; Chesler, 1972; Penfold & Walker, 1983).
A diagnosis of mental illness can stand in isolation from its social context,
which means, in practical terms, that clients' past lives become separated
from their present realities. The fact that they have a history of childhood
trauma is considered a tragic but separate event that is unrelated to the
symptoms of a mental disorder. The multidimensional model, presented
in Chapter 2, reconnects these two events, not necessarily in a causal
manner, but certainly in a relationship in which one reality is understood
as having an impact on the other. The synthesis of these two facts (diagnosis and social context) is central to the provision of real, meaningful
help.

In order to respond effectively to clients' experiences of child abuse,
mental health professionals need to understand the significance of what
clients tell us about their backgrounds as they "speak" to us in a variety

of creative, and often disguised, ways. This does not imply that we should "push" our hypotheses on clients (to do so is unethical), just that we must incorporate into our practice skills the ability to see and to hear the signs and symptoms of a traumatic background.

In this chapter, we describe the observable indicators of a history of child abuse. First, we will discuss a proposed new diagnosis, complex posttraumatic stress disorder (complex PTSD). This diagnosis is designed to capture the full picture of an abuse history. Next, we discuss specific behavioral difficulties that create tremendous challenges for survivors and mental health professionals alike: self-harm, suicide, dissociation, and revictimization. Then, we look at physical, emotional, and relational indicators. These three life areas, although overlapping and interrelated, demonstrate the extent of the impact of abuse both to clients themselves and to the mental health professionals who are their helpers.

COMPLEX POSTTRAUMATIC STRESS DISORDER

Judith Herman (1992) and others are proposing a new diagnosis that would capture the many complicated behaviors and symptoms that are unique to clients who have experienced trauma early in life. Although the experiences of war veterans; rape, robbery, and assault victims; natural disaster survivors; and others are related to those of survivors of childhood trauma, the defining factors that separate one diagnosis from another are the age at which the abuse begins, how long it continues, the levels of violence and sadism involved, and finally, whether or not the perpetrator is in a close interpersonal relationship with the child. The diagnosis of complex PTSD is intended to capture the extremes of suffering that occur in adults who have experienced the severest forms of child abuse. Unlike adults, children don't have the protection of mature cognitive capacities to sustain them. Trauma interrupts their development, so they are further handicapped by virtue of the fact that they have missed vital steps on the way to adulthood. There are alterations in the perception of the self and in interpersonal functioning that are not found in classic PTSD. Vulnerability to repeated harm through both self-injury and suicide attempts, as well as at the hands of others, is also not a standard feature of PTSD. Problems with self-regulation (of behavior and emotion); self-definition (guilt, shame, a sense of being evil); and alterations in interpersonal functioning (revictimization, excessive or no sexual activity, serial unhappy relationships) are not well characterized by PTSD (Roth, Newman, Pelcovitz, van der Kolk, & Mandel, 1997).

Complex PTSD is not intended to replace PTSD as a diagnosis; rather, the two are intended to work together (Herman, 1992). Van der Kolk and colleagues (Roth et al., 1997) categorize survivors' symptoms into seven specific categories: (a) alterations in affect regulation (people enter into extreme states of emotion and have no ability to calm themselves); (b) alterations in consciousness (flashbacks, inability to remember, spacing out [dissociating] under stress, emotional numbing); (c) alterations in self-perception (self-blame, guilt, self-hatred, a sense of being nonhuman or apart from the world); (d) alterations in perception of the perpetrator (idealized, all powerful); (e) alterations in relationships with others (isolation, distrust, search for a rescuer); (f) alterations in biological functioning (easy to startle, chronic hyperarousal, hypervigilance, diffuse physical complaints); and (g) alterations in systems of meaning (no sense of future, hopelessness, a sense that life has no purpose). Van der Kolk (undated) argues that the symptoms that cause clients to report a myriad of physical ailments, some of which are medically questionable, are called "somatization disorder" (under the nomenclature of *Diagnostic and Statistical Manual of Mental Disorders,* American Psychiatric Association, 1994). The symptoms that affect people's consciousness are included under the diagnosis of dissociative disorders. Intrusive memories and flashbacks signal PTSD, and those attributes that affect personality and relationships are diagnosed as borderline personality disorder (BPD). When these trauma-related symptoms are separated under different diagnostic schemes, the whole picture is lost. If they are catalogued under one disorder or diagnosis, then the true reality and extent of the effects of child abuse are revealed.

In initial field trials for complex PTSD, it was found that histories of either physical or sexual abuse among women and men survivors are risk factors for the later development of complex PTSD, with those experiencing both sexual and physical abuse being at greatest risk (Roth et al., 1997). PTSD and complex PTSD have also been documented to occur together in individuals with histories of child abuse, and it remains unclear whether complex PTSD is a distinct subtype of PTSD or whether it describes a more severe form of PTSD. Nevertheless, the research supports at least a theoretical understanding of the aftereffects of childhood trauma as conceptualized under this new diagnostic category (Roth et al., 1997).

The introduction of a new diagnosis has implications that go beyond the broadening of academic and clinical knowledge and become, in many senses, political. For example, clients diagnosed with BPD are viewed so negatively by many professional staff that they often receive inadequate or inappropriate treatment and care (Gallop, 1992)—but most of these patients would meet the criteria for complex PTSD. Given the highly negative and pejorative connotations that have become attached to BPD, it is worth seriously considering whether any client with a history of child abuse should receive this diagnosis at all. It seems to make much more sense to begin to use complex PTSD—a diagnosis that more thoroughly captures clients' subjective experience of suffering while at the same time communicating clearly to the mental health professionals who are charged with the responsibility of helping them.

FOUR DEFINING SIGNS

Self-harm, suicide, dissociation, and revictimization are critical areas of observable impact that we need to understand, both from the perspective of their origins in the survivor's past and from the many present-day purposes they serve.

Self-harm. This most troubling behavior is alternatively called "self-injury" or "self-mutilation" (Faye, 1995; Feldman, 1988). Connors (1996) speaks of a continuum of self-harm ranging from chosen body alterations, such as piercing, tattoos, and cosmetic surgery; to indirect self-harm, such as substance abuse, failure to care for one's self (excessive risk taking, accident-proneness, unsafe sex); and finally, to intentional self-injury. The most extreme forms of self-injury are defined as purposeful actions that harm the body and that are outside of the bounds of social acceptability. They may take many forms, including cutting, burning, abrading, or hitting oneself; inserting sharp objects in the anus or vagina; pulling out body hair; or other self-attacking behaviors idiosyncratic to the survivor and his or her abuse history. However, cutting has been found to be the commonest form of self-harm (Arnold, 1995).

Research shows that rates of self-harm among clinical samples of patients with histories of childhood sexual abuse are at least twice that of nonabused comparison groups.[1] These higher rates have also been documented in a community study of male and female college students, and in this case, the researchers eliminated other factors, such as other forms of child abuse and adulthood stressors such as adult physical and sexual assault (Boudewyn & Huser Liem, 1995). Acts of self-harm were reported by 33% of the women and 18% of the men with histories of sexual abuse versus 9% and 7%, respectively, of nonabused participants (Boudewyn & Huser Liem, 1995). Similarly, when women known to self-harm were interviewed, 49% reported a history of child sexual abuse, and 25% had been physically abused (Arnold, 1995).

Although self-injury is often confused with suicide attempts or suicidal gesturing, survivors cognitively distinguish these activities from attempts to kill themselves and may in fact self-injure in order to avoid suicide (Arnold, 1995; Connors, 1996; Himber, 1994; van der Kolk, Perry, & Herman, 1991). Mental health professionals can misunderstand these behaviors, interpreting them as forms of attention seeking and viewing clients as "manipulative" or "bad." It is therefore especially important that we understand the purpose of self-injurious behavior from the perspective of the survivor in order to respond effectively.

Connors (1996) believes that self-injury serves four primary functions: (a) as a reenactment of trauma; (b) as an expression of feelings that are directed either against the self (such as guilt, shame, rage) or intended to fulfill a need for comfort and containment; (c) as a way to regain homeostasis, both emotional and physiological, when self-soothing or a sense of control are impaired; and finally, (d) for the management and maintenance of dissociative processes. In addition, Alexander (1997) found that self-injury was significantly associated with attempts to communicate with or to influence others, with the regulation of emotion, and with the creation of a sense of safety.

In other work, Miller (1994) noted that a few survivors who self-harm are craving arousal. Growing up in an abusive situation is chaotic. Peace, paradoxically, can leave the body longing for an adrenaline rush, with self-harm supplying not only a needed dose of terror but adding other benefits, such as reintroducing chaos into the survivor's environment followed by the attention of medical personnel. In a qualitative study that focused in depth on survivors' own views, Himber (1994) found that cutting served to communicate inner, otherwise invisible, pain.[2] Most survivors, however, reported that the sight of blood was central to the experience. Blood is a powerful life and death symbol, sometimes evoking fear but, in this case, signifying purification or a talisman of protection. The women in this study also reported an analgesic effect during the cutting process, describing themselves merely as observers who dispassionately watched the blood emerge. In these ways, self-harm can take on a life of its own, satisfying a complex set of needs with one swift slash of a razor blade.

Himber's (1994) subjects were clear that cutting was not a dangerous activity, with the exception that some felt the possibility that they might accidentally do more harm than they had intended. Shame was a common hallmark of the aftermath of self-harm, and subjects described themselves as freaks, feeling that they has lost control and committed a bizarre act that others found repulsive.

Time-honored tactics such as no-cutting contracts, the stock-in-trade of some mental health professionals, are experienced by survivors as punitive, because they miss the central point of self-harm—it is a valued (if not preferred) coping mechanism (Arnold, 1995; Himber, 1994). It has become a "best friend" (Miller, 1994, p. 68): dependable, familiar, and unconditionally available when needed. Attempts to forcibly separate survivors from their "friend" only result in retrenchment. Slowly, within the confines of physical, emotional, and relational safety, survivors can experience the benefits of less shaming coping mechanisms, replacing the old behaviors with healthier ones.

Suicide. Although self-harming behaviors are not suicide attempts, people who self-harm can and do commit suicide. In fact, survivors of abuse are more likely to attempt suicide or to present as current suicide risks than comparison groups are (Read, 1998; Stone, 1990). In the midst of both internal and external chaos, survivors may hold dear what is called the "cherished out" (Summit, as quoted in Courtois, 1988, p. 306). If all tactics to gain some measure of control fail, survivors know that there is one sure way they can stop the pain: They can die. Suicidal thoughts become a kind of comforting mantra that some survivors verbalize while others do not. What we observe, however, are clients who use threats of suicide as common interactional currency, punctuating their demands for service, pleas for rescue, fears of abandonment, and other emotionally charged exchanges with the ubiquitous cry, "I'm going to kill myself." Without understanding the cognitive distortions and emotional pain that accompany these messages, professionals can become frustrated and retaliatory. On a more dangerous note, some may begin responding in an offhand manner or ignoring survivors' suicide threats altogether.

It is *essential* that we take clients' statements about suicide seriously. Many survivors may be chronically suicidal but may fluctuate between periods of relative calm and active intent to take their own lives. We also need to understand the link between a history of abuse and suicide risk. In a study of a community sample, sexually abused women were from 20 to 70 times more likely to have attempted suicide, depending on the severity of the abuse. The highest rate of attempts was reported among women who were survivors of sexual abuse that involved penetration (Mullen, Martin, Anderson, Romans, & Herbison, 1994). Van der Kolk and colleagues (1991) found that a history of sexual and physical abuse was strongly related to both self-injurious acts and suicide attempts. Read (1998) found that men and women inpatients who had experienced both sexual and physical abuse were more likely both to have a history of suicide attempts and to be currently at risk. Stone (1990) conducted a longitudinal study of 206 clients diagnosed with BPD. Nineteen clients had committed suicide, of whom eight had histories of incest.

It is difficult working with clients who are at constant risk for suicide. We are required to protect them whenever we can, but this protection, if it is not carefully negotiated, can mean that survivors feel that they have lost control or are trapped in a power struggle. We need to know how to assess for imminent risk and how to tolerate open discussions of suicidal ideation and intention so that clients can feel in control of their destiny as much as possible (see Chapter 12 for a full discussion on assessing suicide risk).

Dissociation. Dissociation occurs when the brain simply cannot handle the stimuli it is receiving and reality splits from consciousness in order to deal with the overload. Splitting experience from consciousness is a protective mechanism that allows the brain to handle the myriad of incoming stimuli that would otherwise overwhelm it. There is also some evidence that dissociation is more likely to occur when violence is interpersonal (van der Kolk et al., 1996). In these instances, in addition to physical pain, terror, hurt, and rage, the child must deal with betrayal (Miller, 1994).

For some understanding of this phenomenon as it occurs under nontraumatizing circumstances, it is useful to employ the metaphor of the daydream, in which the mind slips away into the imagination and awareness of immediate surroundings recedes. "Coming to" a few minutes later, people realize that time has passed. They know that they've been daydreaming, and with some effort, they can recall the specific content. There is also a residual sense of the feelings attached—pleasure, worry, sadness.

Dissociation may involve quite different brain mechanisms than ordinary daydreaming, but some of the observable results seem similar—if more extreme. For example, people who experience dissociation may say that they "lose time" or that they forget a lot. Some may report feeling spacey or disconnected from reality. Whatever the case, the ability to dissociate appears to have been, at least initially, lifesaving for abuse survivors (Miller, 1994).

The analgesic effect survivors feel when they self-harm is one example of dissociation at work, but survivors also numb or space out when they sense they are about to feel intolerable emotion or, more troubling, when they are confronted with real and imminent danger. They may also have what they describe as out-of-body experiences, in which they feel their conscious self exit the corporal body and observe what is happening from a safe distance. In clinical terms, this phenomenon is called "depersonalization." Disturbances in perception, in which survivors feel their vision narrow to a tunnel or images lose their color are called "derealization (Bremner et al., 1998). This alteration of vision is believed to be another example of an adaptive strategy: Abused children have learned to concentrate with great attention on sources of threat. As children grow into adulthood, however, these perceptual distortions are delinked from their original purpose and become overgeneralized responses to nonthreatening events. When survivors seek help from the psychiatric system, professionals can mistake these symptoms for those of schizophrenia, and misdiagnosis can occur.

Dissociation is also thought to interfere with how memories are stored. Traumatic memory is a controversial subject (discussed in full in Chapter 5). Not all survivors are amnesic for their past abuse, but a certain percentage report that they "forgot" what happened. Present clinical understanding is that survivors have not really forgotten per se but instead have filed their trauma memories away in locations that are not easily accessed. Flashbacks (sudden unbidden intrusion into consciousness of forgotten traumatic experience) are thought to result from breaches in the integrity of this protective mechanism.

In extreme circumstances, dissociation interrupts identity formation, shattering the survivor into a number of personalities (sometimes called "alters") who may or may not be aware of each other's existence. These personalities can have different memories depending on when they came into existence and under what circumstances. Dissociative identity disorder (DID) occurs when abuse is severe, sadistic, and prolonged, and when the child has no opportunity for relief or escape. Although some survivors may have dozens or even hundreds of personalities, in most cases only a few constitute a well-formed presence in their adult lives—although even a few can wreak havoc. Putnam (1989) alludes to four major categories of alters: the children (weeping and despairing), the persecutor personalities (internalized representations of the abuser), the protector personalities (strong but also extremely angry), and the competent "host" personality (a spokesperson for the rest). However, there are many other types that may be present, in more or less strength, depending on the nature of the abuse. Aside from having different roles, clients may describe these various selves as being physically different. Some may have exceptional night vision, while others are blind, deaf, or mute. One may self-harm, while another struggles with substance abuse or an eating disorder. Sometimes, the various personalities use different handwriting styles to leave notes or write in their journals, and they occasionally will use different voices, depending on the age or gender of the alter. Many clients with DID have names for their alters. Some are variations on the client's own name, for example, variations on Margaret such as Marg, Marge, Maggie, or Margie—depending on the age of the personality. Others may be named for people encountered while growing up; occasionally, some are celebrities, consistent with the all-encompassing influence of television and movies. Finally, although the overriding symptom present in this disorder is dissociation, clients are also very likely to exhibit other psychiatric problems, such as depression, delusions, anxieties, phobias, hallucinations, thought disorders, suicidal ideation, and even catatonia.

Revictimization. Mental health professionals are often frustrated when survivors expose themselves to dangerous circumstances over and over. In some cases, they even seem to seek out situations where they will be hurt again. Why, we ask ourselves, can they not learn? Of all people, shouldn't they know what and whom to avoid, given their painful pasts? Several theories have been offered to explain the phenomenon of revictimization. Briere (1992) suggests that it is connected to early experiences that establish the association between relationships and maltreatment—survivors assume that this is how the world works. Other authors believe that revictimization can be attributed to disruptions in self-perception that follow childhood trauma, such as low self-esteem and a sense of shame (Beitchman et al., 1992; Briere & Runtz, 1988). Finkelhor (1979) connects it to the high-risk situations traumatized children may find themselves in as they try to escape their abusive homes, and Miller (1994) believes that dissociation is central to what she terms *trauma reenactment syndrome.*

Research has demonstrated an association between histories of child abuse and later revictimization. *Revictimization* is often defined as another form of self-harm or as a failure to self-protect that is related to the child's early inability to defend the boundaries of his or her body (Miller, 1994). In a broad community study, Greenwald, Leitenberg, Cado, and Tarran (1990) found that women sexually abused as children were more likely to be abused in adulthood—even after controlling for family dysfunction. In addition, the risk of rape, sexual harassment, and battering in adulthood was double for women with histories of sexual abuse (Russell, 1986). Research conducted specifically with psychiatric clients offers similar findings (Briere & Runtz, 1988; Briere, Woo, McRae, Foltz, & Sitzman, 1997; Craine, Henson, Colliver, & MacLean, 1988; Russell, 1986). In a study of women inpatients, Lobel (1992) found that 76% of those who had been sexually abused reported that they "repeatedly allowed other people to force them to do things they did not want to do or allowed others to treat them cruelly" (p. 70).

Survivors have learned how to survive but not how to prevent or stop abuse, because as children they were vulnerable, easily overpowered, and outwitted. In addition, they were typically told, "You asked for it. It's your fault. If you tell anyone, I will kill you." When danger threatened, they learned to "go away in their heads" in order to get through the assault. But this talent becomes a liability in adulthood. Exquisitely attuned to any minute sign that an attack is pending, these survivors space out, numb, or switch to another personality, leaving themselves without defense (Miller, 1994).

Revictimization also has a psychodynamic component related to the particular nature of the original abuse. In these circumstances, survivors appear actually to seek out certain situations where they are victimized in strikingly similar ways. These are not conscious actions, and survivors are as puzzled as anyone else as to why they are *always* the ones who find themselves in the same old situations (with a violent partner, in restraints, raped while at a drunken party, assaulted in a dark alley, fired). The connection between the original abuse and subsequent revictimization patterns can be quite close, but it takes full knowledge of the survivor's story to uncover the relationship.

In other instances, the connection between past abuse and present revictimization may be generalized. Self-harm behaviors, substance abuse, and eating disorders relate more to a general air of victimization in a constant replay of the abuses suffered at the hands of perpetrators. The various ways in which clients harm themselves become simply the extension of an abusive life, where survivors take on the role of the perpetrator who is no longer present.

PHYSICAL INDICATORS

Although self-harm, suicide, dissociation, and revictimization are signs that have physical components, the physical indicators described in this section are more narrowly defined as bodily expressions of an abusive past. Mood changes, hunger, thirst, sexual arousal, the urge to go to the bathroom, and many other signals that are the daily unremarked background noise of a normal body become a treacherous minefield of sensation for survivors. Their bodies have become their enemies.

Research has documented the fact that the prolonged anxiety, hypervigilance, and fearfulness associated with early trauma may translate into physical problems sometimes called "somatization." Survivors monitor their bodies closely, searching for signs of abnormality, which are then presented to the medical community as a set of diffuse complaints that demonstrate suffering but yet are difficult to diagnose. Physical problems can include insomnia; headaches; gastrointestinal upsets; and pelvic, abdominal, or back pain (Cunningham, Pearce, & Pearce, 1988; Drossman et al., 1990; Morrison, 1989). Morrison (1989) found that 55% of women being treated for somatic disorders also had a history of childhood sexual abuse. In general population studies, women with histories of sexual abuse reported significantly more physical symptoms than did nonabused comparison subjects, even after researchers controlled for other sources of childhood stress, such as family dysfunction (Bushnell, Wells, & Oakley-Browne, 1992; Greenwald et al., 1990). Similar findings have been noted in studies of people with a psychiatric diagnosis (Bryer, Nelson, Miller, & Krol, 1987; Margo & McLees, 1991; Surrey, Swett, Michaels, & Levin, 1990). Also, in work related to irritable bowel syndrome, Berkley (cited in Levy & Toner, in press) argues that repeated experiences of pain can lead to associative learning, leaving survivors with lower pain thresholds. As a result, they may also be intolerant of what others may experience as nonpainful stimuli. This research is not intended to demonstrate that survivors don't have real, diagnosable physical illnesses or that all people who experience these sorts of complaints are necessarily survivors of childhood trauma; rather, it indicates simply that survivors are more likely to have certain constellations of illnesses and can express emotional pain in terms of physical symptoms.

Survivors may also neglect their body's health by avoiding physicians and dentists, because visits to these professionals are experienced as both invasive and reminiscent of certain forms of sexual abuse. Women may neglect routine preventive health care such as Pap smears, breast examinations, and appropriate prenatal care because they cannot bear to have a relative stranger touching their bodies. In certain instances, they may avoid showers or baths because they fear the vulnerability of nakedness—even when experienced in private.

Some abuse survivors go to the opposite extreme and become heavy users of medical services. They combine their deep need for loving attention with the reality of their physical distress and form a kind of "addiction" to the health care system. Health professionals can't ethically turn these sorts of patients away, even if they suspect that the real source of the problems resides in their mental and emotional lives. Attempts to separate out what is "real" and what is "imagined" are unproductive, because physical, emotional, and mental health are inextricably linked. Survivors feel blamed and judged when they seek medical help and are told that their problems are all in their head. Alternatively, physicians and nurses feel manipulated when survivors present with vague physical symptoms that no amount of treatment seems to relieve. In the midst of these miscommunications, real physical illnesses may be missed or mistreated, and real mental and emotional distress can be ignored.

Substance abuse can precipitate serious health problems while at the same time serving a number of purposes for survivors. Kearney (1998) suggested that drug or alcohol abuse is a form of destructive self-nurturing, relieving—in the short term—overwhelming anxiety and stress. Drugs and alcohol can be used to inhibit internal emotional distress or to suppress painful memories while at the same time providing a sense of euphoria or at least feelings of relative well-being. In certain circumstances, substance abuse may act as a disinhibitor and allow the expression of intense emotions such as rage and sadness.

Eating disorders can also serve certain assumed protective functions for abuse survivors. Both overeating with obesity and undereating hide breasts and the general femaleness of the body. Survivors often erroneously think of this as a safety measure. Anorexia interrupts menstrual flow and returns a woman's body to its prepubescent state, possibly helping survivors to avoid painful reminders of trauma, risk of pregnancy, or objectification as sexual objects. Eating disorders can also provide a limited sense of control over at least one facet of life, in a world that seems totally out of control.

Some of the rare and more difficult behaviors for the medical and psychiatric community to deal with are pseudo-seizures, double-doctoring, and polysurgery. Pseudo-seizures mimic epilepsy, with survivors (in a typical scenario) falling to the ground, shaking, and shuddering. Telltale signs that these are not true epileptic seizures include a lack of incontinence and no postseizure drowsiness (CMEnet, 1999).

Double-doctoring is a particular tactic used by survivors (and others) who choose to modulate their bodily and emotional reactions through the excessive use of prescription drugs. They present themselves to physician after physician, offering a cogent description of the kinds of symptoms that would lead to the prescription they are seeking. Although obtaining drugs is certainly a central goal of this behavior, survivors often derive other benefits as well. For example, their schedule of appointments keeps them busy and offers social interaction in what would otherwise be a life of isolation. The visits also validate their suffering—they feel bad, and attention from a physician confirms that they haven't "made it up."

Polysurgery is a behavior that results in repeated operations, which in rare cases may number in the dozens. Cosmetic surgery is particularly vulnerable to this form of abuse, because society teaches all women to fear the onset of wrinkles or weight gain. Survivors who struggle with a deep rage against their own bodies may transform their loathing into a never-ending quest for perfection, enduring operation after operation (Miller, 1994). Women who are survivors of repeated infant and child rape (among other atrocities) may complain of severe abdominal pain and seek surgery to remove ovaries and uterus because they believe their organs to be the source of their self-loathing.

Although it must be stressed that pseudo-seizures, double-doctoring and polysurgery are relatively rare behaviors, they are nonetheless important because they are particularly difficult to deal with when they do occur. Clients are convinced of the legitimacy of their claims and resist vigorously any contrary opinion, simply moving from practitioner to practitioner until their demands are met. Direct confrontation rarely works, but over time, stressors in the survivors' lives may be lessened through decent housing, a stable income, and, perhaps, therapy—if they will accept such a service—and the behaviors may lessen. An alternative approach is the formation of an alliance of all involved health professionals who can develop a unified helping strategy that protects the health system from further abuse.

EMOTIONAL INDICATORS

Survivors often experience uncontrolled emotion as their most salient indicator that something is deeply wrong. In fact, they often describe emotional pain as worse than physical pain—and that's saying something, given the lives they have led. Van der Kolk (1996a, 1996b) and van der Kolk and colleagues (1996) confirm that affect dysregulation is a central symptom for survivors. Feelings are enemies that arrive unannounced, create havoc in the survivor's internal and external world, and then leave behind a dark hole of nothingness that can feel even worse than the storm that preceded it.

All or Nothing. Sometimes, under conditions of stress, survivors regress and enter childlike emotional states that can last for a considerable period of time. Inpatient psychiatric wards or community group living situations are examples of environments that survivors find especially stressful, likely because of the power dynamics and the complexity of the relationships involved. During these times, survivors are alternately weepy and demanding, or angry and attacking. These troubling behaviors are evidence of the fact that many survivors think and feel in an "all or nothing" mode:

> "You are the most caring and helpful case manager I have ever had. I hate you, you do nothing for me. I'm getting worse."

> "I must be admitted to hospital RIGHT NOW or I will die. You're going to admit me? Leave me alone! I won't stay in this hellhole."

Understandably, mental health professionals find these opposing messages frustrating, and we can erroneously feel that the survivor is trying to trick us. But, from the survivor's viewpoint, the situation is quite different. Once survivors enter a feeling-state, they *know* they will feel the same horrible way forever, unless they take drastic and immediate action—or persuade someone else to do so on their behalf. They are completely lost in the moment, unable to apply logic to the situation and certainly unable to see the inherent conflict in their pleas. Hence, they oscillate between demand and counterdemand, good and bad, love and hate, and hope and despair, with no ability to find, let alone maintain, emotional middle ground.

Fear and Anxiety. Not surprisingly, studies have found that fear is a common emotion among both women and men who have histories of sexual abuse (45% and 18%, respectively; Stein, Golding, Siegel, Burnam, & Sorenson, 1988). Female subjects, many of whom have been victims of male perpetrators as children, report fear of being alone (26%; Stein et al., 1988) and fear of men (22%; Mullen et al., 1994). The fear of being alone is related to the isolation in which the abuse took place—no one saw or heard, and certainly no one stopped the assault. The intense feelings generated as a consequence of abuse may also be magnified when survivors are alone. For example, Lobel (1992) found that 63% of women who had been sexually abused as children reported feeling self-hatred, worthlessness, and guilt, especially when they were by themselves.

Anxiety, as a form of generalized fear, is an emotional burden that most survivors carry. Raised under a constant state of threat, they have come to fear everything, all the time. Anxiety is also thought to be related to the fact that traumatized children have little opportunity to form secure attachments to their principle caregivers, because few are safe enough to trust (Briere, 1992). For example, a community study found that 37% of women with sexual abuse histories also had a diagnosis of anxiety disorder, as opposed to only 14% of nonabused subjects. For the abused men in the sample, the incidence was 18% versus 8% for nonabused controls. When symptoms only were examined (as opposed to a diagnosed disorder), 57% of the female and 39% of the male survivors reported evidence of anxiety (Stein et al., 1988). In a second community sample, 42% of sexually abused women had an anxiety disorder (Mullen et al., 1994). This relationship holds even when researchers controlled for family dysfunction (Greenwald et al., 1990). Clinical studies have also found that psychiatric patients with sexual abuse histories have a higher prevalence of anxiety than do nonabused patients (Mancini, van Ameringen, & MacMillan, 1995; Margo & McLees, 1991; Surrey et al., 1990).

Panic attacks are acute states of anxiety and are terrifying experiences. Seemingly out of the blue, the heart begins to race to the point where it may seem like it will explode. The survivor may feel faint, nauseated, or in danger of losing control of bowels or bladder. Some survivors can link their panic attacks to certain situations or stimuli, whereas others feel that they arrive unbidden. A common result is even further social isolation, as survivors reduce activities in an attempt to avoid bringing on an attack.

Anger. Many survivors seem intensely angry, and research has confirmed this intuitive understanding. In a broad community sample, 54% of women and 40% of men with histories of child sexual abuse reported feelings of anger (Stein et al., 1988). Many survivors deny that they are angry ("I'm fine. Nothing bothers me."), whereas others find their rage so difficult to control that they have acquired histories of verbal or even physical assault. For example, one clinical study found that female incest survivors who were inpatients experienced more agitation and spent more time in seclusion because of assaultive behavior (Beck & van der Kolk, 1987). A clinical study of victimization among female psychiatric emergency room patients found that a history of sexual abuse was related not only to suicide attempts but also to violence against others (Briere et al., 1997).

Despair. Underneath the anger lies profound sadness. Although the clinical and biochemical picture is complex, many clients experience depression as an expression of warring emotions. Rage and deep despair are the culprits. Survivors fear both of these emotions greatly and equally, and they can shut themselves down rather than risk feeling like they are dying—because that's what they believe will happen if they allow themselves to experience emotional pain. Depression is much more than getting the blues. It is an exquisitely painful state that even the most articulate survivor finds hard to describe. *Cognitive distortions,* defined as a constant internal dialogue of self-denigration, are thought to be closely linked to the development and maintenance of a depressive state (Hawton, Salkovskis, Kirk, & Clark, 1989). Drug and alcohol abuse only serve to compound symptoms, and certainly a life of violence and poverty punctuated by admissions to psychiatric hospitals adds to the survivor's feelings of rage and despair.

Hopelessness. Survivors have extreme difficulty thinking of the future. Hope is a word they avoid and an emotion they fear. To hope means to be disappointed and they feel they simply cannot bear to have their hearts broken one more time. They may resist invitations to participate in goal-setting exercises—or they may participate but fail to follow through. They are also likely to live, literally, as if there is no tomorrow—spending their money as soon as they get it, sabotaging referrals to needed services, taking risks, and entering unwise relationships. Although these activities are related to the dynamics of revictimization, they also indicate a way of life that has no belief in the future. In this sense, the term *survivor* is something of a misnomer, because many survivors of childhood trauma never expected to live long enough to become an adult.

Coupled with feelings of hopelessness is a sense of spiritual abandonment. Survivors who have religious backgrounds may rage against God for not saving them. Some may have abandoned burgeoning talents (sports, music, or art), because they seem pointless in the face of the cruelty they have experienced. Others are unable to find comfort anywhere, and the small pleasures of life—a sunny morning, a purring cat—go unnoticed. Survivors have lost their faith in the world because, as they will say, "The world let me down."

RELATIONAL INDICATORS

In the same way they experience problems modulating their emotional lives, survivors are unable to achieve a balance in how close (physically, emotionally, and sexually) they get to other people. Some relate to others in an enmeshed way, mixing up their own needs and feelings with those of their family, friends, neighbors, and acquaintances because they do not have a clear sense of boundaries. This intermingling of emotion, perception, and intention leaves survivors unable to sort out which feelings are their own and which belong to the other person in the relationship. As a result, they are always on the alert for other people's reactions, and they watch carefully for signs of abandonment and betrayal, often misinterpreting straightforward actions as threatening. New acquaintances may find themselves attacked as a result of a raised eyebrow, a smile, or a frown—simple gestures that survivors just know are meant to hurt them. The result of all this emotional drama and enmeshment is what is typically called a "self-fulfilling prophecy." Survivors find themselves victimized, scapegoated, and abandoned—the very things they fear most, which, unaccountably, seem to happen over and over again.

Some give up on relationships altogether and isolate themselves from their fellow human beings as much as possible, preferring the predictability of loneliness to the emotional roller-coaster ride of attempted intimacy. But isolation does not protect them from their own longings, and periodically they will try once again to find a friend or sexual partner, only to have their tender hopes wither when things, yet again, don't work out.

Survivors who have experienced sexual abuse have extreme difficulties in their own sexual lives. Some are repulsed by even the idea of sex and live celibate lives. Others have repressed their sexual urges so completely that they could be considered asexual. Many use their sexuality as an avenue for revictimization, placing themselves in dangerous situations, engaging in unprotected sex, or having sex compulsively with multiple partners. Some may be uncertain of their sexual orientation and not really know if they are gay or straight. A few engage in sexual practices such as prostitution, sadomasochism, or group sex, and some may have perpetrated sexual abuse themselves. Many of these difficult or disturbing expressions of sexuality reflect the nature of the abuse the survivor suffered in childhood (sex coupled with shame, violence, guilt, or pain), and all will interfere with the ability to form healthy intimate relationships.

Sexual dysfunction among survivors has been confirmed in research. For example, a New Zealand study of a broad community sample found that women with histories of sexual abuse reported more disruptions in communication, sexual relations, and intimacy than did nonabused subjects (Mullen et al., 1994). Research conducted among clinical populations shows similar findings (Briere & Runtz, 1988). In addition, fear of sex, loss of enjoyment or interest in sex, and compulsive sexual behaviors have been well documented (Craine et al., 1988; Lobel, 1992). There is also some evidence that sexual dysfunction is higher among survivors who have experienced incest or abuse involving penetration (Beitchman et al., 1992).

All these relational disturbances are fertile ground for a myriad of revictimization scenarios. It is not at all uncommon for survivors to be in relationships that are physically, emotionally, or sexually abusive. Frequently, survivors (or their partners) are involved with the law and may move frequently or experience periods of homelessness. They may also be temporarily absent because of admissions to psychiatric hospitals or jail terms. Into these tumultuous dynamics are born their children. Although many survivors try their best to be good parents, they obviously have a number of strikes against them. They may be at risk of harming their unborn child because of poor nutrition, substance abuse, or the use of prescribed medication not discontinued in time. They may be involved with child welfare authorities and may have lost children to foster or adoptive parents—or even to death, because of their own or an abusive partner's actions. The intergenerational nature of child abuse is a reality, and even though many, if not most, survivors do the best they can for their children—and succeed—the statistics for the population as a whole require professionals to be vigilant. The reporting of suspected child abuse is now mandatory in most jurisdictions.

CONCLUSION

Nothing is ever simple when mental health professionals work with survivors of childhood trauma—neither the factors that precipitate their psychiatric admissions in the first place, the course of their treatment, their discharge plans, nor their life in the community. An additional factor is the wide gulf between survivors' competent facades and their incompetent histories. Survivors can be intelligent, fun-loving, and witty one moment, and pleading for rescue the next, weeping uncontrollably and threatening suicide. As their professional helpers, they can make us feel like we are on a roller-coaster. One day we feel empathy and optimism, and we feel effective in our helping roles. The next day, we feel angry, powerless, manipulated, incompetent, and vengeful. The key is understanding—but we first must learn how to recognize the many signs and symptoms of a traumatic past, and then we must acquire the practice skills to do something about them.

NOTES

1. A detailed review on the association between childhood abuse, self-harm, and suicidality has been produced (Santa Mina & Gallop, 1998).
2. Arnold (1995) reported that the following feelings preceded self-injury: overwhelming emotional pain such as misery, sadness, grief, desperation, or self-hatred (57%); depression or hopelessness (51%); anger, frustration, or a sense of powerlessness (50%); and anxiety, panic, fear, or tension (34%).

REFERENCES

Alexander, L. (1997, November). *Self-injury and its function in a non-clinical population: Preliminary findings.* Paper presented at the meeting of the International Society for Traumatic Stress, Montreal, Canada.

American Psychiatric Association. (1994). *Diagnostic and statistical manual of mental disorders* (4th ed.). Washington, DC: Author.

Arnold, L. (1995). *Women and self-injury, a survey of 76 women: A report on women's experience of self-injury and their views on service provision.* Bristol, UK: Bristol Crisis Service for Women.

Beck, J., & van der Kolk, B. (1987). Reports of childhood incest and current behavior of chronically hospitalized psychotic women. *American Journal of Psychiatry, 144,* 1474-1476.

Beitchman, J. H., Zucker, K. J., Hood, J. E., daCosta, G. A., Akman, D., & Cassavia, E. (1992). A review of the long-term effects of child sexual abuse. *Child Abuse & Neglect, 16,* 101-118.

Boudewyn, A. C., & Huser Liem, J. H. (1995). Childhood sexual abuse as a precursor to depression and self-destructive behavior in adulthood. *Journal of Traumatic Stress, 8,* 445-459.

Breggin, P. (1991). *Toxic psychiatry.* New York: St. Martin's.

Bremner, J. D., Krystal, J., Putnam, F., Southwick, S., Marmar, C., Charney, D., & Mazure, C. (1998). Measurement of dissociative states with the clinician-administered dissociative states scale (CADS). *Journal of Traumatic Stress, 11,* 125-136.

Briere, J. N. (1992). *Child abuse trauma: Theory and treatment of the lasting effects.* Newbury Park, CA: Sage.

Briere, J., & Runtz, M. (1988). Symptomatology associated with childhood sexual victimization in a non-clinical sample. *Child Abuse & Neglect, 12,* 51-59.

Briere, J., Woo, R., McRae, B., Foltz, J., & Sitzman, R. (1997). Lifetime victimization history, demographics, and clinical status in female psychiatric emergency room patients. *Journal of Nervous and Mental Disease, 185,* 95-101.

Bryer, J. B., Nelson, B. A., Miller, J. B., & Krol, P. A. (1987). Childhood sexual and physical abuse as factors in adult psychiatric illness. *American Journal of Psychiatry, 144,* 1426-1430.

Bushnell, J. A., Wells, J. E., & Oakley-Browne, M. A. (1992). Long-term effects of intrafamilial sexual abuse in childhood. *Acta Psychiatrica Scandinavica, 85,* 136-142.

Chesler, P. (1972). *Women and madness.* New York: Avon.

CMEnet. (1999). *Neurological emergencies: Curriculum* [On-line]. Available: www.cme.net.au/curric/neuro/seizure/seiz.htm.

Connors, R. (1996). Self-injury in trauma survivors: 1. Functions and meanings. *American Journal of Orthopsychiatry, 66,* 197-206.

Courtois, C. (1988). *Healing the incest wound: Adult survivors in therapy.* New York: Norton.

Craine, L. S., Henson, C. E., Colliver, J. A., & MacLean, D. G. (1988). Prevalence of a history of sexual abuse among female psychiatric patients in a state hospital system. *Hospital and Community Psychiatry, 39,* 300-304.

Cunningham, J., Pearce, T., & Pearce, P. (1988). Childhood sexual abuse and medical complaints in adult women. *Journal of Interpersonal Violence, 3,* 131-144.

Drossman, D., Leserman, J., Nachman, G., Li, Z., Gluck, H., Toomey, T., & Mitchell, C. (1990). Sexual and physical abuse in women with functional or organic gastrointestinal disorders. *Annals of Internal Medicine, 113,* 828-833.

Faye, P. (1995). Addictive characteristics of the behavior of self-mutilation. *Journal of Psychosocial Nursing, 33,* 36-39.

Feldman, M. (1988). The challenge of self-mutilation: A review. *Comprehensive Psychiatry, 29,* 252-269.

Finkelhor, D. (1979). *Sexually victimized children.* New York: Free Press.

Gallop, R. (1992). Self-destructive and impulsive behavior in the patient with a borderline personality disorder: Rethinking hospital treatment and management. *Archives of Psychiatric Nursing, 6,* 178-182.

Greenwald, E., Leitenberg, H., Cado, S., & Tarran, M. J. (1990). Childhood sexual abuse: Long-term effects on psychological and sexual functioning in a nonclinical and nonstudent sample of adult women. *Child Abuse & Neglect, 14,* 503-513.

Hawton, K., Salkovskis, P., Kirk, J., & Clark, D. (1989). The development and principles of cognitive-behavioral treatments. In K. Hawton, P. Salkovskis, J. Kirk, & D. Clark (Eds.), *Cognitive-behavioral therapy for psychiatric problems: A practical guide* (pp. 1-12). New York: Oxford University Press.

Herman, J. (1992). *Trauma and recovery.* New York: Basic Books.

Himber, J. (1994). Blood rituals: Self-cutting in female psychiatric inpatients. *Psychotherapy, 31,* 620-631.

Kearney, M. (1998). Truthful self-nurturing: A grounded formal theory of women's addiction recovery. *Qualitative Health Research, 8,* 495-512.

Levy, R., & Toner, B. (in press). Gender issues in chronic abdominal pain. In K. W. Olden (Ed.), *Chronic abdominal pain: A comprehensive approach.*

Lobel, C. M. (1992). Relationship between childhood sexual abuse and borderline personality disorder in women psychiatric inpatients. *Journal of Child Sexual Abuse, 1*(1), 63-80.

Mancini, C., van Ameringen, M., & MacMillan, H. (1995). Relationship of childhood sexual and physical abuse to anxiety disorders. *Journal of Nervous and Mental Disease, 183,* 309-314.

Margo, G. M., & McLees, E. M. (1991). Further evidence for the significance of a childhood abuse history in psychiatric inpatients. *Comprehensive Psychiatry, 32,* 362-366.

Miller, D. (1994). *Women who hurt themselves: A book of hope and understanding.* New York: Basic Books.

Morrison, J. (1989). Childhood sexual histories of women with somatization disorder. *American Journal of Psychiatry, 146,* 239-241.

Mullen, P. E., Martin, J. L., Anderson, J. C., Romans, S. E., & Herbison, G. P. (1994). The effect of child sexual abuse on social, interpersonal and sexual function in adult life. *British Journal of Psychiatry, 165,* 35-47.

Penfold, S., & Walker, G. (1983). *Woman and the psychiatric paradox.* Montreal, Canada: Eden Press.

Putnam, F. (1989). *Multiple personality disorder.* New York: Guilford.

Read, J. (1998). Child abuse and severity of disturbance among adult psychiatric inpatients. *Child Abuse & Neglect, 22,* 359-368.

Roth, S., Newman, E., Pelcovitz, D., van der Kolk, B., & Mandel, F. S. (1997). Complex PTSD in victims exposed to sexual and physical abuse: Results from the DSM-IV field trial for posttraumatic stress disorder. *Journal of Traumatic Stress, 10,* 539-555.

Russell, D. E. H. (1986). *The secret trauma: Incest in the lives of girls and women.* New York: Basic Books.

Santa Mina, E., & Gallop, R. (1998). Childhood sexual abuse and physical abuse and adult self-harm and suicidal behaviour: A literature review. *Canadian Journal of Psychiatry, 43,* 793-800.

Stein, J. A., Golding, J. M., Siegel, J. M., Burnam, M. A., & Sorenson, S. B. (1988). Long-term psychological sequelae of child sexual abuse: The Los Angeles epidemiologic catchment area study. In G. E. Wyatt & G. J. Powell (Eds.), *Lasting effects of child sexual abuse* (pp. 135-154). Newbury Park, CA: Sage.

Stone, M. (1990). *The fate of borderline patients: Successful outcome and psychiatric practice.* New York: Guilford.

Surrey, J., Swett, C., Jr., Michaels, A., & Levin, S. (1990). Reported history of physical and sexual abuse and severity of symptomatology in women psychiatric outpatients. *American Journal of Orthopsychiatry, 60,* 412-417.

van der Kolk, B. (undated). *Severe early trauma: Part 1* [Videotape]. Vancouver, Canada: Odin Books.

van der Kolk, B. (1996a). The body keeps score: Approaches to the psychobiology of posttraumatic stress disorder. In B. van der Kolk, A. McFarlane, & L. Weisaeth (Eds.), *Traumatic stress: The effects of overwhelming experience on mind, body and society.* New York: Guilford.

van der Kolk, B. (1996b). The complexity of adaptation to trauma: Self-regulation, stimulus discrimination, and characterological development. In B. van der Kolk, A. McFarlane, & L. Weisaeth (Eds.), *Traumatic stress: The effects of overwhelming experience on mind, body and society.* New York: Guilford.

van der Kolk, B., Pelcovitz, D., Roth, S., Mandel, F. S., McFarlane, A., & Herman, J. (1996). Dissociation, somatization, and affect dysregulation: The complexity of adaptation of trauma. *American Journal of Psychiatry, 153,* 83-93.

van der Kolk, B. A., Perry, J. C., & Herman, J. L. (1991). Childhood origins of self-destructive behaviour. *American Journal of Psychiatry, 148,* 1665-1671.

CHAPTER 5

The Controversy
Surrounding
Traumatic
Memory

In the past several years, there has been considerable attention focused on the nature of traumatic memory. This interest has been generated in part by new scientific knowledge about how memories are stored and recovered. However, the most intense controversy surrounds two terms: *recovered memory* and *false memory syndrome*. Recovered memory describes situations in which people who previously denied having or believed themselves not to have a history of child sexual abuse begin in adulthood to recall that they were indeed abused. Recovered memories drew little attention until adult children began bringing criminal charges or taking their parents to civil court. The False Memory Syndrome Foundation was organized in 1992 and is largely composed of parents who have been accused of sexual

---

AUTHORS' NOTE: Some of the material in this chapter appeared previously in Gallop, Austin, McCay, Bayer, and Peternelj-Taylor (1997).

abuse by their adult children. This organization does not deny the existence of sexual abuse but contends that members' children have not recovered memories at all but are instead suffering from false memory syndrome. Proponents believe that false memory syndrome is created when overzealous, incompetent, or unscrupulous therapists induce clients to believe they were sexually abused (Pope & Brown, 1996). Some parents have gone on to successfully sue therapists, making the case that their incompetence has torn families asunder and created great harm. In addition, a few adult children who initially charged sexual abuse have recanted, although whether they have done so for fear of being ostracized by their families or because of a genuine belief that they were led astray by their therapist is not clear. Whatever the case, some adult children appear to have joined their parents in denouncing their former therapists, arguing that recovered memories don't exist.

False memory syndrome, itself, is not a recognized medical condition, despite its diseaselike name. Nevertheless, it has received substantial media attention. One reason is that adult children's charging their parents with sexual abuse and suing them makes for dramatic news stories. A second reason is that proponents of false memory syndrome give journalists a source of countervailing opinion that can be called on to fulfill their obligation to produce balanced reporting. Previously, sources of opposing views were confined to the inaccurate (child abuse does not exist) or the unpalatable (it does no harm).

This ongoing debate may also reflect the complex social context of childhood trauma, particularly sexual abuse and incest. People seem able to accept that forgetting or amnesia can occur after certain sorts of traumas (traffic accidents, violent crime, and combat). In fact, amnesia is a clinical sign of posttraumatic stress disorder (PTSD) as defined by the *Diagnostic and Statistical Manual of Mental Disorders* (American Psychiatric Association, 1994a). However, the trauma of child abuse seems to be another matter. The wish to deny abuse, particularly incest, is not surprising given the fundamental taboos that exist in nearly all societies. To acknowledge that parents, close relatives, friends, and figures of authority such as priests and teachers can violate the trust of a child in such a fundamental way is a thought that many people do not wish to entertain. And for some mental health professionals, the distress of acknowledging abuse histories in others may resonate with their own fragmented memories of personal trauma. Under the embattled conditions created by the recovered memory versus false memory syndrome debate, defining the true nature of traumatic memory has gone from a somewhat obscure research endeavor to what is often the pivotal issue in highly publicized civil cases in which millions of dollars in awards hang in the balance.

An example of the familial and social divisions that these battles create can be seen in two of the sources of information for this chapter. Jennifer Freyd is a respected academic who has written in the area of traumatic memory. Pamela Freyd is founding member and executive director of the False Memory Syndrome Foundation. This family's story came to light when Pamela Freyd acknowledged that she was the author of an article published under the pseudonym Jane Doe (1991). In this article, Pamela Freyd claimed that Jennifer Freyd, her daughter, had not been sexually abused by her father as she had privately claimed; instead, according to the article, Jennifer was a victim of false memory syndrome. Two years later, Jennifer Freyd broke her silence, maintaining that her experiences were real and her memories accurate (Freyd, 1996).

Researchers and clinicians have also joined the fray. The validity of techniques such as hypnosis, which has been used in adults to surface childhood memories, has been questioned. The degree to which a therapist can influence a client within the therapeutic situation is also at issue. Some authors have written position papers arguing that it is possible to construct false memories. Opponents, determined not to return to the times in which victims of child abuse were uniformly silenced, are reluctant to even consider false memory as a possibility. And researchers line up on both sides, working hard to prove their respective cases.

It is inevitable that mental health professionals will be drawn into the debate. Regardless of which position sounds most credible, it is essential that professional helping activities be based on a sound understanding of this complex subject area. This chapter presents a comprehensive but not exhaustive review of the literature—the controversy has spawned an inordinate amount of writing and research activity. We have chosen to focus on the following areas: memory storage and retrieval; the hypothesized mechanisms of traumatic memory; recovered memories, including the empirical and theoretical basis for understanding why memories may be forgotten; memory and suggestibility; and a discussion of the False Memory Syndrome Foundation's position. Finally, we will provide practical guidelines for mental health professionals working with trauma survivors.

WHY WE NEED TO KNOW ABOUT MEMORY

Evidence of false allegations of childhood sexual abuse is sparse (Everson & Boat, 1989). In psychiatric literature, emphasis has typically been weighted toward concerns of underreporting rather than concerns regarding rampant fabrication. The reality is that most victims of child abuse do not forget the trauma they experienced. In fact, survivors often say they wish they could forget, but they cannot. Nevertheless, credible clinical experience reveals that a certain portion will report forgetting all or part of the trauma and remembering later on. In fact, professionals will observe a wide variation in the nature and type of abuse memories. Some clients will remember very little, and some will recall vague images, smells, or sensations. Others will remember with what appears to be total and vivid recall: dates, times, the clothes they were wearing, the pattern of the wallpaper, and the texture of the bedclothes. Also, clients who interact with professionals over an extended period of time—even when the relationship is not targeted at trauma therapy—may reveal more and more details as the relationship develops. This is not a surprising occurrence, since psychodynamic or insight-oriented therapy has long relied on the expectation that feelings, conflicts, and memories will be uncovered as a safe, trustworthy, and connected environment is created.

These dynamics are the essence of human storytelling. The narrative unfolds over time and builds on previous revelations in ever-evolving patterns of understanding. Personal truth is, in a sense, "acquired" through the process of adult eyes re-creating in hindsight the child's journey. Under these circumstances, both the teller and the listener need to be able to tolerate ambiguity. After all, clients are thinking out loud, struggling forward, then doubling back and retracing the same path as they fight to define the past.

Truth, in its absolute form, is not the goal of this form of personal storytelling. The task of the mental health professional, regardless of role, is to help clients move forward in their lives, not to determine the legal validity of their claims.[1] In this sense, what clients recall is less important than how it is recalled. This is a critical distinction to make and one that is, at first, hard to understand. The typical helping process is focused on how clients view their lives, what meaning they take from events, and how they express their distress. How they recall their pasts reveals both meaning and emotion, and these are the "facts" of the helping endeavor. Evidence of an abusive past may be contained not so much in what clients say but in how they live their lives, the "testimony" of signs and symptoms as discussed in Chapter 4. Thus, it is the more esoteric aspects of memory (meaning and emotion) that professionals must attend to and understand. We also need to know how humans recall both under normal circumstances and under conditions of trauma (Courtois, 1996).

MEMORY STORAGE AND RETRIEVAL

Any discussion of memory must start with the recognition that recall is subjective. Memories are representations of events, not the events themselves. If six witnesses were asked to recall an accident, their descriptions would no doubt reveal commonalities, but there would also be six sets of unique memories. What is remembered is influenced by what is salient and important to each individual both at the time the memory is laid down and when it is later recalled. Men and women, children and adults might remember very different aspects even when they have observed the same situation. "Memories are produced out of experience and, in turn, reshape it" (Antze & Lambek, 1996, p. xii). Different ways of remembering are not equivalent to "making things up" and instead are a reflection of vantage point (attention, background, gender, age, and other unique characteristics).

Memory storage and retrieval processes are complex, but in essence, the specific event (feelings, perceptions, sensation, visual images, sounds) must first be input or encoded in some fashion—just as data are entered into a computer. Then these impressions (memories) are stored in specific areas of the brain ready for later retrieval. Storage is influenced by numerous factors, a few of which are age, context, and stress level. Retrieval processes are also affected by stress and context (who is asking for the material and why). When memories are recalled, the brain must determine what information went into storage, where it went, and which aspects remain available for retrieval.

Memory theorists and researchers believe there are two main kinds of memory. *Declarative* or *explicit* memory refers to the capacity to consciously recall facts and events. For example, a vacation, the name of your first-grade teacher, your address, that there are 100 cents in a dollar.

Nondeclarative or *implicit* memory refers to knowledge of experience without conscious recall.[2] It can include skills such as riding a bike or swimming—you know how to do it, but you can't remember exactly how you learned. Nondeclarative memory also includes emotional associations and conditioned sensory responses (van der Kolk, 1994). For example, the smell of coffee may bring feelings of comfort, but there is no real memory of why this is so. The sound of a police siren may terrify even when adults can't recall much about a childhood spent in a war zone.

These two forms of memory, declarative and nondeclarative, are thought to be mediated by different brain systems. Declarative memory is managed by the hippocampus, which seems to evaluate and sort incoming events, comparing them to previously stored information, called "schema." Language is important to the mechanisms of declarative memory because these processes require words to work effectively. Emotional arousal stimulates other parts of the brain, in particular the thalamus and amygdala. Excessive emotion creates levels of stimulation that interfere with hippocampal functioning, inhibiting the cognitive and sorting capacities required to put information into appropriate schema and into words. More specifically, stress leads to the excretion of adrenal steroid hormones, including human glucocorticoids needed for the "fight or flight" response. Research has shown that sustained or excessive exposure to gluticocortoids appears to lead to damage or atrophy of the hippocampus (Bremner, 1999; Sapolsky, 1996). According to trauma researchers, these neural mechanisms may interfere with the capacity of the brain to store information in declarative memory. Hence, traumatic memories are believed to be stored as somatic sensations and visual images—in nondeclarative memory (van der Kolk, 1994).

TRAUMATIC MEMORY

Authors have suggested that recall of early memories (prior to age 3) is difficult because both the laying down of the memory and the subsequent recall require language to name the event and to describe and share details (Burgess, Hartman, & Clements, 1995; Nelson, 1993). It should also be noted that the hippocampus, critical to declarative memory, does not mature until 3 or 4 years of age. Consequently, trauma experienced by small children will be remembered quite differently than trauma experienced by an adult. Not only are children still in an early developmental stage of personality, but their experience of the world is also limited. Adults have some kind of framework or memory schema already in place to which they can link events and make comparisons, thus creating meaning. Based on these ideas, theorists argue that traumatic memories, no matter what the victim's age, can be stored through nondeclarative processes (sensory and olfactory experiences or visual images). This storage may well be accompanied by amnesia, because the memories were never associated with the brain's cognitive capacity to create meaning (Pillemer & White, 1989; van der Kolk & Fisler, 1995). There is also an emerging body of work that measures and maps associated neurobiological changes in the brain that support these sorts of findings (Pope & Brown, 1996).

Research by Herman and Harvey (1997) provides further evidence for the role of nondeclarative memory, in that it has been demonstrated that the recall of traumatic events occurs over time and often in the context of triggers. Triggers are stimuli, such as smells, sounds, textures, and other sensations, that are reminiscent of trauma experience. They are thought to evoke images of early abuse even when the individual cannot recall the precise experience. Life events and crises, such as illness, job loss, divorce, or the survivor's children's attaining the same age as when the original abuse occurred, are also noted triggers for recall.

These traumatic memory theories were originally presented in research by van der Kolk and Fisler (1995). In their study, abuse victims reported that memories initially returned as visual, olfactory, or sensory experiences and gradually became more explicit over the course of time. Van der Kolk (1994) had argued in earlier work that these sorts of early memories remain fixed and unaltered over time precisely because they are unavailable for the ordinary process of aware recall. Hence, flashbacks—intense and overwhelming emotional, sensory, and visual nondeclarative memory fragments—may haunt survivors, occurring and reoccurring over extended periods of time.

RECOVERED MEMORIES

The idea that some children exposed to abuse early in their lives "forget" what happened is at the base of the concept of recovered memory. How and under what circumstances amnesia occurs is central to traumatic memory research and theory production.

The Research. Evidence for the existence of recovered memory comes from two major sources. First, researchers are expanding their general knowledge about the complex nature of memory. The above discussion of declarative and nondeclarative memory is a case in point. These theories serve to illuminate how various regions of the brain are involved in the acquisition and retrieval of information and how strong emotion can affect the storage and retrieval process. This knowledge has led to the critical distinction between the encoding and retrieval of "ordinary" versus traumatic memories (van der Kolk, 1994; van der Kolk & Fisler, 1995). The second source of knowledge is credible empirical evidence showing that child sexual abuse can be forgotten, sometimes for years. For example, Whitfield (1998) reviewed 36 studies examining this question and found that from 16% to 78% of trauma victims reported experiencing some degree of amnesia, ranging from partial to total. Williams (1994) interviewed 129 women who had been treated for sexual abuse as children in the emergency room of a local hospital. Seventeen to 20 years after the abuse, she asked them to participate in her follow-up study of patients who had received care at this specific hospital during a 3-year period (1973 to 1975)—without mention of the fact that the research was looking at recall of sexual abuse. As part of a questionnaire, the women were asked detailed questions about a history of child abuse. Overall, 49 participants (38%) were unable to recall the abuse that had brought them to the emergency room, even though there was written evidence in hospital reports that abuse had occurred. Of the women who were aged 4 to 6 years at the time of the abuse, 62% did not recall the original event; of those who were 4 or under, 55% did not recall. In other research, 42 victims of a confessed and convicted child molester were interviewed, and 47% reported a period of time in which they had no recall of events (Grassian & Holtzen, 1996). In a large self-report study, researchers selected a random nonclinical sample of 498 people. Of the 113 who reported a history of child abuse, 42% said that they had experienced partial amnesia and 20% total amnesia for traumatic events (Elliott & Briere, 1995). A questionnaire developed by Briere and Conte (1993) found that 267 (59%) of participants with a sexual abuse history indicated that they had, at some point in their life, forgotten the experience.

In earlier work, Herman and Schatzow (1987) treated 53 incest survivors with group therapy. Fourteen of the women had experienced severe memory loss related to sexual abuse, and 19 had experienced moderate loss. The treatment intervention stimulated memory, and eventually the women began to recall the abuse. In this instance, family members or other reliable sources verified events in 75% of the cases.

Research findings such as these have led to theories of a continuum of recall. For example, in the clinical evaluation of 77 psychiatric patients with a history of childhood trauma, 53% claimed to have never forgotten, 17% reported a mixture of continuous memory and delayed recall, and 16% reported periods of complete amnesia followed by recall (Herman & Harvey, 1997).

This work represents compelling evidence for the existence of recovered memories, and new work is added regularly. However, methodological critiques exist. For example, Pope and Hudson (1995) suggest that there is often no way to tell if research subjects have actually forgotten events or if they simply have chosen not to tell. For example, Williams's (1994) participants may have not wanted to talk about their early experience, or they may have been diverted away from the topic because the true nature of the study was not revealed. Also, they may have been experiencing normal childhood forgetting rather than amnesia as a consequence of trauma. Pope and Hudson (1995) argue that just because people forget childhood trauma does not mean that there are special brain processes in place that mediate memories laid down under conditions of high emotion. They also challenge the validity of Herman and Schatzow's (1987) findings, pointing to the fact that some of the case examples used were composite (an amalgam of several of the women's stories) and that, in a few instances, the corroborating evidence was inferred. For example, the researchers concluded that one subject's memories must be accurate, because another sibling had also been abused. Certainly, all study of traumatic memory suffers from one overriding problem—child abuse typically occurs in secret and isolation. Often, only the child and the perpetrator know for sure what happened.

Explanatory Theories. Lego (1996) and Williams (1994) build on exactly this point in the development of their theory of traumatic memory. They suggest that notions of simple forgetting or repression[3] may be inadequate to describe the kind of fragmentation and lack of recall that occurs under traumatic conditions. Dissociation, these authors say, more accurately encompasses the processes of forgetting early child abuse—particularly sexual abuse that occurs under threat and in private. The shaming aspect of this form of abuse evokes feelings of fear, humiliation, and guilt. These emotional forces may combine to produce defenses in children that enable them to disengage (dissociate) from the event by altering their state of consciousness (Herman, 1992). Although repression refers to the burial of memories, dissociation occurs at the time of the event, potentially affecting how memories are stored. Dissociation may also be related to the eventual development of complex PTSD (Terr, 1994). Because dissociation is believed to interfere with storage, events cannot be forgotten in the traditional sense. The mechanisms of dissociation also fit well with research evidence that shows that later recall of traumatic material is fragmentary and vague and evolves over time.

Freyd (1996) offers cognitive explanations for dissociation and subsequent forgetting. She suggests that dissociation keeps traumatic information from interfering with the mechanisms that control attachment behavior. She suggests that by blocking knowledge of abuse, children avoid linking the parent with the abusive behavior. In fact, research has shown that, when the perpetrator is trusted and known to the victim, the psychological impact is devastating (Feinauer, 1989). As a result, Freyd (1996) and others (Herman, 1992) argue that forgetting or dissociation serves as a protective mechanism, preventing loss of the fundamental role of caregiver in the life and development of the child. According to Herman (1992), the child must split off the abuse from the abuser because this process is essential to survival. The child needs to "take the evil of the abuser into herself and thereby preserve the primary attachment to her parents" (p. 105). Freyd calls this dynamic "betrayal trauma" and states that the abuse information must be blocked partially or in whole, depending on individual circumstances. Coercion, threats, prohibitions, and intimidation enhance the likelihood of forgetting (Elliott, 1997).

MEMORY AND SUGGESTIBILITY

Research on eyewitness accounts is the main source of information on how memory may be subject to suggestion. Elizabeth Loftus, a well-known researcher in this area, has demonstrated that adult subjects

shown videotapes of an auto accident are vulnerable to misinforma-
tion—for example, suggestions after the viewing that a stop sign was
present when none appeared in the film can affect how the subjects describe what they saw. Eyewitnesses to real events and crimes appear to be
less vulnerable to suggestion, perhaps because the stakes are higher. It
also should be noted that even in laboratory experiments, research subjects couldn't be convinced that, for example, a robbery occurred when
they actually watched a tape of an assault. There is also some evidence
that small children can be convinced that an event occurred when it did
not if the "pseudomemory" is suggested over and over again or if misleading postevent information is provided (Ceci & Bruck, 1993; Loftus
& Ketcham, 1994). However, these kinds of findings do not hold up well
when the children are older. Overall, research on memory and suggestibility offers mixed results, with factors such as the age of the research
subject, his or her relationship to the person making the suggestions,
whether or not the event is witnessed or personally experienced, and how
the subject is subsequently questioned about what happened all affecting
results (Pope & Brown, 1996).

THE FALSE MEMORY SYNDROME FOUNDATION

False memory is defined as a "recalled" experience of child abuse that
never actually occurred. False memory is *not* "making it up," exaggerat-
ing, or appropriating someone else's story, as is sometimes erroneously
thought. According to Lego (1996), false memory occurs when a vulnerable or suggestible client is "unwittingly coached by a respected authority
figure" (p. 110)—typically a therapist. False Memory Syndrome Foundation members do not believe that clients are seeking to deceive deliberately. Instead, they are victims who have had inaccurate ideas implanted
in their minds so that they honestly believe that they were abused as children, when in fact they were not.

One obvious challenge to the False Memory Syndrome Foundation's
credibility is that it is, in fact, a sophisticated haven for perpetrators. In
her article "How Do We Know We're Not Representing Pedophiles?"
Pamela Freyd argued that simply looking at the membership is proof:
"We are a good looking bunch of people: graying hair, well-dressed,
healthy, smiling. . . . Just about every person who has attended is someone

you would likely find interesting and want to count as a friend" (Freyd, as quoted in Pope & Brown, 1996, p. 76). Perhaps as an antidote to this form of naive response, the Foundation has developed an extensive list of researchers and academics on its Scientific and Professional Advisory Board to lend credence to its arguments.

Although it has been difficult to find acceptable methodologies capable of proving that forgotten child abuse actually happened, the False Memory Syndrome Foundation has had the even more difficult task of proving that remembered abuse did not happen. As a result, it asserts in blanket fashion that there is no such thing as recovered memory—children who have had horrible things happen to them are incapable of forgetting. Proponents of this position also argue that there is little or no evidence that traumatic memories are stored in a unique way (Loftus, Polonsky, & Fullilove, 1994).

To test the notion of false memory syndrome, Hovdestad and Kristiansen (1996) compared sexual abuse survivors who had always remembered the abuse with survivors who had recovered memories, using the four symptom clusters that are said to be associated with false memory syndrome: (a) the victim's strongly held belief that the trauma occurred, along with denial by the perpetrator; (b) disruption in relationships with the perpetrator or other people who don't believe the victim; (c) irregular or discontinuous symptoms of distress; and (d) specific characteristics of the therapy experience (e.g., therapy was sought for nonabuse issues, but the therapist used suggestive techniques and focused on abuse). These investigators hypothesized that if recovered memories are false, then the two groups (continuous memory and recovered memory) should have different scores on the four symptom clusters. However, results showed no difference between groups. In addition, in the few systematic studies of "retractors" (people who recant and say that their recovered memories were indeed false), researchers found that these subjects also did not fit the false memory syndrome cluster profile, in that they reported questioning their memories of abuse all along (Hovdestad & Kristiansen, 1996).

Much of the evidence for false memory cited by the Foundation is based on the type of eyewitness research that demonstrates that memories can be created in laboratory situations. Central to the Foundation's case is an experiment in which several children were persuaded by older relatives that they had been lost in a shopping mall at an earlier age (Loftus & Ketcham, 1994). This experiment is said to prove that memories can be implanted in children by a trusted authority figure. The obvious critique of this work is that the experience of being lost hardly equates to the trauma of severe child abuse. From the False Memory Syndrome Foundation's perspective, this point only serves to prove its case: Atrocities such as rape and incest are such salient events that no child could ever forget them. It is important to note that experiments that attempted to implant more traumalike memories (e.g., memories of a rectal enema) have failed (Pope, 1996).

The False Memory Syndrome Foundation has had a substantial impact on the field of trauma therapy and on mental health in general. For example, in a recent survey of the beliefs, attitudes, and educational needs of 1,701 psychiatric nurses, subjects were asked about false memory syndrome (Gallop et al., 1997). Seventy-five percent of participants reported that they had heard about false memory, and of this group, 80% wrote comments regarding their thoughts on the matter. The majority believed that false memory syndrome, although rare, could occur and was a consequence of incompetent and unethical therapists. They also worried that attention to false memory would silence or revictimize people who had true abuse histories. Although the nurses supported the principle of routine inquiry about a history of child abuse for psychiatric clients, they expressed concern about suggesting it as a possibility when clients had made no mention of abuse or had denied experiences of trauma. They felt very strongly that it was their role to follow the client's lead and also to proceed at a pace set by the client. This position was almost unanimously endorsed in the sample, despite comments by many nurses that childhood trauma seemed so widespread among psychiatric clients that they assumed it to be part of clients' histories unless told otherwise (Gallop, McCay, Austin, Bayer, & Peternelj-Taylor, 1998).

The comments from these nurses hold great wisdom. There is no question that incompetent therapists exist and that clients have been harmed by their practices. Claims made by the False Memory Foundation have challenged mental health professionals to become more knowledgeable and skilled in the area of child abuse, thereby achieving at least one laudable outcome: All clients benefit if their professional helpers are good at their jobs.

PRACTICE ISSUES FOR
MENTAL HEALTH PROFESSIONALS

One of the most important services professionals can provide is to take clients seriously and to value what they have to say. Helping relationships provide a safe place where memories are shared and stories told. However, professionals are not in a position to confirm or deny what clients say when, as is so often the case, corroborating evidence is not available. Although the false memory debate has illuminated this aspect of the helping process in a critical way, neutrality is simply good practice in any client-professional encounter. For example, if a client tells us that his or her parents favored an older brother, we don't argue, nor do we seek out evidence to prove or disprove the story. Instead, we accept that this is the client's subjective reality; by listening attentively to what is being said, we create a climate of trust and safety, which is the foundation for human growth.

This principle of supportive neutrality remains true in the case of childhood trauma (Courtois, 1996). Professionals must neither suggest nor dismiss abuse. In addition, numerous authors discourage the use of extreme efforts to ferret out forgotten or missing information and state that memory recovery and the use of memory recovery techniques should not be the focus of therapy (Brown, 1995). The American Psychiatric Association (1994b) emphasized the need for training, knowledge, and experience for clinicians who wish to use specialized techniques such as hypnosis or Amytal (amobarbitol, a drug thought to aid the recovery of memory). The American Psychiatric Association also stresses a neutral, nonjudgmental, and empathic attitude toward reported memories of sexual abuse and adds that assumptions regarding the causes of any patient's difficulties interferes with accurate assessment and appropriate treatment.

Practice guidelines advising appropriate and ethical helping processes for clients who may be recovering memories of trauma have now been developed (see Courtois, 1997, 1999; Pope & Brown, 1996). The guidelines that follow result from our own clinical experience and are intended to assist mental health professionals to practice safely and competently:

1. Stay informed. Trauma and traumatic memory is a rapidly expanding field, and professionals need to take advantage of new knowledge and educational opportunities such as courses, seminars, and

workshops. We need to know both what to do and how to do it. There-fore, it is important to balance formal academic learning with hands-on skills development experiences.

2. Know what is realistic for our role and skill level. As profession-als, we must recognize both our capabilities and our limitations, as well as the strictures of our particular practice setting. Becoming a therapist who specializes in treating survivors of childhood trauma requires ad-vanced clinical training. However, this does not mean that nontherapist mental health professionals cannot be extremely helpful and supportive as memories emerge. Psychiatric nurses, case managers, housing and hostel workers, and many other professionals (clergy, police, lawyers, physicians) can provide both validation and safety. They may also be central in facilitating the capacity of clients to start the work of healing and recovery.

3. Work within the prescribed ethical and conduct guidelines of our professional associations. We need to be aware if there is a position pa-per on trauma and recovered memory particular to our professional role and take its suggestions into account in our practice approach.

4. Seek advice and supervision from peers, managers, consultants, and other experts. Wise professionals value opportunities to talk through problems or concerns, and in most clinical situations, such consulta-tions are critical to accountability.

5. Although it may make sense in certain settings to always inquire about an abusive past, when, where, and how to ask is a complicated matter (please see Chapter 6 for a full discussion). Not all psychiatric clients have a history of abuse, and some will not disclose on first ques-tioning. We cannot assume that because a person denies a history of abuse, none has occurred. Similarly, we cannot assume that abuse will eventually be disclosed. People may not remember, or they may have had previous experiences of disclosure where they were disbelieved, ig-nored, or humiliated. Some clients need to test the water and offer a par-tial or disguised disclosure that can be used to check how the recipient of this knowledge responds (Limandri, 1989).

6. Don't push recall. Clients will remember when they need to and at a pace they can handle. Also, we must recognize that additional memo-ries, which may or may not include abuse experiences, will surface if

there is an ongoing client-professional relationship. Often, these are not recovered memories per se but are more detailed descriptions of events already known to the client. Nonetheless, it is important for professionals to understand the nature of triggers, their impact on everyday functioning, and their role in memory recovery.

7. Be aware of biases and assumptions. The beliefs that psychiatric clients always have a history of abuse, that all men are violent, that family members should be viewed with suspicion (or should be held above suspicion), that abuse can't have occurred if there is no corroborating evidence, and that abuse that happened long ago can't affect the present are examples of positions that are not supported by scientific evidence. Professionals must be careful not to jump to conclusions or form opinions too early in the client-professional relationship. A professional's credibility is based on careful assessments and well-thought-out treatment plans that respond to the uniqueness of each client's circumstance (Pope & Brown, 1996).

8. Make documentation a regular part of practice. Accountable professionals keep notes, often following prescribed clinical templates, that describe what is happening in the helping relationship and how work is progressing. If a history of trauma is emerging, recall can be tracked through documentation, which not only aids in clarifying professional thinking but also serves as a legal record of the helping process. It is here, in our notes, that evidence of our thoughtful and unbiased work can be found.

9. Stay within the helping frame (as discussed in Chapter 7). Mental health professionals have a valuable role to play in clients' lives as prescribed by the boundaries of the helping frame. This role does not included persuading clients to confront or charge their abusers. If clients wish to take this step, professionals can offer support, information, and resources, but the decision to proceed must be entirely the client's.

CONCLUSION

Most survivors of childhood trauma do not forget what happened to them, but some do. As professionals, we must be aware that traumatic amnesia can and does occur, but even if we strongly suspect a history of abuse, our job is to wait for clients to remember. In this chapter, we outlined some of the central issues associated with recovered memory and false memory syndrome. It is important to point out that knowledge in this field is rapidly expanding and that new information is emerging regularly. It may be difficult to keep up, but we must be prepared to rise to the challenge if we are to practice in a credible and competent manner.

NOTES

1. Some mental health professionals may act as expert witnesses or as assessors for the purposes of legal action. At these times, they may be testifying as to the credibility of the client's claims. However, even in these circumstances, responsible expert testimony must take into account *how* the client recalls, not just *what* the client recalls.

2. Nondeclarative memory is sometimes called "procedural memory" (Pope & Brown, 1996).

3. *Repression* is defined as a kind of motivated forgetting and, as such, is a psychodynamic defense against knowing, because to know would bring great pain and sadness (Loftus & Loftus, as cited in Pope & Brown, 1996).

REFERENCES

American Psychiatric Association. (1994a). *Diagnostic and statistical manual of mental disorders* (4th ed.). Washington, DC: Author.

American Psychiatric Association. (1994b). *Interim report of the working group on investigation of memories of childhood abuse.* Washington, DC: Author.

Antze, P., & Lambek, M. (Eds.). (1996). *Tense past: Cultural essays in trauma and memory.* New York: Routledge.

Bremner, J. D. (1999). Does stress damage the brain? *Biological Psychiatry, 45,* 797-805.

Briere, J., & Conte, J. (1993). Self-reported amnesia for abuse in adults molested as children. *Journal of Traumatic Stress, 6,* 21-31.

Brown, D. (1995). Pseudomemories: The standard of science and the standard of care in trauma treatment. *American Journal of Clinical Hypnosis, 37,* 1-23.

Burgess, A. W., Hartman, C. R., & Clements, P. T., Jr. (1995). Biology of memory and childhood trauma. *Journal of Psychosocial Nursing, 33*(3), 16-26.

Ceci, S., & Bruck, M. (1993). The suggestibility of the child witness: A historical review and synthesis. *Psychological Bulletin, 113,* 403-439.

Courtois, C. A. (1996). Informed clinical practice and the delayed memory controversy. In M. Conway (Ed.), *False and recovered memories* (pp. 206-229). Oxford, UK: Oxford University Press.

Courtois, C. (1997). Guidelines for treatment of adults abused or possibly abused as children. *American Journal of Psychotherapy, 51,* 497-510.

Courtois, C. (1999). *Recollections of sexual abuse: Treatment principles and guidelines.* New York: Norton.

Doe, J. [Pamela Freyd]. (1991). How could this happen? In E. Goldstein & K. Farmer (Eds.), *Confabulations: Creating false memories, destroying families* (pp. 27-60). Boca Raton, FL: SIRS Books.

Elliott, D. M. (1997). Traumatic events: Prevalence and delayed recall in the general population. *Journal of Consulting and Clinical Psychology, 65,* 811-820.

Elliott, D. M., & Briere, J. (1995). Posttraumatic stress associated with delayed recall of sexual abuse: A general population study. *Journal of Traumatic Stress, 8,* 629-647.

Everson, M., & Boat, B. (1989). False allegations of sexual abuse by children and adolescents. *Journal of the American Academy of Child and Adolescent Psychiatry, 28,* 230-235.

Feinauer, L. (1989). Comparison of long-term effects of child abuse by type of abuse and by relationship of the offender to the victim. *American Journal of Family Therapy, 17,* 48-56.

Freyd, J. (1996). *Betrayal trauma theory: The logic of forgetting abuse.* Cambridge, MA: Harvard University Press.

Gallop, R., Austin, W., McCay, E., Bayer, M., & Peternelj-Taylor, C. (1997). Nurses' views regarding false memory syndrome. *Archives of Psychiatric Nursing, 11,* 257-263.

Gallop, R., McCay, E., Austin, W., Bayer, M., & Peternelj-Taylor, C. (1998). A survey of psychiatric nurses regarding working with clients who have a history of sexual abuse. *Journal of the American Psychiatric Nursing Association, 4,* 9-17 .

Grassian, S., & Holtzen, D. (1996, July). *Memory of sexual abuse by a parish priest.* Paper presented at Trauma and Memory: An International Research Conference, Portsmouth, NH.

Herman, J. L. (1992). *Trauma and recovery.* New York: Basic Books.

Herman, J. L., & Harvey, M. R. (1997). Adult memories of childhood trauma: A naturalistic clinical study. *Journal of Traumatic Stress, 10,* 557-571.

Herman, J. L., & Schatzow, E. (1987). Recovery and verification of memories of childhood sexual trauma. *Psychoanalytic Psychology, 4*(1), 1-14.

Hovdestad, W. E., & Kristiansen, C. M. (1996). A field study of "false memory syndrome": Construct validity and incidence. *The Journal of Psychiatry & Law, 24,* 299-338.

Lego, S. (1996). Repressed memory and false memory. *Archives of Psychiatric Nursing, 10,* 110-115.

Limandri, B. J. (1989). Disclosure of stigmatizing conditions: The discloser's perspective. *Archives of Psychiatric Nursing, 3,* 69-78.

Loftus, E., & Ketcham, K. (1994). *The myth of repressed memory: False memories and allegations of sexual abuse.* New York: St. Martin's.

Loftus, E., Polonsky, S., & Fullilove, M. (1994). Memories of childhood sexual abuse: Remembering and repressing. *Psychology of Women Quarterly, 18,* 67-84.

Nelson, L. (1993). The psychological and social origins of autobiographical memory. *Psychological Science, 4,* 7-14.

Pillemer, D. B., & White, S. H. (1989). Childhood events recalled by children and adults. *Advances in Child Development and Behavior, 21,* 297-340.

Pope, H. G., Jr., & Hudson, J. I. (1995). Can memories of childhood sexual abuse be repressed? *Psychological Medicine, 25,* 121-126.

Pope, K. (1996). Memory, abuse and science: Questioning claims about the false memory epidemic. *American Psychologist, 51,* 957-974.

Pope, K., & Brown, L. (1996). *Recovered memories of abuse: Assessment, therapy, forensics.* Washington, DC: American Psychological Association.

Roe, C. M., & Schwartz, M. F. (1996). Characteristics of previously forgotten memories of sexual abuse: A descriptive study. *Journal of Psychiatry & Law, 24,* 189-206.

Salpolsky, R. (1996). Why stress is bad for the brain. *Science, 273,* 748-750.

Terr, L. (1994). *Unchained memories.* New York: Basic Books.

van der Kolk, B. A. (1994). The body keeps the score: Memory and the evolving psychobiology of posttraumatic stress. *Harvard Review of Psychiatry, 1,* 253-265.

van der Kolk, B. A., & Fisler, R. (1995). Dissociation and the fragmentary nature of traumatic memories: Overview and exploratory study. *Journal of Traumatic Stress, 8,* 505-525.

Whitfield, C. (1998). Trauma and memory: Clinical and legal understanding of traumatic memory. In A. Burgess (Ed.), *Advanced practice psychiatric nursing* (pp. 171-186). Stamford, CT: Appleton & Lange.

Williams, L. M. (1994). Recall of childhood trauma: A prospective study of women's memories of child sexual abuse. *Journal of Consulting and Clinical Psychology, 62,* 1167-1176.

CHAPTER 6

Asking
About Abuse

The documented prevalence of histories of childhood trauma among psychiatric clients has led many researchers and clinicians to recommend that questions about an abusive past become a routine part of any mental health assessment or admission history. The reason for this recommendation is obvious. Information about childhood trauma is critical to the development of appropriate treatment plans and therapeutic interventions. It is also important in group housing situations and in case management agencies, where knowledge of past abuse experiences helps staff make appropriate referrals and assist clients to adjust to the complexity of relationships with fellow residents. Research evidence also suggests that disclosure itself, if handled sensitively and with skill, can be an empowering process (Doob, 1992; Urbancic, 1992). Breaking the pattern of silence and denial may also help decrease chronicity as well as interrupt the cycle of revictimization so often seen in survivors of childhood trauma.

The decision to inquire about a history of abuse must be based on sound reasoning. Mental health professionals need to think through their motivations for asking and know how they are going to use the information they receive. We also need to know how to ask about an abusive past and how to respond sensitively to disclosure. This chapter is intended as a guide to help professionals decide when it is appropriate to ask and when it is not. We will also provide examples of how to introduce the topic and how to ask respectfully. Obviously, professionals who work in mental health settings where childhood trauma is the focus of their helping activities must be well versed in these skills. However, professionals who see clients on a regular basis for reasons unrelated to abuse (vocational counseling, housing support, skills teaching, social recreational activities) also create ongoing relationships in which, over time, clients come to feel safe. As trust grows, there is a distinct possibility that they may want to share a secret—something they have told no one else. Because clients disclose even when no direct inquiry is made, mental health professionals in all sorts of roles need to know how to respond. As a final note, we have chosen to focus primarily on inquiring about sexual abuse, because herein lies the most discomfort. Asking about childhood physical abuse, while important, appears to generate less conflict and to arouse less anxiety among professionals.

WHY PROFESSIONALS RESIST ASKING

Despite increasing awareness that many people requesting mental health services have histories of childhood trauma and evidence that this knowledge is necessary for the development of appropriate helping plans and interventions, many professionals don't know about their clients' abuse backgrounds. Jacobson and Herald (1990) reported that 44% of their research subjects who had sexual abuse histories had never spoken of their experiences to anyone. Other studies have found that when clients were asked directly about their pasts for the purposes of research, they often disclosed abuse information that had never been documented in their clinical charts, despite formal mental health assessments (Briere & Runtz, 1987; Briere & Zaidi, 1989). One reason for this discrepancy is that clients often don't tell spontaneously. For example, in a national survey of the general population, researchers found that 42% of men and 33% of women reported that they had never told anyone that they had been sexually abused (Finkelhor, Hotaling, Lewis, & Smith, 1990). Recent work continues to provide evidence that mental health professionals are not inquiring about or are unaware of the abuse histories of their clients (Wurr & Partridge, 1996). A review of 53 charts with admission forms that asked about a history of trauma found that in 36 charts, admitting psychiatrists had recorded no abuse information (Read & Fraser, 1998). Although it is possible that the question was asked and the answer not documented, these charts had very few other blank areas. In a second study of a hospital setting, the majority of patients could not remember being asked, even though questions about abuse were part of the standard nursing history template (DiNunzio, 1998).

Some research evidence suggests that mental health professionals are uncomfortable discussing sexual abuse, primarily because this topic has not been incorporated into their academic or clinical teaching (Briere & Zaidi, 1989; Bryer, Nelson, Miller, & Krol, 1987; Herman, 1986; Jacobson & Richardson, 1987). A survey of American general hospital psychiatric units revealed that as few as 30% of staff had specialized training in the area (Mitchell, Grindel, & Laurenzano, 1996). In a large Canadian study of psychiatric nurses and nursing assistants, 50% of participants reported that they did not feel competent to help survivors of abuse (Gallop, McCay, Austin, Bayer, & Peternelj-Taylor, 1998). Sixty-five percent acknowledged limited abilities in initiating and discussing sexual abuse, and 80% were unsure about how to proceed when planning helping strategies. Participants also indicated uncertainty regarding their professional authority and role and expressed fears about planting ideas in their clients' heads (Gallop et al., 1998). When asked how they had learned about caring for sexually abused clients, 80% indicated that their knowledge had been acquired through self-study. Only 40% had learned about the topic in basic nursing programs, and an even smaller number referred to in-service training programs or conferences as sources of information.

In a study that looked at nurses' own experiences of abuse in relation to their attitudes and practices when caring for sexually abused clients, it was found that both abused and nonabused professionals generally supported routine inquiry (62% and 63%, respectively). However, they voiced many concerns about the practice (Gallop, McKeever, Toner, Lancee, & Lueck, 1995). Respondents worried that sexual abuse is too sensitive a topic for initial assessments and believed that discussions should be postponed until professionals have had the opportunity to establish relationships with clients. Some of the nurses felt that discussing sexual abuse was simply too intimate and should be avoided altogether. Most, whether abused or not, expressed discomfort when listening to abuse histories, not only because of their own lack of training but also because of the nature of the topic. In some cases, the professionals' own abuse histories interfered with their capacity to listen, but almost all respondents reported feeling distressed and angry, in combination with great sympathy, as they heard their clients' stories (Gallop et al., 1995).

Research has also documented professionals' failure to incorporate clients' sexual abuse experiences into diagnostic assessments and treatment plans. In a study conducted in an outpatient department of a large urban teaching hospital, inquiry about abuse had been mandated, and all professionals' work was carefully reviewed by attending psychiatrists or the clinic director. Findings clearly indicated that, although abuse backgrounds were elicited, the resulting information was not integrated into assessments or treatment plans in 90% of cases (Eilenberg, Fullilove, Goldman, & Mellman, 1996).

RESEARCH ON THE ASKING PROCESS

Although there is evidence that simply asking about sexual abuse is anxiety provoking for mental health professionals, little attention has been devoted to the inquiry process itself. In work that discusses the generic problem of asking about a stigmatizing health condition, Limandri (1989) found anecdotal evidence that showed that sexual abuse survivors refrain from disclosing to others because of a pervasive sense of shame. Abuse was considered the most stigmatizing problem of all and, as a result, the most difficult to talk about. Disclosures were characterized by an initial offering of small clues, which the client then used to evaluate whether or not the listener was someone who was safe. *Safety* has been defined as both a supportive environment and a competent listener who can respond appropriately when clients express painful feelings of fear, neediness, and vulnerability (Lister, 1982).

Unfortunately, many clients may have long histories of attempting to tell professionals, only to find that they were met with disbelief, blame, or aversion, causing them to describe the disclosure experience as traumatizing in itself (Limandri, 1989; Lister, 1982). Thus, it is not surprising that although some researchers believe disclosure is therapeutic, they simultaneously caution that professionals must have the skill and knowledge required to inquire appropriately and then to listen with caring and sensitivity (Doob, 1992; Hall, Sachs, Rayens, & Lutenbacher, 1993; Herman, 1986; Lister, 1982; Urbancic, 1992; Wingerson, 1992). If disclosures are disbelieved or discounted, professionals are not just being unhelpful, they are harming their client through further revictimization.

In research that examines what clients think of the questioning process (DiNunzio, 1998; Engels, 1997), participants expressed concern about how their histories of sexual abuse would be used to help them during their hospital admission, reinforcing other literature that suggests that, when inquiry occurs, the resulting information needs to be integrated into diagnoses, therapeutic interventions, and treatment plans (Doob, 1992). Engels (1997) interviewed 19 women about their experiences of being asked about their abuse backgrounds. Many suggested that being offered a choice of whether or not to answer would have made them feel more comfortable. They also reported that even well-handled inquiries elicited a multitude of disturbing feelings: guilt, shame, fear, anger, pain, vulnerability, and sadness. These feelings led to behaviors such as self-harm, dissociation, and flashbacks, further confirming the need for a safe environment and skilled professionals who can take the necessary time to listen with caring. In other research, clients reported discomfort at the rushed atmosphere during assessment, especially on admission to hospital, and felt that professionals often treated abuse inquiries as just another task to be completed, rather than an invitation to disclose intimate, terrifying, and heart-rending information that was supposed to be central to their treatment (DiNunzio, 1998). Respondents in all these studies listed skill, privacy, compassion, understanding, respect, and a nonjudgmental stance as crucial ingredients in the disclosure encounter.

ASKING ABOUT ABUSE

Given the high prevalence rates of childhood trauma among psychiatric clients, it seems only sensible that inquiry should be mandated in all mental health settings. After all, it is unethical to ignore suffering, and clients "tell" all the time, in their life experiences, their behaviors, and their symptoms. In addition, knowing about an abuse history is central to understanding clients' other problems and is an important ingredient in comprehensive treatment plans and competent referrals. Indeed, many mental health settings have moved to mandate inquiry; however, as research shows, this tactic does not ensure that the questions will be asked or the resulting information used. Although many professionals are uncomfortable with or avoid altogether questions about childhood trauma, others take the other extreme and argue that asking about abuse is like asking about anything else in mental health—symptoms, recent stressful events, medication compliance, sleeping patterns—and that to treat it as a special topic is to increase the stigma and secrecy. Though well-meaning, this stance neglects the knowledge, skill, and sensitivity required, and it risks minimizing the impact of disclosure on both the client and the professional listener. How professionals ask and how they respond can have profound effects on clients, and a mishandled inquiry or reaction can lead to harm. Asking about an abuse history should be neither an "always" nor a "never" decision; instead, inquiry should be subject to organizational and professional judgment.

To Ask or Not To Ask?

Mandated inquiry has its pitfalls and may not be appropriate under all circumstances. On the other hand, avoiding asking altogether is not helpful either. The following questions require thoughtful answers before professionals can make a firm decision about whether or not to ask.

1. *Why is it important for me to know?* This question speaks to the setting and the role of the professional. It asks what there is about the service offered that makes it imperative for this kind of information to be collected and incorporated into helping strategies. For example, professionals who provide short-term crisis services may decide that knowing about an abusive background helps them understand clients' current difficulties and assists them in making appropriate referrals. On the other hand, the nature of the work is typically short-term, oriented to the present, and focused on problem solving. Perhaps there is not enough time to respond with sensitivity, or there is a reasonable expectation that the crisis state will escalate if inquiries about abuse are made. These are judgment calls that require sharp individual and organizational thinking to ensure that policies fit clients' needs, as defined within the context of the service offered.

2. What am I going to do with the information? As research has demonstrated, it is not uncommon for information about clients' histories of childhood trauma to be gathered and then not used. Given that disclosing or talking about abuse can trigger disturbing behavioral responses and given that it can be emotionally difficult for professionals to hear stories of abuse, it only makes sense to have a clear understanding of how the material is to be used before everyone is put to the trouble of gathering it. It is also questionable practice from the perspective of client privacy to retain such intimate details in formal documentation when, in fact, there was no real reason for asking in the first place. On the other hand, if helping strategies are to be planned and implemented within the context of clients' experiences of trauma, then it becomes necessary to ensure that the information is available—insofar as clients are willing to disclose. In any setting, it is not only important for clients to know what information is being documented and how it will be used, but also who else has access to it.

The documentation of abuse can have significant legal ramifications—for example, records can be subpoenaed for court cases. Mental health organizations need to be clear on the legislation in their jurisdiction and have written policies on recording. Professionals and clients in any setting—housing, vocational, case management, counseling, and hospital—need to know that the confidentiality of records cannot always be protected. In addition, the content and style of notes must be sensitive—at all times—especially because clients themselves may read what has been written about them, given that, in most instances, they have the legal right to view their own records.

3. Can I explain to clients why I am asking? One of the first signs that professionals have not carefully thought through the reasons why they are asking about abuse histories, or perhaps one of the reasons why they don't ask at all, is that they are unsure themselves why they are inquiring. As a result, they are not prepared to field questions from clients as to their motives. If, however, the reasons behind the inquiry are well defined, clients' questions and concerns can be discussed openly.

4. Do I know how to ask? Asking clients about their abuse histories includes three components. First, professionals must explain why they are asking. Second, they must tell clients what use will be made of the information. Finally, they need to offer clients the opportunity to decline to answer. The following is a sample of how to approach an inquiry:

> I would like to ask you some questions about a history of physical or sexual abuse. First, I would like to tell you why we ask these questions. As you may be aware, many people who have mental health difficulties or seek help from a service such as this one have been physically or sexually abused either as a child or adult. These experiences may be related to their mental health problems or current difficulties. This information will help us in planning your treatment with you. You do not have to answer these questions, and, if you do choose to answer, you can tell me as much or as little as you feel comfortable with. Can I proceed?

The specific nature of inquiry will vary according to the setting and its purposes. Some settings may prefer to use a shorter questionnaire format such as Hoff's victimization assessment tool (see Appendix A, p. 117; Hoff, 1992). This tool screens not only for past histories of abuse but also for current self-harm activity and the potential for assault, because these behaviors can be part of the aftermath of childhood trauma.

If services are focused specifically on trauma, initial assessments may be quite detailed (e.g., see the Sexual Victimization Interview [Russell, 1986] and the Briere history of physical abuse [Briere, 1992]). When extensive history taking is involved, it is useful to obtain other information about the abuse event not immediately revealed by the client. For example, supplementary questions may relate to when the incidents began; who the perpetrator was; and the frequency, severity, and duration of the abuse—important factors in assessing impact. However, clients must set the pace of disclosure, and their comfort, sense of safety, and willingness to elaborate must not only be respected but even take precedence over the interests of obtaining a complete history. It is also crucial that professionals not actively elicit emotional responses during the initial assessment phase. Clients need to maintain as much emotional distance from the material as possible in the interests of safety and containment.

When a research protocol underlies clinical work, it becomes important for the integrity of the study findings that professionals take additional time to define clearly what is meant by sexual or physical abuse. General questions, such as "Have you ever been sexually abused?" tend to generate more false negatives—clients answer "no" when in fact they have been abused—either because of their wish to minimize their experiences or because they aren't sure whether or not what happened would qualify as abuse. As pointed out previously, professionals who work in longer-term clinical or treatment roles tend not to mind if clients choose not to disclose when first asked, because their main concern is the safety and security of the developing therapeutic relationship. Disclosure, when and if it occurs, is expected to unfold over time. However, the demands of research dictate that questioning must be precise and detailed to ensure the highest level of accuracy in clients' answers and thus in the study's findings. In addition, the many approval processes attached to research endeavors must have been completed before any data are gathered: an ethics review, full disclosure of the nature of the research, and signed consents from subjects. In this type of focused questioning, specific examples of behaviors will likely be used to indicate clearly what is meant. For example,

> Before you were 14 (some settings will use an older age), did you have any sexual experiences with an adult or someone at least 5 years older than you? By this we mean sexual encounters, including being touched, being asked to touch another, being fondled, or being kissed in a sexual manner by family members (including father, mother, stepparents, brothers, grandparents, cousins, uncles, etc.) or by non-family members (including neighbors, priests, teachers, strangers, etc.).
>
> Before age 14, did any of the above individuals try to have or succeed in having sexual intercourse with you?
>
> During adolescence, were you a victim of sexual assault?
>
> During adulthood, have you been a victim of sexual assault?
>
> During childhood or adulthood, have you been a victim of physical assault?
>
> Are you currently in a physically and/or sexually abusive relationship?
>
> Is there anything else you think it would be useful for us to know about your history of physical and/or sexual abuse?

If this type of questioning does double duty as a data-gathering instrument for research and as an initial clinical assessment, the emotional fallout evoked in clients can be handled within the client-professional relationship. However, if these questions are being asked solely for the purposes of research, then the researchers themselves need to be skilled in handling the aftermath of disclosure. Some research protocols include provisions for referrals to therapists or require interviewers to provide respondents with a list of available resources to ensure that they have somewhere to turn if they become overwhelmed. Research subjects should also be assured that they can refuse to answer any and all questions and that they can stop the interview at any time if they begin to feel over-whelmed. Placing the client in firm control of the pacing of the interview serves to reconcile the demands for precision in data collection with the ethical goal of safety and security for respondents.

5. Do I have the time to ask? As the many examples of inquiry de-scribed previously show, asking about abuse takes time, as does hearing disclosure. In addition, knowledge of an abuse history may lead to fur-ther inquiry about sleep difficulties, problems of nightmares and flash-backs, concerns about feeling safe in coed accommodation, and many other details that assist in proper treatment planning—and these supple-mentary questions also take time (Gallop et al., 1998). If admitting or as-sessment procedures are rushed, as is so often the case in present-day mental health services, it may be wiser to postpone asking until later in the process. On the other hand, if this information is required immedi-ately for treatment decision making, or if an abuse history is a program-matic entrance requirement, a simple "yes" or "no" answer may suffice, as long as professionals are aware that a "no" answer may mean either that abuse has not occurred or that the client does not wish to disclose at this time.

6. Is there a private place where I can ask these questions? Privacy can be one of the first casualties of the search for economy and efficiency in mental health care. In many overloaded emergency and admitting de-partments, space allotments typically take into account some level of physical privacy but disregard the fact that conversations can readily be overheard. In the same fashion, underfunded housing programs, case management services, hostels, or drop-in centers save money by not pro-viding offices (although staff may share a desk and a phone). Case man-agers frequently meet their clients in restaurants, shopping malls, and coffee shops. These conditions mean that there is very little secluded space for clients to talk about sensitive issues. Sometimes, professionals can be under pressure to get the job done, so they ask their questions and collect the needed information anyway. Sensitive organizational policies must allow for appropriate scheduling of assessments and the provision of some private interview space for those instances when intimate questions need to be asked. Alternatively, professionals and their organizations may decide that they simply cannot offer the appropriate conditions for disclosure and may instead put mechanisms into place to refer clients to other services where this particular need can be met. Either approach is valid insofar as it is thought through.

7. *Is this the right time to ask?* Disclosure must be viewed in the context of other factors in the client's life. If he or she is in the middle of a crisis that demands immediate attention or is paralyzed by depression, inquiry needs to be delayed. Some clients will say that now is not the time, because they have the care of their children to think of and they just can't "lose it." Others will say that they have abuse in their backgrounds but that they don't want to dig it up all over again. These assertions must be respected.

For clients who have been diagnosed with a psychotic disorder, inquiry about abuse needs to occur when they are at their strongest and when they are fully in control. Even then, if disclosure is not handled with great care and at a slow pace, there is the very real possibility that the emotions elicited will precipitate a breakdown.

8. *Do I know what to do if the client says, "Yes, I have been abused?"* Asking the question is one thing. Responding to disclosure is quite another. The remainder of this text is focused on how to be helpful once disclosure is made, but there are some basic skills professionals must employ:

1. Listen with attention. Let clients talk. Disclosure may be detailed or may be confined to a few terse words. Concentrate on what is being said. If you must take notes, warn clients in advance of the assessment or initial interview that this is a requirement and then take notes in a manner that doesn't compromise attentiveness to what is being said.

2. Remain neutral. There is no need to confirm or deny what clients are saying; instead, simply listen to their perceptions of what happened. Professionals also need to know that it is unethical to try to "open clients up" or to probe with a barrage of questions designed to access memories that are presently unavailable or that clients don't wish to reveal. Clients must be free to tell as much or as little as they themselves deem appropriate.

3. Remain calm. Clients with abuse experiences have extreme difficulty managing their own emotional states. They also fear that they will be rejected and abandoned when they tell their shameful secret, and because they are attuned to any clue that indicates distress, they may stop disclosure in an effort to "take care" of the listening professional's feelings. Professionals need to communicate in both direct and indirect ways that they can handle disclosure. Clients require the safety of a calm, even demeanor—with listening professionals neither reacting in obvious shock or offering excessive sympathy. A comment such as "Your father should be put in jail for what he did!" while seemingly sympathetic, is absolutely terrifying to clients, because it signals that they are losing control of what will be done with the information they have provided. Neutral but empathetic statements such as "I admire your courage for telling me" or "I'm sad to hear that" allow professionals to acknowledge the anger and sorrow clients feel without opening the door to an escalated emotional reaction.

4. Create containment. Initial disclosures are typically characterized by parameters such as time constraints, the newness of the information, and the early stage of the client-professional relationship—natural boundaries that can serve the goal of containment. Although clients need some time to reveal even basic facts, there should be no invitation to go on and on and on. Disclosures, understandably, can trigger extremely disturbing emotional and cognitive states, and clients do not yet have the skills to calm themselves down. Bringing closure to the interaction needs to be timed so that enough material has been revealed for clients to know that they are understood, but not so much that they begin to lose themselves in reliving traumatic events. Ideally, professionals should signal the end of this part of the assessment by explaining exactly how the disclosure will be integrated into treatment plans. Professionals can make a statement such as, "Thank you for telling me. While you are in the program (at the hospital), we can work with you to help you deal with these sorts of problems—if that's what you want."

In instances where disclosure has been spontaneous (the professional didn't ask about an abusive past, but clients felt the need to tell anyway), it can be important to ask why they have chosen to tell now and what they would like done with the information. For some, just being heard is all that is wanted. Later, they may wish to take action to resolve their feelings, but not at this moment in time. Professionals must respect these wishes. Given clients' past experiences of powerlessness and betrayal, providing as much control as possible over what happens after disclosure is critical. For those who appear to be seeking a next step, it is important to clarify whether or not they have discussed the matter with other professionals. If not, clearly, it is appropriate to suggest that these experiences are something they may wish to talk over with a therapist, and, with permission, a referral may be arranged.

9. Do I know about resources for clients? Professionals may gather information about clients' abuse backgrounds even if they themselves will not be providing direct help for this problem. For example, professionals whose main role is to make referrals (crisis workers, discharge planners) need to know about an abusive past so that they can work with clients to ensure that they find housing and generic community- or hospital-based mental health services that are sensitive to their backgrounds, as well as specialized counseling or therapy that can deal directly with the problem. However, clients have to agree (typically in writing) to having this, as well as other information, shared.

Many counseling agencies provide service brochures and encourage direct self-referral. Having these materials available provides clients with control over the decision of whether or not to seek further help. Professionals should also know whether services are covered by health insurance or require direct payment—a critical decision-making factor for clients who live in poverty. Clients should also have access to a list of emergency resources—waiting lists for services can be long, and crises may arise before they are able to access help.

10. Do I know how these disclosures will affect me? Professionals who choose to work in the area of trauma should not do so lightly. Disclosures of abuse can be harrowing. The level of sadistic cruelty that adults are capable of leveling at vulnerable children knows no bounds, and, although not all disclosures involve the extremes of abuse, no professional emerges from any such process unchanged. Some of us have an innate capacity for self-protection, but most of us must develop these skills. We need the support of one another in our professional environments, and we must have access to supervisory resources and other experts to deal with the complex countertransference responses that can occur. The inescapable reality is that we must care for ourselves or we will lose our ability to be helpful. Risks such as burnout, secondary trauma, and vicarious traumatization are discussed in full in Chapter 15.

Given the prevalence of childhood trauma in the general population, it is likely that many health professionals will themselves have personal histories of abuse. Inevitably, these experiences will affect our responses to disclosure, particularly if professionals have intense unrealized feelings and have not sought personal counseling (Gallop et al., 1995). Although professionals with abuse backgrounds may share some similarities with their clients, each person's history is unique and must be respected as such. It can never be assumed that we automatically know what clients are feeling or what actions they wish to take. In fact, disclosure of *any* personal information on the part of the professional needs to be a thoughtful and purposeful activity, not an impulsive decision. Thus, it is very rarely appropriate to speak of our own abuse histories to clients. Even though we may think that this information will create an empathic atmosphere of shared experience, it is the client's story that is the focus of the helping relationship. Our own disclosures can leave them with the impression that we have enough difficulties of our own to deal with and that their pain is just one more burden we bear.

11. Am I in a position to help? We are personally and professionally attuned to clients' cries for help. How can we not reach out? But good intention is no substitute for knowledge and skill. Trauma therapy is highly skilled work. A professional's role may be either to provide help directly or, if we do not have the necessary training or appropriate mandate, to refer clients to suitable resources. Either tactic ensures that we are doing what we are supposed to: relieving suffering. In this process, however, it is important that we do not rush in with offers of help when we are not qualified or when we are working in roles that do not include responding to trauma. Obvious questions to ask under these circumstances are: Do I have the knowledge and skills? Does my workplace support trauma work? Do I have access to supervision? Do I understand the risks to myself? Do I know of resources that can help this client more effectively than I can? As mental health professionals, it is our responsibility to know our individual strengths and limitations and to work within the scope of our service environment.

CONCLUSION

The prevalence of histories of childhood trauma among people who have a psychiatric diagnosis is high, but routine inquiry has the potential of revictimizing survivors if it is not handled sensitively. Unskilled professionals who lack the knowledge and comfort to discuss abuse histories may do real harm by disconfirming, ignoring, or minimizing these experiences. As professionals and the mental health organizations that employ them become more aware of the impact of abuse on mental health, the likelihood of mandated inquiry in all sorts of settings will increase. Under these circumstances, all direct-service staff and their supervisors and managers must have the opportunity to acquire the necessary skills to ask with sensitivity, to respond to disclosures with empathy, and to actively include this information in treatment plans. As soon as disclosure occurs, the world is never the same. But it can be an empowering step for clients if the surrounding environment is supportive and if the listening professional is well trained.

REFERENCES

Briere, J. N. (1992). *Child abuse trauma: Theory and treatment of the lasting effects.* Newbury Park, CA: Sage.

Briere, J., & Runtz, M. (1987). Post sexual abuse trauma: Data and implications for clinical practice. *Journal of Interpersonal Violence, 2,* 367-379.

Briere, J., & Zaidi, L. Y. (1989). Sexual abuse histories and sequelae in female psychiatric emergency room patients. *American Journal of Psychiatry, 146,* 1602-1606.

Bryer, J., Nelson, B., Miller, J., & Krol, P. (1987). Childhood sexual and physical abuse as factors in adult psychiatric illness. *American Journal of Psychiatry, 144,* 1426-1430.

DiNunzio, R. (1998). *Asking and talking about a history of childhood sexual abuse.* Unpublished master's thesis, University of Toronto, Toronto, Canada.

Doob, D. (1992). Female sexual abuse survivors as patients: Avoiding retraumatization. *Archives of Psychiatric Nursing, 6,* 245-251.

Eilenberg, J., Fullilove, M. T., Goldman, R. G., & Mellman, L. (1996). Quality and use of trauma histories obtained from psychiatric outpatients through mandated inquiry. *Psychiatric Services, 47,* 165-169.

Engels, S. (1997). *Routine inquiry about childhood sexual abuse: Perceptions of women hospitalized in psychiatric settings.* Unpublished master's thesis, University of Toronto, Toronto, Canada.

Finkelhor, D., Hotaling, G., Lewis, I. A., & Smith, C. (1990). Sexual abuse in a national survey of adult men and women: Prevalence, characteristics, and risk factors. *Child Abuse & Neglect, 14,* 19-28.

Gallop, R., McCay, E., Austin, W., Bayer, M., & Peternelj-Taylor, C. (1998). A survey of psychiatric nurses regarding working with clients who have a history of sexual abuse. *Journal of the American Psychiatric Nursing Association, 4,* 9-17.

Gallop, R., McKeever, P., Toner, B., Lancee, W., & Lueck, M. (1995). Inquiring about childhood sexual abuse as part of the nursing history: Opinions of abused and nonabused nurses. *Archives of Psychiatric Nursing, 9,* 146-151.

Hall, L. A., Sachs, B., Rayens, M. K., & Lutenbacher, M. (1993). Childhood physical and sexual abuse: Their relationship with depressive symptoms in adulthood. *IMAGE: Journal of Nursing Scholarship, 25,* 317-323.

Herman, J. L. (1986). Histories of violence in an outpatient population: An exploratory study. *American Journal of Orthopsychiatry, 56,* 137-141.

Hoff, L. A. (1992). Battered women: Understanding, identification, and assessment—A psychosociocultural perspective: Part 1. *Journal of the American Academy of Nurse Practitioners, 4,* 148-155.

Jacobson, A., & Herald, C. (1990). The relevance of childhood sexual abuse to adult psychiatric inpatient care. *Hospital and Community Psychiatry, 41,* 154-158.

Jacobson, A., & Richardson, B. (1987). Assault experiences of 100 psychiatric inpatients: Evidence of the need for routine inquiry. *American Journal of Psychiatry, 144,* 908-913.

Limandri, B. J. (1989). Disclosure of stigmatizing conditions: The discloser's perspective. *Archives of Psychiatric Nursing, 3,* 69-78.

Lister, E. D. (1982). Forced silence: A neglected dimension of trauma. *American Journal of Psychiatry, 139,* 872-876.

Mitchell, D., Grindel, C. G., & Laurenzano, C. (1996). Sexual abuse assessment on admission by nursing staff in general hospital psychiatric settings. *Psychiatric Services, 47,* 159-164.

Read, J., & Fraser, A. (1998). Abuse histories of psychiatric inpatients: To ask or not to ask? *Psychiatric Services, 49,* 355-359.

Russell, D. E. H. (1986). *The secret trauma: Incest in the lives of girls and women.* New York: Basic Books.

Urbancic, J. C. (1992). Empowerment support with adult female survivors of childhood incest: Part 2. Application of Orem's methods of helping. *Archives of Psychiatric Nursing, 6,* 282-286.

Wingerson, N. (1992). Psychic loss in adult survivors of father-daughter incest. *Archives of Psychiatric Nursing, 6,* 239-244.

Wurr, C., & Partridge, I. (1996). The prevalence of a history of acute sexual abuse in an inpatient population. *Child Abuse & Neglect, 20,* 867-872.

APPENDIX A

Hoff's Scale:
Suggested Screening
Questions for
Victimization
and Violence

1. Have you ever been troubled or injured by any kind of abuse
   or violence? (e.g., hit by a partner, forced sex)
   Yes _____ No _____ Not Sure _____ Refused _____
   If yes, check one:
   By someone in your family _____
   By an acquaintance or stranger _____
   Describe:_____

2. If yes, has something like this ever happened before?
   Yes _____ No _____ If yes, when? _____
   Describe:_____

3. Do you have anyone you can turn to or rely on now to protect
   you from possible further injury?
   Yes _____ No _____ If yes, who? _____

117

4. Do you feel so badly now that you have thought of hurting yourself/suicide?

Yes _____ No _____

If yes, what have you thought about doing?

5. Are you so angry about what's happened that you have considered hurting someone else?

Yes _____ No _____ If yes, describe briefly:_____

_____

_____

SOURCE: Reprinted with permission from Hoff (1992).

PART 2

EFFECTIVE INTERVENTIONS

CHAPTER 7

Understanding Power

Power exists in all relationships, and its expression can take multiple forms. Survivors, however, know only one form: power that harms, wounds, humiliates, and conquers. This type of power is called "dominance" and is characterized by its win-lose quality and by the application of coercion or force. The strong can impose their will upon the more vulnerable, and there is very little to stop them. Sociologists argue that most of us think of power in the narrow terms of dominance, neglecting its more benign face. Although it is true that power can injure and damage, it can also nurture, inspire, and heal (Wartenberg, 1990).

Mental health professionals are powerful because we are educated, employed, and occupy a role in society that is valued. We are also powerful within the context of the relationships that we create with our clients. Yet power as a central theme in the mental health field is rarely discussed. Confronting it is critical for two important reasons. First, clients who are survivors of childhood abuse have experienced the misuse of power in many cruel ways, and they are finely attuned to its presence in helping relationships. Second, there is a hidden but unresolved tension between mental health laws that provide for involuntary commitment and the view that true help can only be offered (or received) on a voluntary basis.

MENTAL HEALTH LAWS AS "POWER OVER"

Mental health laws provide mechanisms that can force hospitalization and treatment on clients if they pose a danger to themselves or others. In addition, some states and provinces have what are called community committal laws whereby clients are required to take their psychiatric medications as a condition of continued residence in the community; if they do not, they can be returned to the hospital. These laws are examples of "power over," in that they prescribe a socially sanctioned form of power that is wielded from above and accompanied by force to obtain compliance. Most survivors of child abuse do not have a diagnosis of mental illness and thus need not concern themselves with these kinds of laws, but survivors who have the severest symptoms must be aware of how they can be affected.

The power of mental health laws is often criticized as being excessive and open to misuse, serving primarily to control patients and clients rather than help them (Breggin, 1991; Szasz, 1974). Indeed, the use of force is contrary to the common definition of *help*, which is based on altruistic concern for another's well-being and voluntary participation. Former mental patients, now calling themselves "consumers" and "psychiatric survivors," protest that laws that allow psychiatrists to "lock them up" are an infringement upon their civil rights (Boudreau & Lambert, 1993). In addition, those who have experienced involuntary commitment, forced treatment, and mechanical restraint identify these measures as traumatizing, with many feeling that they have been harmed, not helped (Everett, 1994). However, some family members of the mentally ill and, indeed, the majority of the general public believe that society is justified in forcing clients to accept psychiatric treatment both because clients' judgment is impaired by illness and because taking such measures is "for their own good." These disparate views point to an unresolved dilemma that is central to the provision of mental health services: Can help be forced on people and still be called "help"?

Although psychiatrists usually bear the brunt of the criticism for forcing treatment, the reality is that all professionals who work in the mental health system have a part to play—whether advising commitment, carrying out the order, or simply witnessing the event. Forced treatment is power-as-dominance in action, and as a result, it is traumatizing for everyone involved—patients, families, professionals, and police. Identifying the social control role of the mental health system is, in some senses, liberating. It allows for an open discussion of the reality that, under certain extreme conditions, mental health professionals can have their clients committed, treated against their will, or mechanically restrained. Stating this fact defines the outer boundary of the voluntary mental health helping relationship. Insofar as relationships between professionals and clients remain voluntary, help as it is traditionally understood can be provided. When conditions for legal commitment are met, this relationship changes to one of control. This is a painful burden that needs to be acknowledged and expressed, because force is *never* the preferred course of action and should represent absolutely the last resort. Professionals must grapple with the reality that they are invested with the power to use force—and that this power, even when used as a last resort and with utmost wisdom, is an immense responsibility.

Although it may be somewhat of an oversimplification, generally speaking, community mental health settings, rehabilitation programs, and outpatient departments have wider latitude to create and maintain voluntary helping relationships with their clients—insofar as they are not working under community committal laws or with mandated clients.[1] Institutional and hospital inpatient settings have a more limited opportunity, because one of their primary roles is to admit and detain people under commitment orders. Box 7.1 contains two diagrams that represent the "voluntary helping frame" in community and outpatient settings versus hospitals and institutions.[2] Their purpose is to demonstrate that in both instances, help can occur but that help is of a different sort and focus when the voluntary helping frame is restricted.

THE VOLUNTARY HELPING FRAME, OR "POWER WITH"

As these diagrams point out, involuntary commitment is a salient influence in the mental health system as a whole and, as such, cannot be denied or ignored. However, as professionals, we can work with our cli-

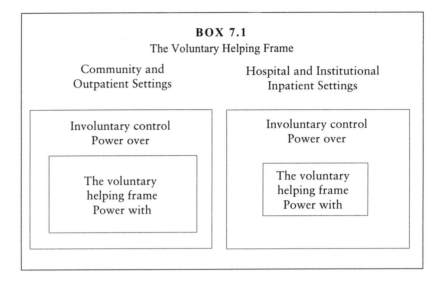

ents to ensure that our relations remain within the voluntary helping frame as much as possible. In order to do this, we must focus on assisting clients to grow, change, develop, and recover—with the ultimate goal of avoiding, on a permanent basis, the possibility of involuntary commitment.

Transformative power, as opposed to dominance, nurtures, inspires, or heals. It is "the constitution of the other as a more independent being as a result of the relationship itself" (Wartenberg, 1990, p. 206). We have chosen to call this type of power "power with" in contrast to "power over" in line with terminology used by Miller and Stiver (1997). Transformative power relationships, like dominant ones, include by definition a power imbalance. However, with transformative power, the focus is the nature and quality of the helping relationship itself. The tactics employed are intended to create a client-professional environment characterized by continuous learning, ongoing skills development, choice, and the dignity of risk combined with natural consequences. The goal of transformative power is mutual liberation—from dependency (for the client) and from being depended upon (for the professional).

HEALTHY "POWER WITH" RELATIONSHIPS

Creating healthy "power with" relationships within the voluntary helping frame, and with psychiatric clients who also have histories of childhood trauma, is particularly daunting because a principal indicator of childhood trauma is the inability to relate well to others.

As social beings, people are engaged in relationships most of the time. However, for mental health professionals, building healthy relationships must become a conscious, purposeful activity that integrates substantial theoretical knowledge along with the application of practical skills. Miller and Stiver (1997) point to the centrality of *mutual empathy,* defined as hearing, seeing, and knowing how another feels and responding in a manner that mirrors understanding. The resulting connection creates growth. Abuse disconnects survivors from the possibility of creating mutual empathy, because their feelings are consistently ignored.

In our many and varied roles as mental health professionals, we have a responsibility to understand the importance of relationship building in our ability to be effective helpers. Positive client-professional relationships have a number of necessary components: mutual respect, clear communication, permeable boundaries, authenticity, and accountability (the parameters of the helping frame).

Mutual Respect. By definition, there is dual presence in any relationship— a "me" and a "you." Respect begins with the ability see the "me" that is in "you," to recognize in another the humanness that resides within one's self. It is also an emotional connection that says, "I see qualities and capabilities in you that I value and admire." Although respect is most often discussed as a component of individual relationships, it is also part of a broader worldview characterized by the belief that all people are worthy. However, respect is not only belief—it is belief coupled with action. Congruence of thought and action is integral to the building of a respectful relationship.

Although respect can be communicated through learned techniques and practice methods, it is most consistently conveyed in the small unaware spaces of human interaction such as eye contact, body language, and tone of voice. In fact, these minute gestures are often attended to much more closely than more obvious forms of communication. We must continually examine our relational stance, because we are communicating with clients at all times and at all levels—and respect must reside in each and every nuance.

Respect must also be *mutual*. It is not enough for us to demonstrate respect for our clients—we must also demand respect in return. Obviously, an important step is to go first. Clients are far more likely to respond to professionals in a respectful manner if they feel respected themselves. But modeling, all by itself, is insufficient. We should be prepared to have direct conversations with clients about our expectations, conversations that should include an outline of our own commitment to respect and of what behaviors we in turn require. Although respectful behavior is often defined in the negative—what clients should not do—with abuse survivors, it must also be defined in the positive—what they should do. For example, survivors have learned to suppress their own needs and to do as they are told, particularly in the face of authority. Respect, under these circumstances, can mean asking clients to reveal their needs honestly or to say "no" when they disagree. These sorts of open exchanges produce a respectful atmosphere in and of themselves. They also create a context in which inadvertent breaches, by either professional or client, can be confronted and corrective action taken. In summary, respect is the cornerstone of "power with" and the foundation upon which healthy relationships are created. Without it, not much else works.

Clear Communication. Working with clients who have histories of child abuse in combination with a psychiatric diagnosis can teach professionals important lessons regarding clear communication, principally because speaking and being heard are absolutely central for people who have been forcibly silenced. As a result of their backgrounds, many survivors have developed habits that can inhibit clear communication. First, a history of child abuse can leave survivors highly anxious and unable to attend well to what others are saying. They may also dissociate or "space out" and be unable to recall what was said. Some may have developed short-term memory problems as a consequence of electroconvulsive therapy. Others may require an adjustment to their psychiatric medications so that they are alert enough to participate in conversation. Still others will have evolved a particular style of speaking through which they defend against further hurt by filling up the air with incessant and pressured talk, to the point that it is difficult for professionals to find any pause in which to take a conversational turn. Finally, people who have lived lives of neglect, abuse, poverty, and institutionalization may not have developed the words to convey what they mean. This idea goes beyond the concept of limited vocabulary and speaks to an inability to connect thoughts and feelings with words—another hallmark of a severe abuse background. As a consequence, some survivors' conversations may seem impoverished and at odds with their level of intellect and richness of personality.

Given these sorts of problems, it is important for professionals to attend to even the smallest components of communication. In some cases, we will find ourselves actively teaching clients how to initiate and maintain the normal turn taking of conversational flow. We also need to check regularly that we understand clearly what clients are trying to say, from the perspective of both content and meaning. This is no simple task, because these sorts of ongoing probes for clarity fly in the face of conventional conversation. Nevertheless, providing real help demands that we understand who our clients are, how they think, and what they value. Conversely, it is wise to check that clients hear and understand what is being said to them, given that "spacing out" or "forgetting" are common defense mechanisms. Although these conversational stops and starts may at first seem artificial and tedious, they will net substantial benefits in the long run, because understanding is a second foundational component of a "power with" relationship.

Permeable Boundaries. Survivors of childhood trauma have had their physical, emotional, and relational boundaries breached early and often. As a result, they have trouble judging where "self" ends and "other" begins. A boundary is defined as the ability to establish and maintain a clear division between "me" and "you" whereby those things that are mine (body, thoughts, feelings, opinions, actions) are known to be owned and protected by me, and those things that are yours are known to be owned and protected by you. A permeable boundary relates to an ability to judge accurately under what conditions it is safe to reveal personal information or to allow people to be close—physically, emotionally, or relationally.

Establishing and maintaining clear boundaries is a hard task and tends to be a skill set that develops and improves as people grow and mature.

However, survivors of child abuse have particular problems because they know that the world is a dangerous place and see harm as a natural consequence of human contact. Although some survivors may isolate almost all the time and others may regularly repeat their victimization, most alternate between these two relational stances, demonstrating a deep yearning for, combined with a terror of, human intimacy.

Alternation between fear ("I need you, don't leave me") and defensive anger ("I hate you because I know you will hurt me") wreaks havoc with establishing a healthy client-professional relationship. Clients may be clingy and demanding one day (or hour), angry and blaming the next. They may continually test the relationship in disconcerting ways, such as bringing gifts; pushing for more and more time; asking to become a friend; or, in some cases, becoming overtly sexual. Some professionals react in ways that are not mindful of their own boundaries—by rescuing; becoming angry; blurring the delineation between their private and professional roles; or, in extreme cases, becoming sexually involved with clients.

Professionals have typically defended against these sorts of boundary violations by erecting barriers expressed as formal rules and regulations that define, on our behalf, a wide social distance between ourselves and our clients. Certainly, staff in hospitals and institutions tend to have more formal relationships with their clients (patients), while at the other extreme, some community professionals virtually live with their clients, as with supportive housing or group home programs. Professionals who work in small towns or rural areas may know their clients on a number of levels, making the maintenance of clear boundaries an exceptionally tricky exercise requiring great skill and self-insight.

The key to establishing boundaries is self-awareness on the part of the professional coupled with a self-reflective practice stance. Professional supervision is also necessary for those moments when the objective opinion of a less involved colleague or manager can help disentangle personal emotions from professional responsibilities (see Chapter 15 for a fuller discussion of the role of supervision). Maintaining boundaries will be a never-ending struggle when helping survivors of child abuse, and continuous learning is to be expected. However, it is important to understand that low-level boundary violations—inviting clients to lunch, hiring them to help out in the home, or reserving the last appointment of the day for one "special" client—while sometimes interpreted as extra dedication, have been demonstrated to have the potential to escalate to the level of exploitation and abuse (Dolan, 1992).

Authenticity. Authenticity is defined as being your genuine self most of the time. This is a deceptively simple definition for such a complex endeavor. First, in order to *be* ourselves, we must *know* ourselves, and this is a lifelong journey. Second, we must consistently express our genuine self both personally and professionally. Third, we must attune ourselves to our environments so we can modify the expression of our "self" to meet situational demands. Although a discussion of boundaries asks that professionals understand and maintain the division between our personal and professional roles, authenticity demands that we remain essentially the same person in either circumstance.

Authenticity in common terms means "what you see is what you get," and it is essential to the relationship-building enterprise because it creates an atmosphere of trust. People who are honestly themselves can be "known" in a way that is comforting and predictable, especially important factors for clients whose lives typify chaos and betrayal. There is, however, no easy recipe for accessing and expressing one's genuine self— and for doing so in tune with one's context. This skill, like so many others in the helping professions, is one that is developed over time in concert with ongoing study and practice.

Accountability. A functioning healthy relationship is based on a form of unwritten social contract, in this case a power contract (Everett, 2000) whereby those involved are held accountable to each other. A power contract means that each person agrees to contribute his or her own individual expertise, talent, or capability to the relationship so that both can benefit. The idea of a contract does not mean that the participating parties are necessarily equal—just that each has a contribution to make that is valued.

Accountability is a difficult concept for abuse survivors, because they typically see others as controlling their behavior but fail to recognize that they can have an effect themselves. In our professional helping roles, we are responsible for ensuring that clients understand that they have a part to play in the power contract. First, they need to understand why professionals need information from them, how it will be used, and what the consequences will be if it is withheld. Professionals and clients will also want to discuss how they will divide responsibilities. For example, the professional's responsibility may be to make appropriate referrals, whereas the client's role is to turn up at the appointments. The key ingredient in these sorts of discussions is transparency. Why information is needed, what tasks have to be done, who will do them and by when, what will happen if they are not done—all are details that define points of accountability within the power contract. They also serve to bring to mutual awareness necessary obligations and responsibilities that *both* parties must fulfill in order for the contract to work. These activities establish the parameters of the voluntary helping frame clearly and with limited ambiguity.

LIBERATION TACTICS

The ultimate goal of creating healthy relationships is to promote clients' greater independence. Although a healthy relationship and a clearly defined helping frame are the incubators for change, professionals also need to focus on forward movement, often described as growth and development or as healing and recovery, depending on the preferred perspective.

When first learning about liberation tactics (often called "empowerment"), some professionals ask, "Does this mean we let clients do whatever they want, whenever they want?" This question neglects the mutuality of client-professional relationships and ignores the critical process of negotiation. Neither client nor professional has all the answers. Each perspective has value, and through a process of negotiation, client and professional can eventually come to a mutual understanding of the best course of action to achieve positive change.

The tactics employed to help clients move forward under a "power with" or liberation paradigm are those that emphasize continuous learning, skills development, choice and the dignity of risk, and the power of natural consequences to create an internalized sense of self-discipline.

Continuous Learning. Adults who are survivors of child abuse learn that it is dangerous to question, analyze, and—in extreme cases—even to think or feel. Experiences such early apprehension—conducted by child welfare agencies; incarceration in youth correctional centers; and, eventually, admissions to psychiatric hospitals—acclimatizes survivors to lives in which regimen predominates. They learn that it is always someone else who decides what is "best" and that they have no choice. A liberation paradigm demands that professionals share information openly with clients and create barrier-free access (insofar as we are able) to available resources. But beyond these more instrumental offerings is the nurturance of an overall continuous learning atmosphere, one in which questions are welcomed, information is actively shared and analyzed, options are explored, and choices are weighed.

It is important, however, for professionals to recognize how difficult it will be for clients to begin to think for themselves and to become active, reflective participants in the decisions that relate to their own lives. In fact, some may retreat from this challenge because it is just too frightening. Others may insist that they *need* to be taken care of, especially in light of the fact that a history of abuse means that they were never cared for as children. These sorts of resistances are real and point to a need for professionals to proceed slowly—but proceed we must, because with encouragement, most clients can in time become more active in their own care.

Skills Teaching. In order for clients to grow and develop, they must discard old habits and learn new skills. The professional role in this process is as model, active teacher, and coach. An appropriate beginning place is to acknowledge the skills that clients already have. Sometimes these are obvious and positive, such as a sense of humor or a generous nature. Other abilities are less obvious and often relate to survival techniques that have developed under conditions of extreme duress. These coping mechanisms may serve the client in the short term, but they create other problems in the long term. For example, self-harm as a coping mechanism is often misinterpreted as a suicide attempt and may precipitate multiple involuntary admissions to the hospital. Substance abuse serves to deaden overwhelming emotion but leads directly to relationship problems, job loss, or trouble with the law. Other sorts of survival skills relate to managing the stress of poverty, substandard housing, or threats of violence. Sometimes, we have a hard time imagining what our clients' lives are really like, and we can make the mistake of assuming that we know what they need to learn. For example, a considerable amount of skill-teaching energy is spent showing clients how to budget money without any acknowledgment that they may have little discretionary income, how to do laundry when they have no access to affordable facilities, or how to shop for food when their accommodation offers no secure storage. These well-meaning activities neglect the context of clients' lives and, further, negate the value of the survival skills (both positive and negative) that they have developed on their own.

New, healthier coping mechanisms have to meet the goals of the old survival skills. These goals most often relate to basic human needs such as needs to be heard and understood; to achieve physical, emotional, and relational safety; to receive loving attention; to release anger effectively; and to modulate excessive emotion. The most important concern, from a liberation perspective, is to teach skills within the past and present context of clients' lives. Professionals must also build upon the skill base that clients already have, and finally, we must create an atmosphere of acceptance and high expectation where sincere effort and successive approximations are acknowledged and rewarded until the new skill is acquired. This last point is critical because it speaks to a level of optimism that this client group is often denied. They *can* learn new ways of being in the world. It may take time, and progress may be slow, but professionals who work within a liberation paradigm must maintain an optimistic focus on forward movement—despite difficulties and setbacks.

Choice and the Dignity of Risk. When clients have access to information and resources, they are more likely to make informed choices, but there is no guarantee that the choices they make will be the right ones. Even more disconcerting is the possibility that they may choose a course of action that appears to defy logic. However, clients have the right to be wrong—even to do dumb things—as long as they are not placing themselves or others in danger. Gadacz (1994) calls this "the dignity of risk," and it is central to the right to choose. Clients must be able to risk failure if they are to become independent beings.

The dignity of risk is often denied vulnerable groups. As professionals, we may equate our own career success with the success of our clients and may see our clients' mistakes as our own. Some mental health professionals work in settings where they are covertly blamed if clients make "wrong" choices, behave badly, or fail to comply. Others have been taught to prevent pain—at all costs—and there is no question that making a mistake hurts. However, mistakes are focused points of learning that can spur growth and development. Also, what at first appeared to have been a mistake may in the end turn out to be the right choice. Who is to know for sure without taking the time to try? We must also respect a client's right to be right—and our own right to be wrong. The professional role is to guide clients through the choosing process, not to make their choices for them.

Self-discipline. Survivors of child abuse have been harshly treated as a consequence of living—beaten, exploited, humiliated, and harmed, often by someone who was supposed to love and care for them. They grew up with an all-too-clear understanding of the pain of arbitrary punishment but with no knowledge of discipline.

Discipline is a form of training in which children (and adults) learn what they have done wrong, why it is wrong, and what they can do to solve the problem. Discipline leaves dignity intact. Consequences for wrongdoing are natural or are at least in proportion to the agreed-upon transgression. A liberation paradigm means that professionals must help clients achieve a sense of internalized self-discipline. Self-discipline is developed through experience and over time, often through making mistakes or taking poorly thought-out risks. In order for us to help clients develop their own sense of discipline, we must accord them not only the right to be wrong, but also the right to experience the consequences.

Coloroso (1995) proposes a four-step process to the development of self-discipline. Although her ideas are intended to help parents deal with children, they are nonetheless instructive because they help adult clients retrace a missed developmental step. Clients are typically poor self-observers and may not know the effect they have on others. Also, because they experience the world as dangerous, they can assume an all-encompassing self-defensive posture that seems merely good sense to them but that looks and feels to others like an attack. In addition, they have learned bad habits and hurtful behaviors from their abusers. Thus, the first step in teaching self-discipline is to let clients know what they have done wrong—in clear, straightforward, but neutral terms. Second, they need to know that the consequences for their actions and the difficulties they create are theirs to own. No one else is to blame. It is important to emphasize that, although they have learned these troubling behaviors as a result of past circumstances that were *not their fault,* nonetheless, what they say and do in the present is indisputably their responsibility. Third, clients need to be offered ideas and resources that will help them solve their own problems, and fourth, they must be given the opportunity to follow through on the solutions they devise. If they do not take action, they need to have a chance to experience the consequences, and then the conversation can begin again. This final step, although not always necessary, is called the "second-chance policy."

When this model is applied to adult survivors of trauma who also have psychiatric diagnoses, it is obvious that there are some commonly held beliefs that must be confronted. For example, it is typical to excuse behaviors that would otherwise not be tolerated because they are thought to be manifestations of mental illness. This perspective tends to mix up symptoms with behaviors. For example, a symptom of schizophrenia is hearing voices, but a behavior is assaulting a family member; a symptom of the aftermath of child abuse is mood swings, whereas a behavior is screaming insults. Making this distinction is crucial because it allows clients to take ownership of their own behaviors. Ownership places responsibility (and thus control) in their hands. A second belief is that symptoms, as the manifestations of disease, are beyond control. However, people who suffer from chronic physical conditions learn that there are many helpful strategies designed to manage the ups and downs of their illness. There is no reason why people with mental illness cannot learn similar strategies. A third belief is that clients should, at all times and under all circumstances, be protected from the consequences of their own actions because they are "sick." In truth, the natural consequences for bad or unwise behavior in adulthood can be painful and costly. For example, clients may choose to be sexually active without protection, risking sexually transmitted diseases or unwanted pregnancy. Other clients may choose not to pay their rent, risking eviction and homelessness. Still others may discontinue helpful medication or refuse to care for themselves emotionally, resulting in mental deterioration and subsequent admission to the hospital. These are only some of the many difficult choices that adult clients make, and allowing them the freedom to make them constitutes perhaps the greatest challenge to our commitment to a liberation paradigm. In these difficult instances, the professional role, insofar as the relationship remains voluntary, is to reiterate the four steps toward developing self-discipline: Tell clients exactly what they are doing wrong, ensure that they understand that they are completely responsible for their own actions, point out that there are healthier choices that they could make (along with offering resources), and give them a chance to follow through. Should they choose to continue their unwise, neglectful, or just plain bad behavior, the professional role is to allow the consequences to rest on their shoulders, acknowledge the pain they are feeling, and ask, "Is there anything you would like to do differently next time?"

Because this process is difficult and because monitoring the level of risk involved is critical, it is important that professionals maintain, at all times, close contact with their colleagues, managers, and supervisors. From time to time, clients may appear ready to cross the line from unwise to illegal, from competent to psychotic, from anger to assault, or from suicidal ideation to suicidal actions. In these instances, the "natural" consequences have gone beyond painful and have become dangerous or even life threatening. If clients refuse to draw back from this line and work on methods to regain control over their own symptoms and behaviors, it will be necessary to invoke the power that mental health laws accord us and use involuntary hospitalization as a containment strategy. However, we must not make these crucial judgments in isolation; instead, we should involve our clients (insofar as they are capable), supportive family and friends (if we have permission), and our colleagues and managers. Once the decision is made, there are precise legally defined steps that must be followed, orders to be written and signed by the appropriate authority, and forms to be completed, all accompanied by extensive clinical documentation. These actions are also carried out in concert with specific organizational policies and directives. At these times, accountability is crucial, because professionals and clients have now entered the involuntary helping frame, the boundaries of which are prescribed by law. Mistakes expose both the professional and his or her organization to extensive liability and can result in lawsuits, sanctions by funding agencies, dismissal for the professional, and any number of other penalties. Working within the confines of mental health law means that mental health professionals, as well as the police and the courts, are its stewards. Most of us who work with survivors of the severest forms of abuse who also have a diagnosis of mental illness will eventually either witness or be directly involved in the process of involuntary commitment. We, like our clients, must "own" the responsibility for our actions when we invoke the power we hold.

As a final note, there are things and circumstances over which no one has control. Clients do not "own" racism or gender discrimination. They are not responsible for their own poverty or for the fact that they have been victimized. However, survivors of abuse have learned that there is absolutely nothing over which they have control. The point of self-discipline is to bring clients to conscious awareness that there are areas in their lives where they have choice and control—but they also have responsibility and must face consequences. Nowhere is the foundation of a healthy relationship more crucial. Clients may become angry when they are not saved from the consequences of their own behavior. Professionals, who are trained to help and protect, may feel guilty for not responding to pleas for rescue. A relational atmosphere of respect, open communication, permeable boundaries, authenticity, and mutual accountability offers professionals and clients the best opportunity to work through these difficulties. And if we are successful, clients will emerge as stronger, more independent beings, and we will gain confidence in our own professional capabilities and skills.

USING "POWER OVER" RESPONSIBLY

Although clients have fairly wide latitude to make mistakes and take risks when they are within the voluntary helping frame, mental health legislation defines the types of risks they must be prevented from taking. Such legislation also defines the ways and means professionals can use to ensure that clients do not take these risks.

A "power with" liberation paradigm means that we work openly with clients so that they understand the mental health laws that affect them; where our own professional obligations lie; and under what specific circumstances involuntary commitment, forced treatment, or mechanical restraint can occur. However, these sorts of conversations are rarely held. Professionals may feel that openly discussing such issues will contaminate a "power with" relationship. Indeed, this sort of discussion may be unnecessary for clients whose problems are such that they are likely never to be committed. However, most mental health professionals who serve survivors of severe child abuse work in settings where clients have either already experienced involuntary treatment or are at future risk. Paradoxically, the best chance for clients and professionals to remain within the voluntary helping frame is to address proactively under exactly what conditions the force of mental health laws can be invoked.

Although there may be a number of ways to introduce this topic to clients, this is one instance when the formality of a written contractual agreement is invaluable. Appendix A (p. 139) is a template that professionals and clients might find helpful. Note that this form of contract is also useful in inpatient settings where mechanical restraint is a possibility; in housing where evictions occur; and in situations where clients are also parents, and professionals are required to report suspected child abuse. It is important that this contract be negotiated at a time of calm *before* crises occur. The answers to the questions are recorded, and both professional and client retain copies.

CONCLUSION

This chapter began by acknowledging the "power over" nature of the mental health system. Under certain legally defined circumstances, professionals can force clients who are judged to be a danger to themselves or others into the hospital and, if necessary, can treat them against their will. There are, nonetheless, substantial opportunities for professionals to provide services within a voluntary helping framework. By creating "power with" relationships and utilizing liberation tactics, professionals and clients can maintain an optimistic focus on growth and development, with the ultimate goal of being released from dependence on the "power over" capacities of the mental health system.

NOTES

1. These are people who *must* receive mental health services as a condition of parole or probation.

2. The therapeutic frame is a concept that relates to the parameters of therapy and the therapeutic relationship (Pearlman & Saakvitne, 1995). However, it translates well as a way of describing the tasks, roles, responsibilities, and boundaries of general mental health

helping activities and relationships. Hence, we have borrowed the idea and called it the
"helping frame."

REFERENCES

Boudreau, F., & Lambert, P. (1993). Compulsory treatment? 2. The collision of views and
complexities involved: Is it "the best possible alternative?" *Canadian Journal of
Community Mental Health, 12*(1), 79-96.
Breggin, P. (1991). *Toxic psychiatry.* New York: St. Martin's.
Coloroso, B. (1995). *Kids are worth it: Giving your child the gift of inner discipline.* Toronto, Canada: Somerville House.
Dolan, Y. (1992). *Resolving sexual abuse: Solution-focused therapy and Ericksonian hyp-
nosis for adult survivors.* New York: Norton.
Everett, B. (1994). Something is happening: The contemporary consumer and psychiatric
survivor movement in historical context. *Journal of Mind and Behavior, 15*(1/2),
55-70.
Everett, B. (2000). *A fragile revolution: Consumers and psychiatric survivors confront the
power of the mental health system.* Waterloo, Canada: Wilfrid Laurier University
Press.
Gadacz, R. (1994). *Re-thinking disability: New structures, new relationships.* Edmonton,
Canada: University of Alberta Press.
Miller, J. B., & Stiver, I. P. (1997). *The healing connection: How women form relationships
in therapy and in life.* Boston: Beacon Press.
Pearlman, L. A., & Saakvitne, K. (1995). *Trauma and the therapist: Countertransference
and vicarious traumatization in psychotherapy with incest survivors.* New York:
Norton.
Szasz, T. (1974). *The myth of mental illness.* New York: Harper & Row Evanston.
Wartenberg, T. (1990). *The forms of power: From domination to transformation.* Philadel-
phia: Temple University Press.

Contract

Question 1 is designed to confront the feared possibility head-on, but in a way that requires clients to reflect upon and describe in some detail what they have experienced when they have lost control. This question asks clients to imagine that an involuntary admission is imminent.

1. What specifically is happening for you when you know you can no longer avoid an involuntary admission (eviction, mechanical restraint, abusing).

    What are you doing? What are you saying? What are you feeling?

    What are others observing you doing/saying/feeling?

    What do you (client) need to do?

    What can I (as a professional) do to help at this time? Note: It is important to discuss real legal, ethical limitations to the professional role at this point.

Question 2 takes a step backward in an effort to point out that losing control is a process and that there are points along the way where steps can be taken to avoid what clients often feel is inevitable.

2. What *specifically* is happening for you when you know you are beginning to escalate toward the point where you might require an admission?

    What are you doing? What are you saying? What are you feeling?

    What are others observing you doing/saying/feeling?

    What do you (client) need to do to prevent things from going further?

    How can I (as a professional) support you in preventing an admission?

Question 3 asks clients to imagine that an admission has occurred, and ways of getting through the experience are being examined.

3. If, despite all our efforts, an involuntary admission occurs . . .

    What do you (client) need to do to support yourself through it?

    What would you like my role (as a professional) to be? (Again, it may be important to be honest about the limitations of the professional role under these circumstances.)

Question 4 is more of an empathetic statement in preparation for looking back on the imagined event in order to find ways to prevent further involuntary admissions, even before the symptoms or behaviors listed in Question 1 begin to appear.

4. Involuntary admissions are painful for everyone. It hurts me to see this happen to you, and I know it hurts you to go through it.

What do you need to do so that it won't happen again?

How can I help (as a professional) so that it won't happen again?

The benefits of this sort of formal contractual approach are numerous. First, it is written so that clients and professionals can return to it in times of crisis, when emotions are high and judgment is likely to be off. Second, it demonstrates that involuntary admissions don't "just happen." Instead, they occur as part of a process that has knowable and potentially avoidable steps. Third, it emphasizes the centrality of the client-professional partnership by highlighting the mutuality of our obligations. As such, it becomes a tool that can build "power with" relationships, in and of itself. It also demonstrates that clients can retain a certain level of control, even during what is typically viewed as an out-of-control situation. Finally, and perhaps most important, it provides a vision of the future when, with sufficient change and growth, an involuntary admission can successfully be avoided. Clients may not immediately acquire the necessary skills to completely liberate themselves from this specter, but over time, they can work step by step toward this ideal goal.

CHAPTER 8

The Healing and Recovery Process

When mental health professionals first confront the sheer extent of child abuse among psychiatric clients, they can be forgiven for feeling overwhelmed. The fact that clients have actually lived through these experiences seems miracle enough. Shouldn't they now be left in peace? Why drive them onward to confront the past, to make changes, to achieve goals? Who are we to ask more, when they have suffered so much?

The answers are complex. For those of us who work with survivors of childhood trauma, the clearest understanding we have is that many do not survive the terrors of abuse. They die, by their own or another's hand, or else they give up, becoming the "undead"—lost in helplessness and hopelessness until their physical being collapses under the weight of their rage and sorrow. But there are legions of others who continue to hold on and struggle, living through each fresh disaster, apparently none the wiser, but nevertheless alive. O'Connell Higgins (1994) asks, "What are the silken threads that hold a web of hope in a gale of hate?" (p. xi). The puzzle of the resilience of the human spirit has typically been the province of philosophers and poets, but it is also central to the helping process. The reality that fuels optimism is that, despite all odds, people can and do recover from experiences of child abuse, and for the men and women who choose careers in the helping professions, there is no greater reward than seeing clients overcome their suffering and begin to live, often for the first time, the kind of lives they desire.

Healing and recovery is now conceptualized as a staged process, with the early phases focused on the development of clients' fundamental skills related to acknowledging the abuse in the first place and establishing safety and containment (Chu, 1998). Many mental health professionals are not and will never become trauma therapists, yet they employ many of the same skills and take at least some of the same initial steps with clients. This chapter outlines the healing and recovery journey in its entirety in order to demystify the therapeutic process and to contextualize the value in what all professionals do—regardless of role. Understanding the complete journey helps psychiatric nurses, case managers, social workers, physicians, and other nontherapist professionals modulate their own helping strategies to suit the various stages clients may be in. It also highlights the integral role every mental health professional plays in his or her client's growth and development.

HOW DOES TALKING HELP?

Not everyone who has a traumatic past develops a diagnosable psychiatric disorder. But for those who do, van der Kolk, van der Hart, and Marmar (1996) argue that the many troubling symptoms are a result of once-useful coping strategies continuing to control the present. Over time, these strategies have begun to take on lives of their own, principally because their existence has become divorced from the traumatic past that created them. When assessed and treated in isolation, such symptoms and behaviors do indeed appear to be evidence of madness.

Human beings need to make sense out of their lives almost as much as they need air to breathe. The process of therapy reconnects clients' present behavior with their past experiences, rendering it—and themselves—intelligible. Their stories—"this is what happened to me, this is what I did to try and protect myself, this is why *now* I think and behave the way I do"—constitute the construction of rational meaning, which in turn shines a bright, normalizing light on the selves they have become. Slowly, it all begins to make sense, tragic, painful, horrifying sense to be sure, but sense nonetheless. They are who they are because of what has happened to them. Making sense, in words, in the presence of another human being who understands and confirms that sense, is the healing miracle of therapy.

THERAPY DEFINED

Therapy is a seemingly mysterious process, subject to a number of erroneous beliefs that may be shared by therapists and clients alike (Ross, 1995). Therapists are not friends, nor are they sharing a spiritual journey with their clients. They are not substitute parents, and the process of therapy is not a form of reparenting. They are not involved in their clients' personal lives, nor are they healing saints deserving of worship. In fact, therapists do not heal their clients; clients heal themselves. Likewise, they cannot fill up the achingly empty spaces inside clients with bottomless caring. Finally, they are not silent and blank screens upon which clients project their "fantasies." Instead, they are active, interested, committed partners engaged in an adult-to-adult dialogue that struggles with the creation of a mutual understanding of the client's life experience and worldview. During this process, therapists' main responsibility is to "manage" the structural rules of healthy human interaction in the here and now. To do so, they focus not so much on what is being said as on how it is said, remembered, and felt. In short, they see, hear, and speak in the language of emotion and relationship—an odd and secret tongue that most clients have either never learned or have taught themselves to disregard, because to them, feelings and relationships represent immeasurable pain.

THE THERAPEUTIC TASKS OF RECOVERY

The central task of recovery is, paradoxically, not to reject clients' cruel pasts but instead to help clients "own" the abuse they have experienced and to integrate this knowledge into their self-concept. In doing so, survivors relegate their trauma to a place where it becomes a historical event no longer capable of controlling the present. As their abuse recedes into the background of their lives, they gain the abilities to engage fully in current activities and relationships and to respond to internal and external stimuli effectively. But how exactly is this accomplished?

Models of therapy, as discussed in the following chapter, set out a conceptual structure that guides clinicians' actions along a particular pathway. However, clients are not bound by the same tenets and will heal in their own way and in their own time. Miller (1994) conceptualized the healing process as a series of concentric circles, with the outer circle representing the maximum distance between the client's hidden injured self and the people around him or her. As healing proceeds, the therapeutic relationship deepens, allowing the therapist to move closer to the hidden self. In the inner and final circle, clients reveal the extent of their shame and their pain in safety, thereby laying the groundwork to learn how to protect themselves and how to be close to others.

Herman (1992) was among the first authors to describe the healing process as a set of steps. Although her idea of stages of recovery must be viewed as merely an approximation of how healing proceeds, with each survivor's therapeutic process unfolding uniquely, she nonetheless adds invaluable information to our understanding. Her clearest message is that people can and do recover. Survivors are disbelieving, especially during the early stages of recovery, but they are typically (and often secretly) heartened by the idea that the process they are entering has a step-by-step predictability to it—along with a positive prognosis. We have expanded upon Herman's early work, and as a result, the following steps are more numerous than she proposes, but they align very closely with her views, and we owe a debt to the inspiration her writing provided.

The first point that Herman makes, and one that is echoed repeatedly in this book, is that healing *cannot* take place in isolation. Because it was in personal relationships that the trouble began, we need personal relationships in order to heal (Bradshaw, 1988). A client adds in her own words, "A fragile ego left alone, remains fragile" (Recovering Patient, 1986, p. 69). Therefore, the tenets of a healthy relationship as described in Chapter 7 are presumed to be the basis of each healing journey.

A second point, somewhat embedded in Herman's work but deserving of more emphasis, is the role of information and education. Clients need to know, generally, about the topic of child abuse, the observable emotional and physiological aftereffects, the associated psychiatric diagnoses, and various treatment options—as well as the merits and drawbacks of each. Additional and valued sources of information are survivors' own accounts of their healing journeys (Chase, 1987; Fraser, 1987; Green, 1992; Vale Allen, 1980), survivor newsletters (e.g., *The Healing Woman*),[1] Internet sites and chat lines, workbooks (Davis, 1990; Edwards & Derouard, 1995), films, and art. Although it is true that many clients may initially resist exploring these options, often as a defense against acknowledging their own painful pasts, we nonetheless need to make resources available that they can access when they feel ready. In addition, our willingness to share information and knowledge openly sets a respectful tone that conveys a clear message to the client: "I see you as a thinking, as well as a feeling human being. Ultimately, you are in charge of your own health and recovery and in order to do an effective job, you need to learn all you can."

A third point, implied in almost all work that addresses trauma treatment and specifically addressed in our multidimensional model (Chapter 2), is the necessity to view clients in context. Neither the clients themselves nor the life problems they face exist as discrete, unconnected entities. Instead, they are embedded in historical, racial, gender, cultural, social, and political realities that deeply affect both clients and professionals alike, as well as the nature of the various helping strategies that have evolved, and there are subtle (and sometimes not so subtle) pressures to leave things "just the way they are." Trauma therapists are keenly aware that they are engaged in a political act that challenges existing power structures, taboos, and stereotypes. Clients, too, often feel that their "truth" is one that nobody particularly wants to hear. Therapy, and indeed all helping processes in the mental health system, must acknowledge clients as whole human beings. They have a past; they have a racial and gender identity; they have a sexual orientation; and they have been shaped by ethnic, cultural, and social forces. These multifaceted "locations" deeply affect how problems are expressed, recognized, and dealt with—by the clients themselves, by their friends and family, and by the mental health professionals who are responsible for helping them. In addition, clients often see what has happened to them as an isolated instance and, as a consequence, as being their own fault because they are "bad" people. However, as they learn that child abuse also has a social context, that certain vulnerable groups are more likely to be victimized, that abuse is not new and not unique, and that powerful forces exist to ensure that survivors remain silent, they begin to see their own experiences as part of a much larger truth that, once recognized, apportions blame much differently than what they had originally supposed. They also learn the most powerful message of all: They are not alone. Child abuse is a social fact that harms the whole person, and it is the whole person that must heal. Attempting to fix bits and pieces of the wounded human or to change parts and portions of his or her life simply will not work.

A healthy therapeutic relationship; the ongoing sharing of resources, information, and knowledge; and a larger social and political perspective are the background against which the work of recovery takes place. Although the tasks of healing can quite adequately be conceptualized as steps, these three critical ingredients must be present and in operation throughout the entire healing journey. All mental health professionals, not just therapists, can participate in the creation of a strong foundation for their clients' recovery.

Step 1: Readiness. Survivors, like anyone else, can be confused about exactly what the demands of therapy are and how the process unfolds. Although it is our belief that all survivors want to heal from the abuse that they have suffered, some are ready to make a commitment to this most difficult personal journey, and others are not. De Shazer (as cited in O'Connell, 1998) makes the distinction between a visitor, a complainant, and a customer. Visitors are clients who don't feel that they have a problem or who don't want to be in therapy. Typically, these are clients who have been forced into treatment by the court system as a condition of probation or parole. They may also be people who have been "brought" to therapy by a worried spouse or relative. The bottom line is that they simply don't see the value of being there and would prefer to be somewhere else.

However, survivors of child abuse are usually sure that they have a problem, but they may not think of it as *their* problem. These clients are called complainants. They believe that life would improve if their mother (father, sister, brother, children, partner) would change, if they were to find the right combination of medications, meet the right mate, obtain the perfect housing situation—the wish list can go on and on. In other words, their problems are seen as existing outside of their personal control, and as a result, they are seeking solutions in their external environment.

Customers are clients who recognize that they have a problem and acknowledge that they are the ones who have to do something about it. They are also willing to invest a considerable amount of time and energy in the healing process. Both visitors and complainants may, over time, become customers if the therapist is able to find a benefit that they can both agree upon and work toward—but it is a mistake to treat these three sorts of clients in the same manner. Customers are ready to commit to therapy, and visitors and complainants are not—and may never be. During the readiness phase, therapists must assess which type of client has presented for treatment, bring his or her objections out into the open as soon as possible, find common ground for work (if it can be found), and refer those who do not want to be in therapy to other, more appropriate services—without recrimination or blame.

There are some caveats to this process that are particular both to survivors who have psychiatric diagnoses and to therapists who work within the confines of the mental health system. First, this is a client group that, almost by definition, is likely to be suspicious and to back off initially; however, they may very well be willing to engage in the therapeutic process if they are clear about what it entails and are given time to adjust to its demands. Second, in some specialized forensic mental health settings, clients are forced into therapy because of their involvement with the law, and therapists need to develop a fairly sophisticated set of skills specifically focused on making customers out of visitors and complainants. Under these circumstances, therapists take a much more active role in engaging unwilling clients in the therapeutic process, because neither they nor their clients have the freedom to give up. Third, there may be no other, "more appropriate" services to which clients who don't want therapy can be referred. In these instances, therapists often adjust their services in order to meet their client's needs. In fact, therapists may see this flexibility as a bonus in that they can balance their client ratio, serving some clients who are deep in the emotional demands of therapy and others who prefer more practical, less intense forms of help.

Step 2: Believe. Once it has been determined that a client is ready to begin therapy, the next step is to create an environment where clients understand that what they say is believed. Survivors can be accused, and sometimes accuse themselves, of "making up" stories of abuse and trauma. The reality is that *no one* wants to believe that children are raped, tortured, beaten, starved, abandoned, or subjected to a variety of impossible cruelties bounded only by the perpetrator's sadistic imagination. The family is the sacred foundation of our culture. Mom loves Dad; Dad loves

Mom. Together, they raise lovely children who take their place in the adult world as fine, upstanding citizens ready to raise their own children in the same warm traditions. This picture is highly valued, and in instances where it proves not to be true, we are so shocked that we may disregard the evidence of our own eyes and ears. Thus, the beginning point for a healing and recovery journey is to believe what clients say—even as they struggle to believe themselves. Trauma therapists know that bad things can happen to children, and this knowledge, though never forced on clients, is subtly but clearly reflected in how therapists listen and respond. Even though it is the therapist's task to remain neutral, neither confirming nor denying any particular memory, the fact that therapists know that what clients are saying *could* be true constitutes a form of nonverbal permission for continued exploration. The powerful message is, "Maybe it's true and maybe it's not, and we all hope that it's not—but maybe, just maybe it is." Trauma therapists challenge the cultural myth that the family is universally benign by acknowledging that although we all wish that the myth were true, if it is not, then therapy is the place where it is all right to talk about what happened.

Step 3: Safety. Healing cannot begin if clients are still battling daily with traumatizing events and occurrences. Chapter 10 covers this step in depth because, as with the first two steps, it is one in which all mental health professionals can participate. For the moment, however, it is important to note that the establishment of safety and control is an essential task in the journey. Sometimes, clients (and some professionals) want to skip this time-consuming step, wishing to rush forward in an effort to resolve problems as soon as possible. Those who do rush ahead learn early that nothing of value is accomplished unless, first and foremost, issues of safety are thoroughly addressed.

Friends and family are also essential at this point because they provide an opportunity for lifelong support and continuity. If clients take no other step but to begin to value and work toward safety for themselves, then they have laid the necessary groundwork for further growth and development, whether or not a therapist is ever part of their journey.

Step 4: The Story. Clients tell their stories all the time. Sometimes they tell in words, but mostly they tell in behaviors. Telling about the abuse will not be contained wholly within therapy, and in the many instances where there is no therapist, it will never be part of a formal therapeutic process. It is simply human to want to tell sympathetic others what has happened, and thus it is important for all mental health professionals to understand how, within the confines of our role and practice setting, we can listen, hear, and understand—with sensitivity. Chapter 11 is devoted to this step.

Step 5: Anger and Sadness. Intertwined with the telling of the story in therapy is the recovery of the client's emotional life. Although all mental health professionals can assist in the creation of safety, and though most will at some time in their careers hear stories of abuse, it is from this point onward that the therapist's specialized knowledge and training come most heavily into play.

Over the course of their childhoods, clients learned to fear emotion because they were consistently overwhelmed—by anger, fear, terror, intense longing, shame, guilt, loneliness—but perhaps most of all by sadness. Emotion has come to represent an unpredictable source of deep pain that must be avoided at all costs. Clients will have developed an array of techniques to manage their emotional lives in ways that may temporarily protect them from pain, but when they burst out of control, these techniques are typically labeled "symptoms" by psychiatry and are seen as bizarre, frightening, or disgusting by the rest of the world. Clients, too, feel that they are abnormal and have somehow missed knowing what everyone else magically understands—how to relate to others, how to be happy, and how to be at peace.

Anger can be thought of as a demonstration emotion. It is there to signal that something is wrong—you have been hurt or frightened, or you feel guilty or are sad. In a healthy world, anger allows for an immediate release of energy in preparation for a calmer exploration of the underlying emotion that triggered it in the first place. However, when children are hurt repeatedly and in absolutely terrifying ways, along with the direct or indirect admonition that they must never tell (in word or deed) what is happening, anger cannot do its work. In some cases, it becomes suppressed and turned inward, perhaps so completely that the child, and subsequently the adult, appears shut-down and inert, exhibiting the symptoms of deep depression. Anger, when it is acknowledged at all, is converted into a steady stream of self-denigrating ruminations or attempts to destroy the self through suicidal thoughts and actions. Alternatively, survivors may have grown up expressing their anger outwardly (when out of the presence of the abuser). They rage repeatedly, seemingly without provocation, and certainly ineffectively. Although some may have actually harmed others, most have simply exhibited an ongoing pattern of overreaction and verbal attack, alienating themselves in school, in their housing or employment situations, and in their personal relationships—to the extent that they may find that they are either completely alone or embroiled in one damaging relationship after another.

These never-angry or always-angry people have one thing in common. They are trapped by an unexpressed grief so deep that they fear they will drown in their own tears if they let anyone (including themselves) know how they really feel. A childhood full of trauma and terror prevents the direct expression of sadness as well as anger. Grief is especially likely to be stored up, gaining power year after year, until survivors feel they will burst with the pain.

This step in the healing process involves introducing clients to the language of emotion, the range of emotional possibilities available, and the rules by which they are governed. It is characterized by somewhat intellectual or even educational discussions, because clients are nowhere near strong enough to enter the internal storage vaults overflowing with unexpressed anger and grief. One of the central tasks that occurs during this stage is encouraging clients to begin to express their anger in ways that will keep them and the people they care about safe. Sometimes, they need only acknowledge that they *are* angry. In other cases, they need to learn to respect the anger that seems to rule their lives. They need to know that anger is like fire—out of control, it destroys; used with control and wisdom, it serves basic human needs.

Step 6: Mourning the Losses. Survivors of childhood trauma have lost a lot. They have lost a childhood. If the perpetrator was a parent, they have lost the experience of receiving and giving love to one of the most important people in their past. They may have lost contact with brothers and sisters or have seriously damaged relationships that they quite rightly fear may never heal. They may have lost the opportunity to complete their education and to acquire the "normal" memories of school and adolescence. As time has worn on, those with the severest symptoms have had to struggle with a diagnosis of mental illness and, perhaps, impaired memory from repeated courses of electroconvulsive therapy or, in some cases, damage from the side effects of psychotropic medication (e.g., tardive dyskinesia). Others bear the scars associated with self-mutilation or have physical deficits because of serious but failed suicide attempts. Some have lost their health as their body has struggled to tell in the language of disease and illness what they have not been able to say in words. Survivors look back on numerous failed relationships, friends who have drifted or been driven away, and the many peers they once knew who are now dead because, unlike them, they did not survive. Some may have lost children to the authorities, and others realize they will never have children, either because the time has passed or because they know they simply cannot trust themselves to provide the necessary care. They have also lost less tangible possessions that are nonetheless experienced as real: innocence, opportunity, optimism, pride, and belief in the future. And beyond this long and daunting list, there appears one loss greater than all the others: Survivors have lost a particular kind of hope associated with the dreams of what might have been.

Mourning these losses is the one step that is least amenable to being thought of as a step. It is frequently lengthy and can arise at any time throughout the remainder of the healing process—and on into the future—but the frequency and the intensity of the sad moments will abate over time. This step is the most painful one for clients, as they mourn the death of hope—a naive hope to be sure, based on magical beliefs and fantasy—but one that is fervently and tenaciously held because it holds out the faint chance that some way, somehow, the past can be made right. Although this time is a particularly difficult one for clients, it is also hard on therapists. Having encouraged clients to regain a sense of their emotional life and having introduced them to anger and sadness, therapists cannot flinch in the face of the raw expression of pain that these emotions evoke. As with any death (and clients are mourning multiple deaths), there is an immediacy, a realness of emotion so completely honest and undefended that it is heartrending to watch. It is also a time when there is not much therapists can do to ameliorate the pain—other than to be there; to walk through the experience with clients; and, when moved to do so, to weep with them. However, just being there is not to be disparaged. In many senses, it is the most powerful yet the simplest gift anyone can give.

Step 7: Telling a New Truth. This step is closely connected to the previous one. Here, clients replace the dead hopes of the past with new, more realistic hopes for the future. With the strength they have acquired through the healing accomplished to date, they are now ready to face some obvious but painful truths: "No one is coming to rescue you. No one can make this better but you. Life is not fair. You can't change the past; you can only shape the future." To some degree, these realizations are what we all face as we disconnect from the emotional bumps and bruises of childhood and revise the idealized view of our parents. As with so many of the other tasks of healing, survivors cope with more shock and more disappointment than would be experienced by those who have not had their experiences—but they are at least now grappling with a common developmental task that signals the onset of maturity. Perhaps the most difficult realization during this period surrounds the ongoing role that abuse has played in their lives. As they begin to recognize the value of taking responsibility for their own behavior, some state that they feel ashamed that they weren't able to just "get over it" and that they have instead, through their own actions, created life problem after life problem, making their burdens even greater. Others feel that their obvious distress at least served as a sign to the rest of the world that they needed care and attention. How will they find the love they crave if they are healthy and well? Still others believe that their own healing means that they are somehow condoning the injustice of the abuse: "I didn't create this mess, so why do I have to clean it up?" And finally, a few feel that they must have some sort of revenge—a public acknowledgment that they were wronged, a conviction in criminal court, or a civil judgment.

However, survivors are typically terrified of confronting their abusers. Also, in many cases, the perpetrator has died, moved away, or can't be found. In other cases, there may be no acceptable legal avenue to take. In reality, only a very few survivors actually charge their abusers, and even fewer obtain a conviction. The therapist's task under any of these circumstances is to unlink the process of healing and recovery from a search for justice.[2] Although it makes sense intellectually that healing would proceed faster and more thoroughly if survivors could satisfy themselves that justice has been done, the reality is that they must heal and recover no matter what occurs. This point is crucial, because some survivors will block progress as they struggle with the problem of how to exact revenge. Sometimes it is useful to ask them to imagine that it is the day after they have witnessed the abuser sentenced in court (die a horrible death, lose all of his or her money—whatever the desired revenge is). As they enter the fantasy, survivors may be able to imagine complete humiliation for the perpetrator, but the most common conclusion they reach is that revenge does not give them what they truly want—to have their lives back. No matter what happens to the perpetrators, survivors still have to pick up the pieces and build their own futures. In short, this is a phase in the recovery process where clients face the fact that there is no way around and no way out. They must go forward, and every step toward new life must be taken by them, and only them. Slowly, the bad news ("No one is going to rescue me") is replaced by the good news ("From here on, *my* life is going to be lived *my* way").

Step 8: Defining a New Self. At this point, clients begin to ask some central questions, not the least of which is, "If my life is to be lived my way, who am I and what do I want?" Although the therapist may all along have raised the issue of the pervasiveness of the perpetrator's influence and how it has controlled the survivor's life, it is at this point that clients really "get" what this means. With some horror, they begin to recognize the shadow of the perpetrator as it is expressed within them (the bits and pieces of their personhood that think and behave like the abuser). They may also recognize that the perpetrator has represented such an over-arching presence in their lives that there is a substantial hole to fill should they begin to separate their own sense of self from the perpetrator-defined self that they have for so long accepted as the truth. The process of defining "Who am I?" is an almost cliched developmental phase that all adults must confront sooner or later. However, as with the previous step, survivors have a harder time, because the trauma bond that binds them to the abuser (or abusers) is so much stronger and all encompassing.

During this stage, clients struggle with all sorts of big questions, such as, "Why did I survive? What contribution can I make to the world? What do I believe in? What are my political views? Who do I admire and why? What is my sexual orientation? What sort of people do I want as friends? Are there family members I want in my life? Who do I want as a life partner—do I want a life partner?" Because their experiences have taught them that asking questions is a dangerous activity, survivors will likely enter this stage feeling the twin emotions of exhilaration and trepidation. Also, the survivor's role, by definition, is to make it through to the next moment. Thinking about tomorrow, let alone next year, is a new and frightening experience. Survivors have learned long ago to put their dreams away, because they never come true. Reflecting upon themselves is also a new experience. Beginning statements with "I want . . . I believe . . . I don't like . . . " will seem remarkably bold—at first—but within the safety of the therapeutic relationship, survivors soon learn to hear and appreciate the power in their voices. The therapist's role at this point is to support a healthful process of self-discovery and introspection by allowing substantial time to explore these big questions without imposing his or her own views or moving too quickly to resolution. This kind of questioning signals the onset of a cycle of self-reinvention, a process that will likely repeat itself at critical junctures throughout the client's adult life. Both the questions and the answers are expected to evolve and shift over time. The key is to support the client's newfound ability to question and to think in future-oriented terms—and to use sentences that begin with that most powerful word, *I*. This is the point in the recovery process where survivors learn to dream again.

Step 9: Social and Spiritual Reconnection. Asking the big questions of "Who am I?" and "What do I want in life?" prepares clients for the final step in the recovery process: to take what they have learned and put it into practice. Although clients have been trying out their new skills all along, this is the stage where they bring it all together and begin to work on making their dreams come true. Abuse isolates, and survivors often feel that they have been set apart from the rest of the world. Many will repeat some form of the following kinds of assertions: "I'm different. My abuse was so much worse than anyone else's. No one will ever understand me. If anyone ever got to know the real me, they would hate me. I'm so alone. I feel as if I'm inside a glass jar—I can see other people and they can see me, but we just can't connect." Most survivors both fear and long for intimacy. As they strengthen their sense of self and become more adept at maintaining their own boundaries and keeping themselves safe in relationships, they become capable of connecting with others in healthful ways. They also become more discriminating. Old "friends"—people from earlier, less healthy periods—may drop away as survivors become less tolerant of behaviors they themselves once exhibited. This constitutes yet another form of loss but one that somehow seems easier to bear because survivors have now acquired a taste for the power of their own growth and development. Although they may always be tentative and nervous in new situations, as healing and recovery proceed, they will slowly begin to meet people who add to rather than detract from their social lives. At this point, the therapist's role is to support the development of positive relationships. In order to do so, therapists may reiterate the value of boundaries, counteract the survivor's oversensitivity by offering insight into how "normal" people behave, discuss an awakening sexuality or a newly contained one, make information and resources available that teach the mechanics of dating and making friends, and support the survivor's newfound independence as he or she struggles to form adult relationships with friends and family.

Closely connected to the formation of individual relationships is the search for community. Communities are no longer defined exclusively by geographical location, and many groups create their communities because of their identity (e.g., the women's or the gay community), a shared experience (the psychiatric consumer and survivor community), a creative pursuit (the theatre or arts community), or belief or faith (the Buddhist or Baptist community). The key is the acknowledgment of a set of shared experiences, values, and beliefs that can draw people together and give them a sense of belonging.

An additional therapeutic task is to introduce, or to explore in greater depth, the topic of *spirituality*—defined broadly as those activities or beliefs that feed the soul. Obviously, many survivors may choose to express their spirituality through membership in some form of organized worship, but other pursuits are equally valid—the enjoyment of nature, literature, music, or art; helping others or working for a cause; meditation or yoga; sweet grass ceremonies or sweat lodges—the list is endless and varies from culture to culture. Although it is often the case that survivors live in poverty and under marginal living conditions, the celebration of the spiritual side of life is not tied to money or consumerism. And although we hasten to add that society's obligation is first to feed, clothe, and shelter its more vulnerable citizens, feeding the soul is a dimension of life that is potentially available to everyone, regardless of economic status.

Step 10: Saying Good-Bye. Growth and development are lifelong pursuits, but therapy is not. As survivors reach the conclusion of this part of their life journey, it can be difficult for both client and therapist to end their work. It has been a long struggle that has created a particularly strong bond. Wise therapists introduce the topic of ending right at the beginning, alerting the client to the fact that this is a special sort of relationship, one with a life span.[3] Ending is also a frequent topic throughout the therapeutic process, as therapists continually present clients with a vision of how life will look and feel when the power of the abuse has receded. As the end approaches, it is often helpful to begin to reduce the frequency of sessions to help clients adjust to life after therapy. As the separation process unfolds, most therapists help clients look back to where they were when they entered therapy and help them celebrate their many accomplishments. Some therapists also like to tell clients specifically what the clients have taught them and how they will be using this learning to become a more effective therapist in the future. If therapists intend to retain some form of contact with clients after formal sessions have ended (e.g., receiving an occasional phone call or holiday card), the parameters need to be spelled out clearly.

Also, some clients may want to know if they can return to therapy if, as is so often the case, they feel in need of some support over a life crisis or encounter new memories that they find destabilizing. Some therapists have the freedom to accept clients back for a session or two when needed, as they see fit and as their client load allows. Others work in settings where clients must rerefer themselves to the program as a whole, and then they are assigned to an available therapist—without regard to previous relationships. Whatever the case, clients will want to know what the rules are, because their newfound wellness is often felt to be tentative, and most fear some sort of setback. In fact, one reaction to the ending process may be a sudden recurrence of symptoms or flashbacks, because clients may have begun to equate their own wellness as precipitating yet another loss. Indeed, the close of therapy is a form of loss—but one that is typical of growth and development. Sometimes clients are comforted if they think about the relationship that students have with their teachers—graduation is inevitable. It is the process of saying good-bye to a valuable period in life, even as an exciting future is embraced. Ending therapy has similar bittersweet qualities, but it must be seen as a natural event that is likely to recur in one form or another throughout the client's life.

This is also the time to initiate a conversation about some of the hidden expectations clients may have of their new lives. Survivors often feel (and rightly so) that they have suffered enough. Having survived both the abuse itself and the rigors of therapy, often augmented by the difficulties and stressors inherent in the mental health system, they believe that life should now be continually happy, brimming full of all the good things they so richly deserve. But what they have achieved, though substantial, is not the perfect life of their dreams but the opportunity simply to live a life. Relationships will not always work out, disappointments and failures may still occur, bad days will happen—because these things happen in any life. The close of therapy constitutes just one example of the kind of anxiety-producing change that occurs in the average life. Finally, on the last day, when the inevitable good-byes must be said, therapists and clients may choose to mark the occasion with a small ritual, ceremony, or symbolic exchange of tokens of acknowledgment. In many senses, clients are indeed graduating, and as with any such life passage, it is an occasion deserving of commemoration.

CONCLUSION

Many people recover from the aftereffects of child abuse, and when they do, they will likely engage in a process that resembles the one described in this chapter. Some survivors may complete their journey relatively quickly. Others may take a lifetime. Some may take only a few steps. Everyone is different. The recovery process is not a race or a test. Instead, it parallels the path of human maturation and cannot be rushed. But the road is invariably long and hard—and survivors will need all the help they can get to achieve their destinations. Some survivors will accomplish the tasks of recovery in therapy. But there is no rule that says survivors *must* enter therapy in order to heal. Everyone benefits from human connection, information, and access to resources, as well as support and understanding. All mental health professionals, regardless of formal designation, are trained to provide these key ingredients of well-being, and as a consequence, all have an integral part to play in clients' healing and recovery process.

NOTES

1. *The Healing Woman* newsletter is available by writing to The Healing Woman, P.O. Box 3038, Moss Beach, CA 94038.
2. It is the client's right to decide whether or not to charge the perpetrator. Some clients may find the process empowering, whereas others may find that they are further traumatized. Certainly, the outcome can *never* be guaranteed. During the decision-making process,

therapists may provide information, access to resources, and emotional support, but their stance must be neutral, and their role, as always, must be carried out within the therapeutic frame (Pearlman & Saakvitne, 1995). This does not mean that therapists don't see child abuse as a crime or that they don't deplore the actions of abusers. Instead, it means that they are focused on their job, which is to help clients heal and recover—a process that is independent of whether or not criminal proceedings occur.

3. Fiscal pressures in publicly funded mental health systems have meant that long-term therapy is a very rare luxury. Thus, it is common for therapists and clients to work in specified blocks of time where the end is prescribed. In private practice, however, therapists and clients mutually decide when therapy will end. In either circumstance, the ending tasks are similar.

REFERENCES

Bradshaw, J. (1988). *Healing the shame that binds you.* Deerfield Beach, FL: Health Communications.

Chase, T. (1987). *When rabbit howls.* New York: Jove Books.

Chu, J. (1998). *Rebuilding shattered lives: The responsible treatment of complex post-traumatic and dissociative disorders.* New York: John Wiley.

Davis, L. (1990). *The courage to heal: For women and men survivors of child sexual abuse.* New York: Harper & Row.

Edwards, T., & Derouard, M. (1995). *Hope in healing.* (Available from the authors at 998 Bloor Street West, Box 10546, Toronto, Ontario, Canada M6H 4H9)

Fraser, S. (1987). *My father's house: A memoir of incest and healing.* New York: Harper & Row.

Green, L. (1992). *Ordinary wonders: Living recovery from sexual abuse.* Toronto, Canada: Women's Press.

Herman, J. (1992). *Trauma and recovery.* New York: Basic Books.

Miller, D. (1994). *Women who hurt themselves: A book of hope and understanding.* New York: Basic Books.

O'Connell, B. (1998). *Solution-focused therapy.* Thousand Oaks, CA: Sage.

O'Connell Higgins, G. (1994). *Resilient adults: Overcoming a cruel past.* San Francisco: Jossey-Bass.

Pearlman, L. A., & Saakvitne, K. (1995). *Trauma and the therapist: Countertransference and vicarious traumatization in psychotherapy with incest survivors.* New York: Norton.

Recovering Patient. (1986). Can we talk? The schizophrenic patient in psychotherapy. *American Journal of Psychiatry, 143,* 68-70.

Ross, C. (1995). Current treatment of dissociative identity disorder. In L. Cohen, J. Berzoff, & M. Elin (Eds.), *Dissociative identity disorder: Theoretical and treatment controversies* (pp. 413-434). Northvale, NJ: Jason Aronson.

Vale Allen, C. (1980). *Daddy's girl.* New York: Berkley Books.

van der Kolk, B., van der Hart, O., & Marmar, C. (1996). Dissociation and information processing in posttraumatic stress disorder. In B. van der Kolk, A. McFarlane, & L. Weisaeth (Eds.), *Traumatic stress: The effects of overwhelming experience on mind, body, and society* (pp. 303-327). New York: Guilford.

Treatment Models

A lthough the healing process is never simple, survivors and the mental health professionals who bear witness to their suffering now have access to treatment approaches that provide well-founded hope. Some of us will choose to become trauma specialists and, as such, will come to know these models intimately. However, most mental health professionals won't provide trauma treatment themselves, because it is not their role to do so. Nonetheless, they have a responsibility to acquire at least some knowledge of the various trauma treatment approaches, because they are often in a position to provide information and make referrals. In order to do a good job, we must be informed and educated about what is available, how and why certain approaches work, and what sort of client is likely to benefit. Because it will always be true that no one model works always or works for everyone, this chapter will present a variety of approaches, each with its own merits. Wise professionals study as many models as possible so that they can be fully informed on behalf of their clients and, for those of us who provide treatment directly, so that we can incorporate bits and pieces from each until we have built up a repertoire of helping strategies that can be customized to suit each client's circumstances.

MODELS DEFINED

Models are conceptual constructs, typically based on theories that have been tested empirically in real-world applications. They constitute a "line of thought" that should be considered not as a recipe or blueprint but as a set of guiding principles that are flexible enough to accommodate new knowledge and experience. Models do, however, imply certain belief systems that demand at least some level of acceptance if professionals are to use aspects of them in their practices. The utility of any given model lies in the fact that it represents considerable thought and experimentation, usually communicated in a logical, coherent manner and accompanied by a body of research and critique. In short, models galvanize academic and practice activities and focus them on developing solutions to a set of troubling problems. Also, ideas and findings about effectiveness are generally available in academic literature, so that each model can be used, modified, expanded upon, or rejected as the reading audience sees fit. The various models presented in this chapter are to be seen in the much the same light—as food for thought rather than practice prescriptions. In addition, when evaluating any model, there are some important caveats that should be kept in mind:

1. No one model works for all people under all circumstances.
2. Most models work for some people at some times.
3. The professional him or herself remains the most important "tool" in the helping encounter—regardless of model.
4. Most professionals espouse more than one practice model.
5. Clients (and referring professionals) can and should ask mental health professionals about the types of models they employ and about the assumptions that underlie them.
6. No model will make up for a lack of skills on the part of the professional or a lack of commitment on the part of the client.
7. Practice models should be flexible enough to accommodate clients' individual circumstances and experiences. Neither clients nor professionals should have to remake themselves in uncomfortable ways to fit within a particular model's tenets.

As a final note, the models selected for review are those that are credible and well researched and that also have special modifications to address the needs of survivors of childhood abuse. Obviously, most have a substantial body of literature attached to them, and we cannot pretend to include every nuance here. This chapter gives a brief overview of the salient points of the general model and discusses how it has been adapted for use with survivors. It should also be understood that practitioners of these treatment models have years of training that allow them to use the various techniques with experience and wisdom. What follows constitutes the briefest of introductions, intended to pique interest and, perhaps, to encourage further study.

COGNITIVE-BEHAVIORAL THERAPY

Survivors of child abuse experience both cognitive distortions and behavioral problems. Cognitive-behavioral therapy (CBT) is aimed at restructuring clients' thinking patterns and integrating new learning so that they are able to make positive, real-life behavioral changes outside of the treatment encounter. CBT is an approach grounded in the belief that thinking, emotion, and behavior are interconnected. During childhood, people develop ways of thinking that consist of strongly held views about life, which, in the case of abuse survivors, produce consistently biased judgments (Beck & Freeman, 1990). Padesky and Greenberger (1995) argue for three levels of thinking: (a) cognitive "rules for living," which are called "schema" (e.g., "I am unlovable"); (b) underlying assumptions (e.g., "If people get to know me, they won't like me"); and (c) automatic thoughts (e.g., "I'll never have any friends"). They are also careful not to label clients' thought patterns as "wrong" or "bad"; instead, they emphasize teaching clients how their thoughts can affect their moods, and subsequently, their behaviors (Greenberger & Padesky, 1995).

In other work, not specifically related to trauma survivors but nonetheless relevant, Seligman (1991) examined an important schema dichotomy that he called "optimism versus pessimism." He argued that "finding temporary and specific causes for misfortune is the art of hope" (p. 48). Pessimistic thinking, in which causal attributions are external (e.g., "I can't stop bad things from happening to me"), personal (e.g., "It's all my fault"), permanent (e.g., "This always happens to me"), and pervasive (e.g., "Life is bad"), constitutes a recipe for dysfunction and depression.

CBT is practiced in many iterations, but most are designed to be brief, oriented to the present, and focused on specific problems and thoughts. It is also an approach that doesn't depend on a disease model to explain people's problems, and it seeks not to blame clients for the predicaments in which they find themselves. There are three main approaches: cognitive restructuring (altering negative schema); systematic desensitization (aimed as phobias, intrusive thoughts, or flashbacks); and behavioral problem solving (altering troublesome behaviors; Chambless & Goldstein, 1979).

Cognitive restructuring has received the most attention in work with abuse survivors. For example, Arntz (1994) has employed cognitive restructuring techniques directed at modifying core schema of clients diagnosed with borderline personality disorder (BPD), schema such as "Others are always dangerous. I am powerless. I am bad or evil." Also, Dutton (1992), in her work with battered women, has developed a treatment methodology using modifications of cognitive-behavioral techniques that involve (a) reexperiencing the trauma (remembering, telling about, and feeling the emotions surrounding past experiences of violence);[1] (b) managing stress (teaching patients the skills to deal with excessive emotional arousal); (c) facilitating the expression of emotion (through words, journal writing, screaming, crying); and finally, (d) finding meaning from the victimization (a cognitive restructuring process that integrates trauma experiences into the patient's personal history in a meaningful way). An example of finding meaning might be, "I now know that some relationships can be bad for me, and I intend to value and protect my own safety in the future."

Also, Smucker and Dancu (1999) developed a form of CBT specifically designed for survivors of childhood trauma. Imagery rescripting and reprocessing therapy (IRRT) uses both visualizations and verbal interventions. Conceptually, IRRT is grounded in principles from both cognitive and object relations theory. It includes the therapeutic task of creating a positive internalized image of the therapist within the client. This representation serves not only as a basis for the development of more adaptive schema, but also as a soothing presence that is intended to be the forerunner of a later and more integrated capacity for self-soothing. The ability of clients to calm and comfort themselves is essential in counteracting affect dysregulation.

In IRRT, the entire trauma memory is reactivated as if in the present, and through specific interventions, the client's recurring traumatic imagery and abuse-related beliefs are modified and replaced by more adaptive schema. In therapy, the client first recalls the memories as if he or she were the "Child" he or she used to be. In subsequent imagery sessions, the "Adult" that the client is today enters into the mental picture with the goal of replacing victimization imagery with mastery imagery. This process includes mentally confronting the perpetrator. Later sessions ask the Adult to comfort and nurture the Child. The ultimate goal of IRRT is to help clients get beyond feelings and thoughts that support powerlessness and victimization, accept the trauma as part of their past life experience, and transform it into a meaningful cognitive framework.

Linehan (1993) has adapted many of the processes of CBT and has named her particular model "dialectical behavior therapy" (DBT). The term *dialectical* refers to the paradox that challenges therapists to accept patients as they are while at the same time asking and teaching them to change. DBT evolved as a methodology for the treatment of people diagnosed with BPD who chronically self-harm—a group of clients who are known to have a high incidence of child abuse in their backgrounds. In this author's interpretation of CBT, substantial attention is paid to building a therapeutic relationship, and Linehan addresses what she calls "therapy interfering behaviors." These are the transference issues so prominent in work with survivors of abuse, which she believes are neglected in standard CBT approaches.

Linehan's DBT model emphasizes acceptance and validation of the client's current behaviors. Treatment is directed at reframing self-destructive behavior as a type of habit developed in response to abuse. She describes three bimodal behavioral patterns that require alteration:

1. Emotional vulnerability coupled with invalidation. In this pattern, the survivor is exquisitely sensitive to emotional stimuli but experiences validation only for the most extreme expression of feeling.
2. Helplessness coupled with apparent competency. In this instance, survivors deal with their problems in a passive manner, and although they may

seem competent, this is a facade that denies them the support and comfort they so badly need (e.g., see Gallop, 1992).

3. Unrelenting crisis coupled with inhibited grieving. The survivor lives life in a constant state of upheaval and is unable to attain the peace needed to grieve a history of losses and disappointments.

Finally, in a departure from the exclusive behavioral focus of the general CBT model, DBT emphasizes process (how and why clients do the things they do) over structure (the actual behaviors).

SOLUTION-FOCUSED THERAPY

This approach to therapy has become prominent in many settings both because it addresses new fiscal realities in health care (e.g., managed care) and because long-term therapy models have often failed to prove themselves any more effective than shorter interventions. Clients, too, prefer an approach that promises to get things resolved as quickly as possible (O'Connell, 1998).

Solution-focused therapy, as the name implies, shifts the focus from the problem to the solution. It takes the counterintuitive position that the type of solution that works is not directly defined by the nature of the problem. As a result, solution-focused therapists feel no need to explore in depth the origin of the problem, nor do they assume that a problem of long standing will automatically take a long time to solve. They concentrate on the problem as the client sees it and do not impose their own views as to what broader issues the defined problem might signal. Therapy is seen as merely catalytic, with real and lasting change occurring outside of the therapeutic encounter. In addition, what constitutes change is defined, initiated, and maintained by clients—not by therapists. Some typical questions asked at the beginning include, "What do you want to change? How will you know when it has changed? How will you know that therapy is helping? How can you use the skills you already have to make this change? How will you know we have achieved enough so that you can end therapy?" Obviously, these are questions that define very clearly the therapeutic boundary, and therapists who work in this tradition do not stray into any area of the client's life other than those that the client him- or herself defines. Therapeutic rapport is built through two

central messages: (a) "We only work on the things you say are important," and (b) "You, as a person, don't have to change. You just have to
change what you're doing." Like the questions above, the principles
guiding this form of therapy are straightforward and practical:

The client knows best.
If it isn't broken, don't fix it.
Start with little things—even a small change can lead to bigger change.
If it's working, keep doing it.
If it's not working, stop doing it.

Therapy as conducted within this model is a highly focused activity.
Each session has a prescribed structure, which includes certain questions,
structured exercises, and homework assignments between meetings.
Principal elements in the solution-focused "discourse" include competence talk, exception talk, scaling, and the "miracle question."

Competence Talk. Therapists focus their questioning on the client's
strengths. They ask what's right, not what's wrong, in an effort to capture and utilize the client's own resources for the work ahead. For example, at the very first session, it is assumed that clients have already made
positive changes between the time they called to set up the appointment
and the day of the initial meeting. Solution-focused therapists capture
this energy by asking, "Have you noticed any difference in your problem
since you called? What has helped? What else has helped?" In this way,
both the therapist and the client develop an inventory of skills that the client has already applied to solving the problem, setting a climate of competence right from the outset.

Exception Talk. Therapists ask clients to describe moments when the
problem *isn't* occurring. Again they ask questions that focus on skill.
"How did you manage to do that? What helped you?" These sorts of questions are designed to help clients begin to see themselves as having power
over their problems. Already, they have begun to identify solutions.

Scaling. This is a technique that quantifies movement toward the client's
goals. Typically, therapists use the numbers 0 to 10 as parameters for the
scale: "If 0 describes a time when your problem was at its worst, and 10

means that it has been completely solved, where are you on that scale right now? Where were you last week? Where do you hope to be a week from now?" Scaling is intended to put clients in charge of assessing the severity of their problem and the level of change they are seeking. This technique can also be used to introduce perceptions other than the client's own. For example, the therapist might say, "You feel that you are at level 2 with this problem. Where on the scale would your mother (partner, sister, friend) say you are?" The overall goal is to focus clients' efforts on forward movement in a way that is both tangible and nonthreatening.

The Miracle Question. The centerpiece of the solution-focused technique is a formula question that is intended to engage the client's imagination and orient it toward a better future.

> "Imagine when you go to sleep one night a miracle happens and the problems we've been talking about disappear. As you were asleep, you did not know that a miracle had happened. When you woke up what would be the first signs for you that a miracle had happened?" (O'Connell, 1998, p. 50)

This question helps clients describe new behaviors in detail. It also serves as a technique for helping clients get "unstuck" by showing them what they can do to create change in their lives.

In applying solution-focused therapy to the needs of trauma survivors, Dolan (1992) reinterprets the idea of a client's own resources to include his or her internal as well as external resources. For example, she acknowledges that the telling of the abuse story can, in itself, be retraumatizing and recommends that clients be taught to access their innate skills, which are designed to protect them from overwhelm. First, therapists work with clients to select an object in the immediate environment of the office or meeting space—a plant or picture, perhaps, but something that can be expected to be there each session. This object becomes the client's "symbol of the present" (Dolan, 1992, p. 27). Second, clients are helped to recognize when overwhelm is beginning to occur. The therapist, observing the first signs, asks if clients would like to take a short break from telling the story, focus their attention on their symbol of the present, and describe it in detail.[2] The visual and verbal reminder of the safety of the present, often termed *grounding,* is designed to access the client's own ability to find temporary comfort even in the midst of recalling the traumatic past.

The videotape *Severe Early Trauma: Part 2* (van der Kolk, undated) also provides a number of highly creative exercises that clients can employ during the various tasks and phases of recovery. One example is a "borrow the judgment" task for clients who are prone to placing themselves in unsafe situations. Therapists ask clients to consider borrowing the judgment of a person whom they respect and to use his or her viewpoint to help them out when they are confronted with a risky choice. In other words, they are to look at the situation through another's eyes and decide what that person would or would not do under the circumstances. This sort of metaphor is designed to capitalize on the skills that clients already possess by allowing them to access at critical moments what is in fact their own good sense.

Dolan (1992) also emphasizes the use of "constructive questions," which are designed to help the client and therapist define in a detailed manner exactly what changes must be made—emphasizing the *smallest* increment possible. Survivors of child abuse are typically terrified of losing control and, as a result, will cling rigidly to old patterns of behavior, even those that are harmful. The idea that they need to begin to do some things differently can be so threatening that they find themselves paralyzed. Focusing on identifying the smallest step in the change process can help them begin to take action in a way that is less terrifying. For example, finding appropriate housing may be the first step in a process of creating safety for a client—yet he or she consistently fails to follow through. The problem, according to Dolan's technique, is that the activity has not been broken down into small enough steps. Thus, clients might identify the smallest step as making one phone call to a local housing agency. Others may identify the smallest step as merely looking up the number in the phone book. Whatever the case, once any step is taken, congratulations are in order, because clients have entered into the difficult change process and are on the way to achieving their goal.

EYE MOVEMENT DESENSITIZATION AND REPROCESSING

Discovered by accident in 1987, eye movement desensitization and reprocessing (EMDR) is the latest and, perhaps because of its newness, the most controversial treatment approach. Francine Shapiro noticed that when she moved her eyes in particular patterns while recalling difficult life events, the emotional pain associated with these memories was lessened. She continued to study the phenomenon with Vietnam veterans and initiated a series of research projects that showed positive results. The veterans found that their flashbacks and intrusive thoughts were reduced or eliminated after EMDR treatment. Since that time, thousands of clinicians have been trained in the technique, and numerous research initiatives have, in the main, reported positive results (Shapiro, 1995).

Because the treatment grew out of experience, rather than theory, an explanation of why it seems to work had to be developed after the fact. The accelerated information processing model, in concert with theories regarding how traumatic memories are laid down, proposes that during a traumatic event, the many sensations, impressions, and overwhelming feelings that accompany it are stored in the brain as "frozen" and unprocessed information. This static information subsequently affects survivors' thoughts, feelings, and behaviors when present-day stimuli remind them of their earlier experiences. Survivors respond to current circumstances with rigid ways of feeling and behaving that are directly related to earlier, improperly processed trauma-related information. If these old memories are reprocessed and stored in the brain accompanied by healthier associations, survivors' behaviors will change, and they will be able to live more fully in the present.

Mental health professionals who practice EMDR must first have acquired professional credentials as therapists (a master's level or doctoral degree). In fact, EMDR treatment is typically embedded among the standard processes of a therapeutic encounter, including relationship building and defining the helping frame.

In practical terms, clients are asked to recall a disturbing memory (considerable time is spent deciding which memories to target) and are then led in an eye movement exercise. As they continue to speak about the memory, the therapist stops them at certain points, and the eye movement exercise is repeated. Each time, the client is asked to pick a number on a scale of 0 to 10 that describes his or her level of discomfort. Over time, the number drops as the client becomes desensitized to the memory. At this point, it is likely that statements that are more positive begin to emerge ("I can see now it wasn't my fault," "I did all I could to protect myself"), and the eye movement exercise is repeated. It is thought that the repetition of the eye movements reprocesses (stores) newer, healthier thoughts (associations) in tandem with the old memory, resulting in an immediate sense of relief and a reduction in the power that the memory holds over the survivor's life.

Although some proponents endorse EMDR as a miracle cure, Shapiro (1995) herself warns that we don't really know how it works. In fact, recent research has focused on what is being called the "cognitive dismantling of EMDR," meaning that the various steps in the treatment process have been examined alone and in various combinations to determine which ones are critical to its success. Preliminary findings indicate that EMDR was just as effective when eye movements were eliminated from the treatment process. Authors postulate that the eye movements might not have much to do with the effectiveness of EMDR and, instead, that the repeated exposure to traumatic material in a safe environment is what eventually leads to a reduction in posttraumatic symptoms (Cahill, Carrigan, & Frueh, 1999; Cusack & Spates, 1999). Regardless of the mechanisms, EMDR constitutes one more avenue that therapists may choose to explore in their search for effective help for their clients.

TREATMENT FOR PEOPLE WITH DISSOCIATIVE IDENTITY DISORDER

Traditional treatment techniques have tended to emphasize diagnosis, often including hypnosis to bring the different personalities out into the open; mapping the system (naming each personality and defining how they relate to one another); stabilization; establishing communication and cooperation among the different selves; tracing the memories (which personality remembers what traumatic event); abreaction (the intense emotional release after personalities reveal what happened to them); and fusion (removing the dissociative barriers between the personalities so that they meld into one integrated self; Putnam, 1989).

Over time, the treatment of dissociative identity disorder (DID) has become less focused on searching out all the personalities with the expectation that each must tell his or her horrible story (Segal, 1995). Abreaction can be seen as retraumatizing, and fusion doesn't seem to last. However, it is important that the personalities know each other and learn to value the talents and capacities each brings to the system. The staging of treatment in a step-by-step fashion is paramount in the prevention of overwhelm (Chu, 1998). Putnam's (1989) ideas of establishing stability in the survivor's external world are important, but safety in his or her internal system is also crucial. Often the various personalities are at war with one another and reproduce the abusive dynamics of their childhood in their relationships. Communication and cooperation among the various selves is a critical goal, but clients don't seem to see complete integration as important. In fact, many interpret the idea of integration as killing some of the personalities so that others may live. Although this misconception could be argued against, it is an important point. Most clients with DID have lived all their lives (knowingly or unknowingly) with these internal people. They are, in a sense, family. Certainly, clients want them to behave, to be less angry and "crazy," to be kind to one another and not embarrass themselves, and to stop placing themselves in danger or harming the corporal body that houses them—but they typically don't want them to disappear.

The treatment of DID is a lengthy process. Survivors with this diagnosis have endured the harshest, most sadistic forms of abuse possible, and recovery is painfully slow. Personalities show themselves over time as the therapeutic alliance deepens, and as they do, clients are encouraged to welcome them and introduce them to the newly instilled "family" values of internal and external safety, communication, and cooperation. Dealing with the child personalities of people diagnosed with DID can be particularly difficult for professionals (Chu, 1998). These alters can seem like real children, touchingly vulnerable and in need of protection, and we can feel drawn into parenting scenarios that are not helpful. If we do so, we abandon our therapeutic alliance with the adult who is our client and form bonds with only fragments of his or her person. It is important that we remember that these "children" are part of a whole, and that we continue to support clients in learning the skills to manage their internal "family" dynamics themselves. Complete harmony usually remains a distant hope, but little by little, life calms down as these hidden people (children and adults alike) get to know one another and learn to get along as best they can.

GROUP THERAPY

Survivors of child abuse keenly feel their isolation from the rest of the world. They long for connection with other people and for a place to belong. For this reason, and for more practical reasons such as scarce funding and few trained clinicians, group therapy has developed an important place among credible healing and recovery approaches. The idea that more survivors can be helped by fewer therapists, and at a reduced cost, is paired with clients' needs for connection and community. However, many trauma group therapists recommend that, ideally, clients have an individual case manager or other mental health professional to help provide support for them between sessions (Harris, 1998).

Most trauma therapy groups tend to be time-limited, closed to new members once the group has begun, and of a certain prescribed size, meaning that typically about 8 to 10 members start at the same time and work together for a specified period of time. In between groups, leaders may offer some form of contact for individual members (phone calls, brief meetings), but these contacts tend to be focused solely on how the member can function better in the group context. Usually, members are encouraged to bring most issues (complaints, disclosures, need for more support and feedback) back to the group so that matters can be dealt with employing the expertise of the membership.

The role of the group leader is to facilitate discussion and to manage the relational dynamics in the group. These are complicated tasks, and often two leaders work together, with one directing the content portion of the group (the discussion topic, lesson, or activity), while the other keeps his or her eye on the process (how members are working together, if someone is being left out or becoming overwhelmed). It is highly skilled work that requires rigorous training and ongoing access to clinical supervision.

Typically, each group meeting has a format where clients address specific topics. The leaders plan for each session by developing a rationale (why the topic is important), specifying what is to be achieved (the goals), and providing an outline. Topics for trauma groups can be varied, but topics generally include education about abuse and its long-term effects; how to combat negative self-images; grounding and self-soothing techniques; and lessons about the body, sexuality, nonsexual touch, and other critical subjects. It is not uncommon for group leaders to employ a variety of creative ways to guide the group and encourage interaction (e.g., reading a poem, leading a visualization, showing a short film—the list is bounded only by imagination). The overall goal is to allow members to share their stories and experiences so that they can learn from and support one another through the healing process.

As might be expected, abuse survivors are particularly handicapped in groups because they have learned that love and attention are rare prizes for which they must compete. They fear the authority of the group's leaders, even as they long for their approval. They can also react to their fellow members' disclosures with little empathy and a rather naked desire to one-up one another. In worst-case scenarios, a "hierarchy of suffering" can develop, with members jockeying for position and approval based on ever-heightened, dramatic, and lurid details of their abuse. Group leaders must be skilled and talented people as they manage these difficult dynamics, offering the consistent and clear message that "everyone and everyone's experience matters."

Because survivor groups can suffer from high rates of attrition, some group leaders may decide to call members each week to encourage attendance as a tactic to reduce the drop-out rate. Other leaders see attendance as a member decision and view dropout as a natural protection strategy—the client was simply not ready to go forward at that time. Others may tackle the problem tangentially by reducing barriers to attendance, such as providing transportation money and child care, choosing locations that clients see as safe, running the group at a convenient hour, and providing refreshments.

Although group work is difficult for survivors, those who can tolerate the many inherent anxieties learn valuable lessons about themselves and other survivors—not the least of which is how to begin to manage the dynamics of relating to their fellow human beings. They also benefit from learning how others react to their behaviors, encouraging a more self-reflective stance to the world. Perhaps the most powerful message, however, is the one that tells them they are not alone in their suffering. Others have "been there," and this connecting knowledge allows them to view themselves as a part of, rather than apart from, the world.

SELF-HELP

Perhaps the most famous self-help endeavor[3] is Alcoholics Anonymous (AA) with its now widely disseminated 12-step program. The essence of the 12-step philosophy is that members must acknowledge that their life has spiraled out of control and that a power greater than themselves is at work. Turning their lives over to this higher power is an essential first step as group members work toward admitting where they have gone wrong, deciding what they must do to put things right, and acting on these plans. The central issue for AA members and others who work on 12-step programs is to take responsibility for their own lives and to recognize the impact of their behavior on others. These sorts of groups are not for everyone, but it cannot be denied that they have helped thousands of people.

The inner child work of Alice Miller (1981, 1983, 1984), expanded and popularized by John Bradshaw (1988, 1990) and Charles Whitfield (1991), has spawned a broad self-help movement in which only one of the problems addressed is child abuse. As with any other model, the inner-child therapies have an underlying belief system about how the experience of abuse subsequently affects adults. In essence, inner children are created when parents, who themselves are wounded, project their feelings of inadequacy onto their vulnerable offspring. Children, in turn, are forced to deny what is really happening in an attempt to protect themselves from further harm and to stabilize the parent-child relationship, hoping to avoid complete abandonment. In order to cope with the split between this intense form of denial and what is really happening, the child's "true self" (the inner child) must go into hiding while a "false self" emerges. This false self is constructed mainly of parentally induced self-destructive beliefs and messages. Whenever the inner child attempts to emerge, the false self attacks, resulting in the suppression of grief and a constellation of compensatory symptoms, such as depression, substance abuse, explosive temper, chronic emptiness, suicidal ideation and attempts, and a compulsion to relive the victimization, to name many of the known indicators of an abuse history. Recovery involves discovering and "gently unearthing" the hidden inner child (Whitfield, 1991, p. 29) so it can learn to express itself in a healthy way and resume the developmental tasks that were interrupted by the weight of abuse.

As with therapy, these self-help approaches assume that recovery is best accomplished in the presence of safe, supportive relationships. However, the self-help ethos is based on power equity—no one is seen as having a greater level of expertise or knowledge than anyone else, and healing is achieved among one's peers.

Other types of self-help groups do not espouse either the 12-step program or inner-child work and instead focus on mutual support, empowerment, education, advocacy, and resource and information sharing. Other values remain the same as in any self-help group, with members holding beliefs such as "We're all in this together. Helping others helps me. If others can do it, why can't I? Together we can make a difference." In the psychiatric milieu, groups are based on disorders such as depression or schizophrenia and can include both the client and his or her family and friends as members (Everett, 1994).

In some instances, self-help may be viewed with skepticism in the formal, professionally run mental health system. Sometimes, professionals fear that such groups promote an antipsychiatry viewpoint or disseminate false or misleading information to the membership. These fears are related to the fact that, by definition, self-help does not include a professional presence and is not subject to professional control. Over time, however, most mental health professionals have become more supportive, recognizing the value in mutual aid groups and acknowledging that help can come from many quarters, not just from professionals.

WHEN NOTHING WORKS

One of the messages in this chapter, as well as the previous one, is that treatment, therapy, or self-help is not for everyone. In fact, *help* is not for everyone. By the term *help,* we mean the types of treatments, services, and therapies that urge clients forward by engaging them in the process of taking active, sustained control of their own health and lives. Sometimes, clients simply cannot engage in this sort of helping process for a number of reasons. Clients who are persistently psychotic, high, or drunk cannot take full advantage of help until their symptoms or substance use are under some measure of control. In addition, it is often assumed that clients who have psychotic disorders (schizophrenia especially) are poor candidates for therapy. Indeed, these sorts of clients are extremely emotionally fragile, and professionals must pace their work slowly and cautiously. We must also honor the delusional material as a valid form of communication and engage the client's voices (or hallucinations) in the healing process. Symptoms, which are reframed as important bodily or emotional messages, can become candidates for serious attention, active decoding, and, eventually, action. People with psychotic disorders can and do make significant gains as they learn to respect how their body and mind work and to manage their emotional life with increased maturity.

Another reason clients refuse help is that the approach doesn't meet their needs. If such clients were to be referred to a different kind of service, things might begin to move forward. This rationale is behind the development of a variety of services for people with mental illness. One size (or model) does *not* fit all, and clients benefit if they have a choice. However, some clients have given up—forever. Although this situation is rare, there are people who have entered such deep states of helplessness and hopelessness that no effort, no matter how determined or creative, is likely to reach them. In a similar vein, a few clients may cling to defense mechanisms so rigid and narrow that they repel any attempt at engagement. Although some of the models discussed in this chapter offer a variety of techniques to bypass entrenched defense systems, and each and every one of them should be tried, the reality is that sometimes absolutely nothing works.

Some clients are unable to move forward because they are afraid. They know the level of pain buried deep inside, and no matter how slow the pace or how cautiously the subject of emotion is introduced, they will not risk exploration. In fact, fear is typically the underlying reason for most blocks to forward movement, and the creative ways clients choose to thwart therapeutic engagement are only variations on a theme—"I must protect myself from further harm." Occasionally, the fear is so great that clients remain completely frozen, unable to reach out or to be reached.

Clients can also deny themselves help because they are hiding a shameful secret. These secrets can vary in nature, but a central hallmark is that they are based in reality and they are truly shameful. For example, the client may have abused or may still be abusing his or her own children. Clients who cannot admit that their behavior is harmful and face the consequences cannot grow.

CONCLUSION

Our deepening understanding of the aftermath of child abuse has led to the evolution of helping methodologies that work. Although there are instances where absolutely no approach can induce forward movement, the vast majority of clients change, improve, develop, and grow. The paramount focus of mental health services, no matter what model or approach, must be on positive change—or on healing and recovery in the case of survivors of child abuse. Everyone is capable of growth.

NOTES

1. A favored technique developed in the treatment of Vietnam veterans with symptoms of posttraumatic stress disorder (as well as people experiencing anxiety or phobias) is flooding and systematic desensitization, meaning that patients are placed in a relaxed state while they tell over and over again the "story" of a particular traumatic or frightening event. Each telling of the story escalates in intensity. Over time, the incompatibility of being relaxed while speaking of intensely disturbing events leads to desensitization. We *do not recommend flooding and systematic desensitization for survivors of childhood abuse,* nor does Dutton (1992) recommend this approach for battered women.

2. If clients have not previously selected their symbol of the present, Dolan (1992) advises therapists to simply ask the client to focus on a nearby object for a moment and to describe it in detail.

3. Self-help is sometimes referred to as mutual aid. A favorite self-help saying is, "You alone can do it, but you can't do it alone."

REFERENCES

Arntz, A. (1994). Treatment of borderline personality disorder: A challenge for cognitive-behavioral therapy. *Behavior, Research & Therapy, 32,* 419-430.

Beck, A., & Freeman, A. (1990). *Cognitive therapy of personality disorders.* New York: Guilford.

Bradshaw, J. (1988). *Healing the shame that binds you.* Deerfield Beach, FL: Health Communications.

Bradshaw, J. (1990). *Homecoming: Reclaiming and championing your inner child.* New York: Bantam.

Cahill, S., Carrigan, M., & Frueh, C. (1999). Does EMDR work? And if so, why? A critical review of controlled outcome and dismantling research. *Journal of Anxiety Disorders, 13*(1/2), 5-31.

Chambless, D., & Goldstein, A. (1979). Behavioral psychotherapy. In R. Corsince (Ed.), *Current psychotherapies* (2nd ed., pp. 230-272). Itasca, IL: F. E. Peacock.

Chu, J. (1998). *Rebuilding shattered lives: The responsible treatment of complex post-traumatic and dissociative disorders.* New York: John Wiley.

Cusack, M. A., & Spates, R. (1999). The cognitive dismantling of eye movement desensitization and reprocessing (EMDR) treatment of posttraumatic stress disorder (PTSD). *Journal of Anxiety Disorders, 32*(1/2), 87-99.

Dolan, Y. (1992). *Resolving sexual abuse: Solution-focused therapy and Ericksonian hypnosis for adult survivors.* New York: Norton.

Dutton, M. A. (1992). Assessment and treatment of post-traumatic stress disorder among battered women. In D. Foy (Ed.), *Treating PTSD: Cognitive-behavioral strategies* (pp. 69-98). New York: Guilford.

Everett, B. (Ed). (1994). *You are not alone: A handbook for facilitators of self help and mutual aid support groups.* Toronto, Canada: Mood Disorders Association of Metro Toronto. (Available from the Mood Disorders Association of Metro Toronto, 40 Orchardview Boulevard, Room 222, Toronto, Ontario, Canada M4R 1B9)

Gallop, R. (1992). Self-destructive and impulsive behavior in the patient with a borderline personality disorder: Rethinking hospital treatment and management. *Archives of Psychiatric Nursing, 6,* 178-182.

Greenberger, D., & Padesky, C. (1995). *Mind over mood: Change how you feel by changing the way you think.* New York: Guilford.

Harris, M. (1998). *Trauma recovery and empowerment: A clinician's guide for working with women in groups.* Toronto, Canada: Free Press.

Linehan, M. (1993). *Cognitive-behavioral treatment of borderline personality disorder.* New York: Guilford.

Miller, A. (1981). *The drama of the gifted child.* New York: Basic Books.

Miller, A. (1983). *For your own good: Hidden cruelty in child-rearing and the roots of violence.* New York: Farrar, Straus & Giroux.

Miller, A. (1984). *Thou shalt not be aware: Society's betrayal of the child.* New York: Meridian.

O'Connell, B. (1998). *Solution-focused therapy.* Thousand Oaks, CA: Sage.

Padesky, C., & Greenberger, D. (1995). *Clinician's guide to "Mind Over Mood."* New York: Guilford.

Putnam, F. (1989). *Diagnosis and treatment of multiple personality disorder.* New York: Guilford.

Segal, S. R. (1995). Misalliances and misadventures in the treatment of dissociative disorders. In L. Cohen, J. Berzoff, & M. Elin (Eds.), *Dissociative identity disorder: Theoretical and treatment controversies* (pp. 379-412). Northvale, NJ: Jason Aronson.

Seligman, M. (1991). *Learned optimism.* New York: Knopf.

Shapiro, F. (1995). *Eye movement desensitization and reprocessing: Basic principles, protocols and procedures.* New York: Guilford.

Smucker, M., & Dancu, C. (1999). *Cognitive behavioral therapy for adult survivors of childhood trauma: Imagery rescripting and reprocessing.* Northvale, NJ: Jason Aronson.

van der Kolk, B. (undated). *Severe early trauma: Parts 1-2* [Videotape]. Vancouver, Canada: Odin Books.

Whitfield, C. (1991). *Co-dependence: Healing the human condition.* Deerfield Beach, FL: Health Communications.

CHAPTER 10

Promoting
Client Safety

Safety is the first concrete step in the healing and recovery process. It is the foundation for human
growth, and without it, clients remain "stuck" in unhealthy patterns of
living. Emphasizing safety helps clients understand that the many difficult life changes they must make have a purpose—and that purpose is to
restore a sense of personal power and control (Herman, 1992). All mental health professionals can help clients with this task.

This chapter will concentrate on how mental health professionals, regardless of role, can capture clients' attention and commitment by focusing on relational, emotional, and physical safety. The first two dimensions (relational and emotional safety) are fostered mainly within the
client-professional relationship itself. In real life, these two concepts
overlap, but it is useful to tease them apart so that we can discuss the skills
associated with each. Building healthy relationships is often an unsung
professional activity principally because it is largely invisible, unavailable for inclusion in program statistics, and resistant to measurement and
observation in research. In fact, the only way high-quality client-professional relationships can be "seen" is by the positive outcomes they achieve.

Positive outcomes are contained in activities related to the third dimension, physical safety. Physical safety is created through working with clients to reduce the chaos in their lives. Here, we address clients' practical needs by helping them find safe, affordable housing; providing them with information and resources so they can begin to practice safe sex and improve their general health; and encouraging them to think more critically about the violence likely to be present in their interpersonal relationships.

The final portion of the chapter addresses the topic of safety within the psychiatric inpatient setting. Safety in the context of hospitalization can include the three-dimensional approach described above, but there is an added and salient emphasis on organizational and structural issues that define how professionals carry out their legal responsibilities to keep society safe from patients, and patients safe from themselves, when their symptoms and behaviors are out of control.

RELATIONAL SAFETY

The client-professional relationship is a laboratory in which clients can begin to experience healthy human interaction safely, mediated through the relational components, as discussed in Chapter 7, of mutual respect, clear communication, permeable boundaries, authenticity, and accountability. Through this professionally modulated experience, clients can then branch out and experiment with relationships with family, friends, and lovers.

Safety in the Client-Professional Relationship

The beginning phase of work, regardless of the mental health service paradigm, is a critical moment for the creation of relational safety. There are some specific and straightforward steps we can take in order to address the dimension of safety, and most relate to defining the helping frame.

Long-term experience teaches the wisdom of defining basic relational boundaries right at the outset. With the possible exception of crisis services, where professionals move into a problem-solving mode almost immediately, most client-professional contact is built over a sufficient length of time that spending a few minutes at the beginning to clarify some ground rules does not detract from getting on with the work. In fact, the helping process may be repeatedly interrupted as time goes on if at least some relational parameters are not discussed up front. Although there will be numerous circumstances specific to different mental health services, there are some generic guidelines that should be considered. These guidelines serve to define the helping frame.

Expectations. We can head off numerous predictable threats to relational safety by defining expectations early. These expectations can take many forms. For example, clients benefit from a brief description of the nature of the mental health service being offered. Taking a moment to explain, "This is what we offer. . . . This is what we do. . . . This is what you can expect from us (This is what we expect of you). . . ." exposes misconceptions immediately, allowing them to be discussed openly and, if possible, resolved. It also sets an open, question-and-answer tone that can be built on as the relationship develops.

Other topics that may be relevant are rules of conduct, hours of operation, the length of service (ongoing or time-limited), how and under what circumstances service may be terminated, how often client-professional contact occurs, how documentation is handled, and other parameters of service specific to individual programs or models. The limits of confidentiality should also be explored within the confines of individual circumstances. And, because many clients experience dissociation and can "forget" verbal information, a written statement to accompany these sorts of discussions can be helpful.

Another form of expectation relates to the ability of clients to be attentive and alert during their appointments. The task of establishing a relationship is virtually impossible if clients can't attend to what is going on. Sometimes clients may be overmedicated, and it is appropriate to suggest that they return to their psychiatrist for an assessment in order to recalibrate the amounts or types of medications they are on. Other clients use street drugs or alcohol, and some have lost total control of these self-medicating strategies and have developed full-blown addictions. It may take some time to find specialized help for these problems, but in the meantime, it is perfectly reasonable to set a minimum expectation that clients attend appointments sober and alert.

Survivors of child abuse often also have disturbed sleep patterns. Having been terrorized at night, typically in a bedroom, their bodies refuse to calm down as the evening approaches, and instead, they become especially alert. Clients need to work on establishing more normal day-night patterns over the long term, but in the short term they can start with a little more activity during the day and a little less at night—framed within the expectation that they are required to attend appointments in a more alert state. Sleeping medication may aid this transition, although it may not be appropriate for clients with addiction problems.

Professionals may have also developed other expectations particular to their own personal styles of working. We may want to define how readily available we are in between appointments, how telephone contact works, and upon what schedule we will return clients' phone calls. Others may set specific rules around the cancellation of appointments and how payment is to be made (if applicable). Inpatient staff may want to discuss how much individual time they will have for patients given their other ward duties.

At first, these sorts of discussions may seem unnecessarily time consuming or overly intrusive, but as professional experience is gained, a comfort develops with this necessary beginning phase. The key is neither to overburden the client with a litany of rules and regulations nor to ignore important information that could reasonably be expected to interfere with the health of the client-professional relationship later on.

Touch. Survivors of childhood trauma have had their bodies regularly violated and will have specific and intense feelings about touch. Survivors who are in therapy can expect to have to deal with their fears around touch, and they will be challenged to learn how to experience and tolerate the feelings associated with pleasurable touch (Hunter & Struve, 1998).

However, in any client-professional relationship, the subject of physical touch is loaded and requires substantial up-front discussion before professional and client arrive at a comfortable agreement that suits both. Some clients crave the comfort of nonsexual physical touch and regularly demand hugs. For others, a hug will be interpreted as sexual, no matter how brief or offhand the contact. Others may recoil in horror at the idea of any touch, even a gentle pat on the arm. A few are so reactive that they are in danger of dissociating or lashing out. Openly discussing clients' feelings about touch is essential to clarifying expectations.

As professionals, we have our own feelings about touch. Some of us were raised in homes where physical contact was uncomfortable and typically avoided. Others have had experiences of sexual or physical abuse and share some of the same intense feelings about touch that clients do. If, after careful consideration, we decide that we are simply too uncomfortable to touch or be touched by clients, we will need to communicate our decision sensitively, along with a level of explanation that protects our own boundaries.

On the other hand, some professionals are naturally "touchy" people, seeing nothing but value in physical contact. In these instances, responding in a healthy way to, for example, a request for a hug must first be judged situationally against variables such as the service context, the gender of both the client and the professional, the supposed motivation and tone of the request, and the length of time the client and professional have worked together—to name only a few details to be considered.

Aside from hugs, clients may ask for small loans, invite us to coffee, bring gifts to appointments, or offer to run errands or do small tasks around the office—simple human actions, but ones that are complex within the context of relational safety and the sanctity of a purposeful client-professional relationship. Although therapists' reactions to these sorts of requests are guided by strict ethical rules, other mental health professionals (e.g., case managers; housing, crisis, or community workers) can work in roles and in settings where how to respond is less clearly prescribed. It is helpful to answer a few questions before making a decision:

- Why is my client asking for this?
- Does my organization have a policy around this?
- Would my professional association view responding to this request as unethical?
- How will my relationship with my client be affected if I do/don't do this? In the short term? In the long term?
- What message am I giving my client if I do/don't do this?
- How will my professional colleagues view me if I do/don't do this?
- Is this a matter best discussed in supervision or with a peer?
- What is the best way to tell my client about my decision?

The abilities to pause and reflect and to seek wise counsel are a professional's best friends when trying to decide what course of action to take.

Suicide. Suicidal ideation, suicide threats, and suicide attempts are frequent occurrences among survivors of child abuse. Although mental health laws prescribe the specific actions that must be taken in the event that clients demonstrate firm intentions to kill themselves, real-life situations are rarely that clear-cut. Some clients threaten often and never act. Others say nothing at all and kill themselves. Some make repeated attempts but always call for help at the last moment. Others intend their attempt as a "cry for help" that may, in the end, get the longed-for response—or that may go drastically wrong if they misjudge the lethality of the means they have chosen.

Suicidal threats are familiar interactional currency among survivors, so much so that the threats can begin to take on lives of their own. Most survivors hunger for the loving attention they were denied as children, and depending on their specific experiences of the mental health system, they may have found that the threat of suicide is a valuable technique for focusing attention in their direction. Many survivors have long ago learned to settle for *any* attention at all and may have lost the ability to discriminate between positive and negative attention. Others use the phrase "I want to kill myself" as a coded way of telling professionals and others how bad they feel. Still others use it as a threat: "If you don't talk with me (admit me to hospital, refer me, make that phone call) *right* now, I'm going to kill myself." Survivors don't plot to "manipulate" others, nor do they typically think through the implications of their behavior. However, regardless of the motivations behind a threat of suicide, it is a professional obligation to take clients seriously.

In the beginning stages, it is important to ask clients about their history of suicide ideation, threats, or attempts. The first goal of this conversation is to distinguish between suicide attempts and self-harm, and the second goal is to assess the seriousness of previous suicide attempts (see Chapter 12 for a full discussion). Attempts that were impulsive and private, that employed deadly methods, and that were unsuccessful only because the client was accidentally discovered indicate serious danger.

The role of consultation and supervision cannot be stressed strongly enough during this process. Assessing the level of risk is highly skilled work. Judgments are formal, carry legal weight, and must be made by those who have recognized authority. Negotiated relational ground rules must include a clear, firm discussion about what professionals are required to do by law if clients seriously threaten suicide and refuse to take themselves to the hospital voluntarily. Clients also need to know that once a professional has had to go to the extreme of ordering (or having a colleague order) involuntary commitment, the safety of their working relationship has been breached and will require substantial effort to reestablish.

If clients have stopped to make a phone call or have visited in person in order to threaten suicide, they are obviously of two minds about whether or not to carry through. We can capitalize on this ambivalence by responding, "Do you *really* want to die, or do you want the pain to stop?" The point of this sort of question is to move the client away from the nonproductive dilemma of "How can I get someone to stop me from committing suicide?" toward "How can I comfort myself (or gain access to comfort) when I'm in pain?" Opening up the conversation in this fashion presents clients with an entirely different problem to solve while at the same time appealing to their more rational and competent side. Although no one approach works in all instances, the principle remains the same. Talking about suicide openly and in an empathetic manner gives clients the means to release some of the emotional energy driving the threat. It also allows professionals to remain in the voluntary helping frame, giving us time to assess whether or not other, legally defined actions are required.

These sorts of conversations can lead to the larger task of developing an individualized plan for how clients can keep themselves safe. Such plans involve an inventory of the escalating feelings and behaviors that lead up to overwhelming suicidal feelings, accompanied by specific actions that clients may take in order to soothe and comfort themselves. This kind of discussion is designed to encourage clients to become aware of their own emotions and behaviors and, over the long term, to develop self-soothing skills.

To engage in this sensitive topic area requires that professionals confront their own feelings about suicide. Fears that clients may commit suicide are grounded in reality, and even worse, many mental health professionals have experienced the pain and grief associated with losing a client to suicide. If we are to continue helping, we cannot allow our fears to immobilize us or to render us excessively reactive. Fear is contagious, and clients' anxiety, and thus the chance that they will act impulsively, is only heightened when professionals push the panic button. Talking through our feelings with peers or in supervision is critical, but it is also important to confront the issue directly with clients. Open discussion is a form of safety valve that allows both clients and professionals to shine needed light on the dark ruminations that accompany the suicidal impulse.

Routines. Relational safety requires a certain level of predictability. Routine provides *structure,* which in relational terms refers to the simple rituals that professionals can introduce into the client-professional relationship. For example, we may greet clients in the same fashion, always pause to make tea or coffee before getting down to serious topics, or close meetings in a similar way—a deep breathing exercise, a minute of silent reflection, or simply the ritual of setting the next appointment. Exactly what is done will vary from client to client, but these little routines provide a predictable cadence to client meetings that soothes anxiety. In addition, they are internal to the meeting itself, which can't always be on the same day, at the same time, or even in the same place, given the harried schedules of many hospital and community professionals.

Rituals are both subtle and powerful. They utilize the same mechanisms that are present in early infancy when all information is received through the senses rather than through words—when doing the same thing in the same way at the same place with the same smells in the air and the same sounds in the background communicated predictability. Young children are similarly comforted by hearing the same story or playing the same game repeatedly. Survivors of child abuse are unlikely to have experienced these forms of early safety. Purposefully recreating aspects of them in the present is intended to infuse the client-professional relationship with a sense of calm.

Techniques such as setting ground rules, communicating expectations, negotiating agreements around touch and suicide threats, and using routines set both the boundaries and cadence of the client-professional relationship so that relational safety has space to root and grow. Although these techniques represent basic "ABCs," we can use our creativity to devise other methods, depending on the situation and the individual client. However, the principles that underlie relational safety are likely to remain the same: discussion and negotiation leading toward mutual agreement on the parameters of a healthy, functioning, *safe* relationship.

Safety in Relationships
With Friends and Family

As clients begin their healing and recovery journey, they need the support and understanding of others. No relationship with a mental health professional, regardless of how healthy it is, can substitute for friends and family. The subject of family is especially emotional. A common misunderstanding is that survivors will want to cut off all contact with those family members who have been abusive, but this is likely not to be true. Survivors typically want desperately to maintain contact—but to be kept safe when they do so. It is hard for beginning professionals to understand why survivors expose themselves to the possibility of further hurt, but family bonds—especially those forged under the terrorizing conditions of abuse—are intense and strong. Only in the case of present, ongoing abuse (sexual or physical) must contact stop, and then only with those family members who are perpetrating.[1] Otherwise, discussions are focused on safety and surround issues such as, "Who in your family has not harmed you? What can you do to make that relationship stronger? How can you keep yourself safe when your mother puts you down? When you go home for the holidays, what can you do to protect yourself when you think a fight is about to start?" There are no magic answers to these questions, and each survivor must develop his or her unique plan. At first, most don't do particularly well at keeping themselves safe, but simply raising the topic increases awareness. Over time, plans will slowly evolve as clients come to understand that they are entitled to relational safety and, further, that they have an active role to play in creating it.

Friends are a somewhat less threatening topic, but a gentle approach is still required at this stage. General questions such as "What does friendship mean to you? What qualities do you want in a friend? What do you do to be a good friend?" are useful. Clients often respond with a list of attributes such as "I want someone who will listen to me. I want someone who returns my phone calls. I don't want my friends to judge me or put me down. I don't think a real friend would steal from me." Using this list, survivors can examine some of their present friendships to see if they measure up. Many may not, and this knowledge is painful in itself. A second part of this discussion is the survivor's own behavior. Typically, clients will describe themselves as always giving—sometimes quite literally, giving away money and belongings, and at other times more metaphorically, giving in, compromising, denying their own needs. The message is, "I'll do anything if you don't leave me." In other instances, survivors intersperse their giving with angry attacks, blowing up at friends and threatening retaliation for real or imagined insults. The message here is mixed: "I need you desperately but I'm afraid you'll hurt me." Discussions about the mutuality of friendship are valuable, because they alert survivors to the need to both demand more and give less—in other words, to protect their own boundaries. However, this is a complex concept for people who have never experienced protection, and it is sufficient at the safety stage merely to introduce the idea.

A third aspect of this discussion is the issue of revictimization. Survivors are often quick to form what they will call friendships, only to find out that they have once again chosen someone who hurts or abandons them. Professionals may want to pose questions such as "How long do you think it takes to really get to know someone? What do you need to know about a person before you give your friendship? What are some of the signs that someone isn't a true friend?" Sometimes it helps to make the distinction between friends and acquaintances and to discuss when and with whom it is safe to talk about intimate topics. Survivors often have unrealistic expectations of what adult-to-adult friendships are like, fantasizing that "real" friends are available 24 hours a day, anticipate every need, and respond cheerfully to any and all demands. These expectations are simply a different version of the deep desire for rescue to which all survivors cling.

These beginning relationship skills may seem excessively simplistic, particularly because so many survivors are able to maintain at least the veneer of social capability. However, human relationships are a source of great mystery to them. Part of their isolation stems from the fact that they feel that everyone in the world—but them—knows how to gain the love and attention of caring others. In some senses they are correct. People who have not had their tragic experiences take such a basic relational requirement as safety for granted. But for survivors, keeping themselves safe when in the presence of other humans is a daunting but critical first step toward learning the complex mechanics of healthy and mature relationships.

EMOTIONAL SAFETY

Emotional safety requires first that professionals learn how to manage their *own* emotional reactions so that they can respond with a clear head and with the purposeful nature of their helping role firmly in mind. In other words, we have to learn how to respond to clients' disclosures, behaviors, and symptoms in an empathetic but neutral and nonreactionary manner. Survivors are terrified of emotion, their own and that of others. Not only are they afraid of being overwhelmed by their own feelings, but they also fear disgusting, horrifying, and overwhelming the listening professional. In addition, survivors often disguise how they really feel in order to protect themselves from overwhelm or retaliation. Most will demonstrate mixed-up emotional responses: smiling while they talk of sad events, becoming angry at apparently happy occasions, and feeling guilty for achievements. As professionals, we must make it clear that we are able to tolerate intense emotion and that we will work with survivors to help them contain their feelings. Professionals who adopt a neutral and nonreactionary stance clearly communicate three important messages: "I understand how you feel. I am not overwhelmed by it. I can take care of myself." This stance does not mean that we don't express emotion. Instead, it demands that we use our emotional responses in ways that are accurate to the situation and that mirror clients' true feelings—but in a calm and low-key manner.

Transference and Countertransference. Transference and countertransference are dynamics that are present in all relationships. In the case of the client-professional relationship, *transference* is defined as the individual and idiosyncratic feelings and perceptions arising out of clients' pasts that they transfer onto the professional, without regard to whether or not they accurately reflect present events and circumstances. Often, these feelings are not in the awareness of the client. For example, clients who have been abandoned repeatedly in their lives may interpret a request to change an appointment date as the professional's "underhanded" way of telling them that the professional is leaving them. "Why don't you just come out and say it! You're abandoning me, and you don't want to tell me!" they cry, transferring their fear and mistrust onto us.

Countertransference is defined as the individual and idiosyncratic feelings and perceptions that professionals, in our turn, transfer onto our clients without regard to the fact that ours is a purposeful helping role. In the above example, we may countertransfer our shock at being so thoroughly misunderstood by replying in an exasperated tone, "I was just trying to change the appointment date. Why are you reacting in such a childish manner?"

Countertransference responses are inevitable and can be put to good use in the client-professional relationship if we are prepared to work on understanding their derivation. Supervision can help us to acquire the skills to become aware of and express our own countertransference emotions directly and authentically. The first task is to examine our own reactions and track down the source—are we unable to respond openly to clients because of something in our own background and life experience? Or is our reaction situational—tied to a specific client and a specific encounter or set of encounters? Sometimes, this acknowledgment is openly conveyed to the client; at other times it is talked through with peers or supervisors. Whatever the case, the goal is to reestablish and maintain empathetic connections with clients by finding ways to understand why they behave the way they do. In the case of the request to change the date of an appointment, for example, supervision can help the professional begin to understand his or her frustration at being so quickly misunderstood when, in fact, the real goal was to be helpful, thoughtful, and consistent. The professional may also come to understand the overwhelming fear of abandonment that any change in routine provokes in this client group. This knowledge should allow the reestablishment of an empathic connection, with the professional feeling freer to address the client's concern in an understanding manner: "It must be hard to constantly fear that people are going to disappoint you or let you down."

The consequences of professionals' not addressing their countertransference emotions and behaviors within the client-professional relationship can be extreme, because those who continuously ignore their own feelings eventually find that they have to draw away from clients as a protective measure. In doing so, we sever our empathic connection and move quickly to a harder relational stance. Clients are in danger of becoming an objectified "they," who are labeled as manipulative, demanding, unreasonable, resistant, and incompetent. When this disconnection happens, work turns into a burdensome chore. In some instances, professionals may direct their dissatisfaction inward, berating themselves for their ineffectiveness. In other cases, they may retaliate against clients in indirect ways (missing appointments, failing to return phone calls, speaking in an obviously impatient tone)—ways that may seem unimportant at first but, if left unchecked, could escalate until there is danger of transgressing ethical protocols.

Transparency. As professionals, we have very little choice but to be aware of, and open about, our own feelings. Survivors of child abuse have spent their early years learning to scan their immediate environments for the minutest pieces of information, poised to make instantaneous decisions that may well have meant life or death. This is a client group that will monitor every nuance of the client-professional relationship, searching for indications that their tenuous trust is likely to be betrayed. Everything about the professional will be watched both closely and covertly, making congruence between emotions, words, and deeds absolutely essential. Professionals have to learn to be as transparent as possible.

Transparency is best defined as explaining the reasons for actions before they are taken and revealing thoughts and feelings as they are experienced. This is obviously a tall order. Although we can *try* to explain everything we do, say, and feel, we can't possibly anticipate every reaction that clients might have. As a result, the most efficient tactic is to invite clients to become partners in this endeavor. If clients can agree to ask questions whenever they are puzzled or frightened, they can begin to bring their covert monitoring behaviors out into the open. If clients trust that, when questioned, we will explain ourselves clearly and straightforwardly, they can start to relax at least somewhat. However, they will test this agreement numerous times before they come to trust it.

Testing. When clients test professionals, they do so in disconcerting ways. Survivors often have behavioral problems that provoke a barrage of countertransference emotions. They can frighten, frustrate, hurt, offend, and disgust—equally as well as move us to laughter and tears. Given that it is frequently a professional role to challenge clients to get in touch with their emotions and express them in healthy ways, they are quick to discount us when we don't follow our own advice. Sometimes, professionals adopt an artificially bright and cheery manner, feeling that clients' difficult behavior will stop if they encounter a consistent show of good humor. At other times, we may visibly try to swallow our feelings, pretending that we never get angry or frustrated. Clients' behaviors can escalate under these circumstances, as they continuously push and test in pursuit of an authentic response. The principles of emotional safety demand that we learn the skills to acknowledge that we have feelings, too, and that clients' behavior can have an effect on us. A straightforward, honest response typically reduces clients' anxiety, usually to the point where they can restore the link to more competent internal resources and regain control of their behavior.

Grounding. Clients also need to begin to find ways to contain their symptoms by interrupting lifelong patterns that are no longer serving them. For clients who experience dissociation, as well as overwhelming emotion and flashbacks, it is useful to teach grounding techniques, which are ways to reorient their attention to the present when they begin to feel themselves losing control. For example, we can ask clients to try to maintain eye contact during client-professional meetings. This strategy strengthens the human-to-human connection and helps clients retain a focus on present circumstances—and on the safety of the relationship. Those who fear eye contact because of past abuse experiences (they may have intense feelings of violation or of having their thoughts read) can choose an object, such as a picture, coffee cup, or vase in the professional's office or in the location of the appointment. When "spaceyness" or dissociation begins to occur, we can work with them to ensure that they focus on the chosen object in order to return themselves to the present. Clients may also carry a special possession that serves the same function, for example, by choosing a picture of their own children to remind themselves that they are adults and that the abuse is no longer occurring. The goal of these sorts of techniques is to help clients begin to gain a sense of control over their dissociative symptoms so that they can feel more in charge of their own emotional safety (Chu, 1998).

Self-Soothing. Clients who have abuse histories have not learned how to calm themselves down. For nonabused children, the capacity to self-soothe is acquired over time, starting with the internalization of positive experiences in early childhood. Gradually, even very young children learn to sustain these comforting experiences in the absence of the parent by using substitute objects such as, for example, a quilt to recollect soft touch and comfort. As children mature, more and more abstract notions (a warm bath, a glass of milk, a favorite book) provide this comfort as they learn the habits of self-soothing, as well as how to be alone without being overwhelmed by feelings of anxiety or loss.

For abuse survivors, however, affect dysregulation is something they experience often and fear deeply (van der Kolk et al., 1996). Their unhealthy attempts to calm themselves down result in self-harm, substance abuse, eating disorders, and other behaviors that, paradoxically, create and sustain even more emotional chaos in their lives.

Clients need to be helped to acquire the skills to soothe themselves in healthier ways and to identify their own repertoire of self-soothing strategies. This process is both highly individual and wonderfully creative. One may call a friend, listen to music, or bake cookies, whereas another may scrub the kitchen floor. Groups that teach relaxation skills are also helpful, as are relaxation tapes and exercises. Professionals who have had special guided-imagery training may ask clients to create a "safe place" in their imaginations. When emotion threatens to overwhelm, they can mentally go to their safe place in order to regain control. Others may imagine a locked box where they can store their emotions until they feel more settled. The key is to have many options, because no single strategy works under all conditions.

However, those with the severest of abuse experiences believe that they are not entitled to any sort of kind treatment. It may take some survivors considerable time to begin to incorporate soothing techniques into their repertoire of behaviors, and even more time to test out what works and what doesn't. We must recall that the capacity to self-soothe takes years to develop in the child. Adult clients will internalize this capacity at different rates and have successes and failures along the way. This activity is a natural part of the healing and recovery process, and our ability to patiently support their efforts will enhance growth. As with grounding techniques, the goal of these strategies is for clients to begin to tolerate their own emotions and then to take a more active role in containing them (Courtois, 1999).

PHYSICAL SAFETY

Emotional and relational safety define *how* professionals and clients work together. *What* we do, the actual work of the client-professional relationship, is usually related to attending to clients' physical safety. Many survivors of child abuse who also have psychiatric diagnoses live in poverty and struggle daily with achieving even the basics of life. In 1962 Abraham Maslow developed a set of ideas that are today thoroughly familiar but still wise. He postulated the existence of a hierarchy of human needs, each of which must be met before the next can be considered. At their most basic, human needs involve food, clothing, and shelter. At their most complex, they embody ideas like self-actualization and spiritual fulfillment. Given the prosperous society in which we live, it is often a shock when professionals who have never in their lives gone hungry or wondered where they would sleep begin to realize the extent of the hazards many clients face on a daily basis. Healing and recovery cannot begin before they have met, at least in some fashion, their basic needs.

Housing

In the quest for safety, decent, affordable housing can be called first among equals. Survivors cannot begin their healing journey when homeless or living in the chaos of temporary hostels. Helping clients find and keep housing can be an area of specialization for mental health professionals, as well as a large part of the job requirements for case managers, discharge planners, psychiatric nurses, rehabilitation counselors, and others.

Housing—especially for survivors who live in poverty—is limited, and all too often that which is available is expensive or of poor quality. In addition, economies of scale can mean that a client's only choice may be some form of shared accommodation—a boarding home or rooming house. These forms of housing are often located in unsafe neighborhoods and may be filthy, violent, and run-down, exposing clients to further trauma.

Although rare, some jurisdictions have developed government-funded not-for-profit group homes where professional staff is available, sometimes on a 24-hour basis, to teach residents the skills of daily living. However, even in this Cadillac version, chaos can reign. Professional staff members are charged with the complex task of balancing the needs of the individual resident against those of the group, and there is also no guarantee that residents will respect the physical or emotional safety of their fellows. Nonetheless, this form of group living has its place. Some clients feel they need the presence of staff in their living situation. Others appreciate the fact that either meals are prepared for them or cooking is shared. Young clients who have never lived independently often see a group home as a natural first step on the way to living on their own.

Apartment living, while coveted, offers its own set of challenges. The greatest enemy appears to be loneliness, and clients may compromise their own safety by inviting strangers home, running up phone bills that they can't pay, or isolating to the point that their mental health deteriorates so extensively that they have to be admitted to the hospital. Others may neglect factors like cleanliness or the proper storage of food so that their apartment becomes a health or fire hazard. Each of these activities risks eviction, meaning that certain clients begin to acquire a "bad" reputation, making rehousing them more difficult.

Sometimes clients have other housing choices available to them, such as women-only homes, which can be important to female survivors of abuse. Other accommodations may have a no-drugs-or-alcohol rule, creating a safer environment for people with substance abuse problems. Some homes have been developed by a church or religious order, and certain clients may feel especially at home in these faith-based environments. Still others are defined by a particular model of "therapeutic community."

In order to help in this process, professionals must know local resources extremely well, including the "culture" in the home, the mix of tenants or residents, house rules, staffing levels, quality of food offered (if applicable), temperament of the landlord, referring process, and eviction laws. In cases where clients cannot approach the housing agency or landlord directly, professionals must submit complete and accurate referrals that honestly describe the client's past history—which may or may not include revealing a history of trauma, depending on appropriateness and client permission. However, suppressing facts about clients' behavioral problems in order to pass a rigorous screening process is unethical and dangerous, serving no one in the long run. Finally, wherever possible, it is important that we visit the housing to which we are sending our clients. There is no substitute for firsthand knowledge of the conditions clients must face.

Physical Health

The discussion on the creation of relational safety touches on physical health as it relates to sleeping patterns and drug and alcohol abuse. However, clients have other health needs that must be considered on an individual basis.

Safe Sex. Survivors of sexual abuse, in particular, can engage in sexual practices that endanger their health. These activities can include having unprotected sex, inviting strangers home for sex, working in the sex trades, engaging in sadomasochistic rituals, having sex in bathhouses or public toilets, getting drunk or stoned in unsafe locations, or wandering alleys and parks late at night. Survivors may also be in relationships where physical and sexual violence is common.

Encouraging safe-sex practices is a matter of providing information and education and helping clients access relevant resources, for example, free condoms and dental dams, birth control clinics, and treatment for sexually transmitted diseases. Sexual health for some survivors may include declaring their sexual orientation. Coming-out groups or groups for gays, bisexuals, or lesbians are particularly helpful in these instances.

A small percentage of survivors become sexual abusers. The principle of professional neutrality does not hold true if clients are harming others. Safety applies to *everyone.* Although clients have somewhat more latitude if the only people they are hurting are themselves, they may not under any circumstances, intentionally or through ignorance, harm others. At these times, it is important that we thoroughly understand our legal obligations. Our organization may also have policies to guide action.

General Health Concerns. Some survivors neglect their diet, their physical fitness, and their personal and dental hygiene. Others are heavy smokers. And, of course, many attack their bodies outright, using self-harm behaviors, suicide attempts, drugs, alcohol, and eating disorders to help modulate overwhelming emotion. In addition, the long-term (and sometimes even short-term) use of psychiatric medications can create health concerns of their own that require close monitoring. Years of abuse have taught survivors to hate their bodies. After a time, these indignities add up, creating further and sometimes extremely serious health problems that require ongoing medical attention.

Survivors are often deeply ashamed of their bodies. Conversations regarding their sexual and physical health need to be matter-of-fact and tactful. Framing discussion within the context of safety helps survivors begin to see that there may be a purpose to caring for their bodies. As with the building of relational and emotional safety, achieving physical safety will take time and a clear focus. Professionals who work in nonmedical settings, or whose role is nonmedical, are not qualified to diagnose physical ailments or advise on treatment, but they can help clients gain access to medical and dental resources and, if available, to alternative or culture-based treatments. We can also provide clients with basic information regarding all sorts of nutrition, hygiene, and sexuality issues.

Finding a Physician. Occasionally, clients complain that they have a hard time getting the medical community to take their physical conditions seriously, and they attribute this failure to the stigma associated with their psychiatric diagnosis. Many also have somatic complaints that relate to experiences of abuse, complicating matters further. We can assist clients by supporting them in their quest for a physician who will take them seriously, and independently, we may want to develop a referral list of local facilities or clinics that are sensitive to the needs of survivors in general, but specifically of survivors who also have psychiatric diagnoses. For survivors who are excessive users of medical services (as a tactic for expressing their emotional pain and relieving isolation), now may be the time to obtain permission to speak with all involved medical personnel in order to develop a coordinated plan to deal with legitimate physical concerns while at the same time offering emotional support for those times when the survivor is in danger of misusing medical resources.

Personal Hygiene. As professionals, we may have to struggle with our own shyness regarding the more sensitive aspects of physical health. For example, sometimes clients neglect their personal grooming to the point that they are very hard to be around. Personal hygiene, although a relatively small issue in comparison to other health problems, has substantial social implications for clients while at the same time carrying with it the weight of taboo. Many professionals who deftly handle conversations about safe sex quail at the thought of discussing body odor. For some survivors, neglect of their body has formed part of a defense strategy where they believed that if they made themselves unattractive enough, their abusers would leave them alone. Others were molested or sexually assaulted in the bath or shower and now suffer flashbacks when in similar situations. Some are so socially isolated that they have lost interest in their appearance. Poor hygiene can also indicate that clients have been evicted and are now living on the streets or that their housing is so substandard that it doesn't offer proper bathing facilities. Occasionally, poor hygiene signals the fact that a client has begun to deteriorate mentally. Whatever the case, it is important to explore the topic openly in order to understand what's behind the client's behavior. There are always reasons for the choices clients have made.

Violence in Interpersonal Relationships. If clients are risking their physical safety because they are in violent relationships, we must be careful not to overreact, because an aggressive rescue strategy can place clients in further danger. There are also likely to be complex motivations at work. Some survivors are substantially invested in maintaining their relationship, even if we may judge it to be abhorrent. Their wish, most often, is that their partner stop abusing, not that he or she should leave. As hard as it is, in most instances, the appropriate professional role is to provide information along with access to resources, leaving it up to clients to make their own decisions and take their own actions—when they are ready. However, ongoing consultation with managers or supervisors is important. If the situation escalates to the point that it is reasonable to assume that the client will be seriously harmed or even murdered, if there are children at risk, or if the survivor him- or herself is violent, we are ethically bound to communicate our concerns to the appropriate authorities. Unfortunately, in these complex and tragic circumstances, all too often there is little more that can be done.

SAFETY IN INPATIENT
AND INVOLUNTARY SETTINGS

It is rare for inpatient settings to be devoted to the needs of abuse survivors. Where such services exist, they pose particular challenges for professionals, given the tendency for survivors to regress under conditions where power differentials are so obviously extreme. Safety, in these situations, relates to professionals' abilities to define clear boundaries, set limits in a nonthreatening manner, and contain out-of-control symptoms and behaviors when they erupt. Reasonable accommodations such as women-only wards (given the high incidence of child abuse histories among women psychiatric patients), flexible sleeping times, and the provision of night-lights should be considered. Inpatient staff should also be versed in grounding techniques that assist patients to reorient to the present when experiencing flashbacks or dissociation (Chu, 1998).

Inpatient settings typically have a number of patients who are involuntary, meaning that they are not free to leave and that if it is deemed appropriate, they are treated against their will. Other professionals deal with community treatment orders that allow clients to live outside the hospital only as long as they take their medications. In these circumstances, we labor under the yoke of two masters: laws, which are designed to protect society from patients' symptoms and behaviors, and the patients themselves, who typically resist involuntary treatment vigorously. The collision between these two masters can be brutal, with patients submitting only after a violent struggle with police or hospital staff. In these roles, professionals are often in adversarial relationships with patients, functioning as the "bad guys" because we have to insist that their behaviors be contained and that patients be on treatments that may not have their approval. The nature of this work also means that we see patients at their absolute worst, when they are out of control, angry, manic, or psychotic—a time when it is difficult to form empathetic connections.

Involuntary work environments are extremely challenging because of the social, legal, and organizational structures under which they operate. They are high energy, stressful, demanding, and dangerous, and they are the last resort—often standing between the patient and what is likely to be certain disaster. Relational and emotional safety is difficult, if not impossible, to establish with patients who view professional staff as inherently untrustworthy because they serve the social and structural imperative. Even though professionals may conduct themselves in ways that are entirely respectful, the integral ingredient of mutuality is missing. Help is imposed and is typically experienced as control. Although some patients may, in hindsight, recognize that they (or others) are alive because they were forced into the hospital, very few view the experience as positive (Everett, 2000; Kaltiala-Heino, Laippala, & Salokangas, 1997). It is, after all, a blow dealt by the blunt instrument of law, and as such, it ignores individual freedoms as well as feelings and opinions.

Safety in involuntary and inpatient environments is usually considered a structural issue, covered in formal policies and procedures that speak, in the main, to physical safety. These relate to the conditions and procedures of mechanical restraint; noninjurious physical restraint; incident reports; isolation rooms and their prescribed use; 24-hour observation for patients who are considered to be suicidal; locked wards and bedroom doors that cannot lock; body searches and the confiscation of belongings; procedures for the pursuit of patients who escape; and miscellaneous items such as how staff dispose of needles, whether or not patients are allowed standard cutlery at mealtime, and the secure storage of implements that could become weapons in the wrong hands.

Abuse survivors are at great risk of revictimization in these settings, and it is not clear whether it is possible for them to have a positive experience, voluntary or involuntary (Fromuth & Burkhart, 1992). In a recent study (Gallop, Engels, DiNunzio, & Napravnik, 1999), hospital staff reported that they saw patients' individual needs as secondary to the structural demands of running a ward. The basic reality of involuntary treatment is that it is an avenue of last resort and should be considered only when clients' symptoms or behaviors are out of control or have become life threatening.

CONCLUSION

All mental health professionals, regardless of role or setting, have a part to play in assisting clients to regain power and control in their lives. Through the conceptual framework of relational, emotional, and physical safety, we can help clients lay solid foundations for future growth and development. Some may seek no further help, because they will have accomplished as much as they feel they need to in order to proceed through healing and recovery at their own pace and in their own way. Others, with the help of the freedom that their newfound safety provides, for the first time may want to begin to tell their story.

NOTE

1. If adult clients are still living in abusive family situations, discussions will surround how they can keep themselves safe in the home. Over time, they may develop the courage to leave, but they must not be pushed. In circumstances where the abuse is of a criminal nature (physical or sexual assault), mental health professionals should focus on how survivors can leave safely. However, even with charges laid and convictions obtained, there is no guarantee that the survivor will not return. Healing and recovery cannot proceed until survivors are able to extricate themselves from these actively abusive situations.

REFERENCES

Chu, J. (1998). *Rebuilding shattered lives: The responsible treatment of complex post-traumatic and dissociative disorders.* New York: John Wiley.

Courtois, C. (1999). *Recollections of sexual abuse: Treatment principles and guidelines.* New York: Norton.

Everett, B. (2000). *A fragile revolution: Consumers and psychiatric survivors confront the power of the mental health system.* Waterloo, Canada: Wilfrid Laurier University Press.

Fromuth, M. E., & Burkhart, B. R. (1992). Recovery or recapitulation? An analysis of the impact of psychiatric hospitalization on the child sexual abuse survivor. *Women & Therapy, 12*(3), 81-95.

Gallop, R., Engels, S., DiNunzio, R., & Napravnik, S. (1999). Abused women's concerns about safety and the therapeutic environment during psychiatric hospitalization. *Canadian Journal of Nursing Research, 31,* 53-70.

Herman, J. (1992). *Trauma and recovery.* New York: Basic Books.

Hunter, M., & Struve, J. (1998). *Ethical use of touch in psychotherapy.* Thousand Oaks, CA: Sage.

Kaltiala-Heino, R., Laippala, P., & Salokangas, R. (1997). Impact of coercion on treatment outcomes. *International Journal of Law and Psychiatry, 20*(3), 311-322.

Maslow, A. (1962). *Towards a psychology of being.* Princeton, NJ: Van Nostrand.

van der Kolk, B., Pelcovitz, D., Roth, S., Mandel, F. S., McFarlane, A., & Herman, J. (1996). Dissociation, somatization, and affect dysregulation: The complexity of adaptation to trauma. *American Journal of Psychiatry, 153,* 83-93.

CHAPTER **11**

How to Listen to, Hear, and Understand Clients' Stories

H umans tell stories so that others may know them and so that they may know themselves. Stories both recover and create meaning. They require survivors of childhood trauma to embark on a journey into the past, where they walk in the shoes of their forgotten or denied selves, observing and reporting on what they must have seen, heard, and felt. Tellers mine these manifestations of memory for meanings that could not have been known at the time, given the child's limited cognitive capacities. They also create meanings by superimposing present-day adult knowledge on top of past images so that a series of possible interpretations can be tested out against an internal measure of accuracy.

Although telling one's own story is an essential step in the healing and recovery process, it is important to understand that all stories are uniquely and personally constructed. The pursuit of objective "truth" is

205

beside the point, because the facts of historical human experience can rarely be proven. Instead, the process of storytelling challenges survivors to "name" their own past, in their own way, and at their own pace. This making of meaning is critical to the recovery process. When past traumatic events are given meaning and historical context, they begin to lose their grip on survivors' current-day lives, allowing them to live more fully, and with more control, in the present (van der Kolk, McFarlane, & van der Hart, 1996).

THE TIME AND PLACE FOR STORYTELLING

Survivors of childhood trauma tell their stories all the time. The problem is that they communicate their pain through indirect methods: as symptoms and behaviors instead of in words. Some may not remember much about their childhood and see their own behavior as inexplicable, to themselves as well as to others. Others remember most of their abusive pasts but don't connect them with their current difficulties. Still others recall their pasts but minimize the beatings, abuse, and neglect, saying it was not that bad, was their own fault, or was just the way things were. The mental health system can also sever the past from the present by treating clients' symptoms in isolation.

If survivors are at the point where they feel ready to tell their stories,[1] certain considerations must be taken into account. First, the professionals who are to help guide the storytelling process must have the necessary training. They must also function in a prescribed treatment role; that is, it must be part of their job description to assist in this way. Also, the setting in which they work and their own employment environment must support addressing clients' histories of childhood trauma. Further, they must have taken the necessary preparatory relationship-building steps by addressing with their clients issues of relational, emotional, and physical safety, and they must be prepared to continually revisit these critical aspects of safety throughout the storytelling process. Hearing a client's trauma story is extremely sensitive work, and there are many points along the journey where real harm can be done if we don't thoroughly understand the true nature of the work to be done or if we believe that good intentions can substitute for knowledge and skills.

Finally, it is important to note that even when professionals (for one or more of the above reasons) have decided not to encourage clients to tell their stories, clients often tell anyway. The client-professional bond can be a strong one, and it invites confidences. As a result, all mental health professionals, regardless of training and position, should have at least some understanding of the role of telling stories and of the importance of responding sensitively to disclosures. This chapter describes how to listen to, hear, and understand survivors' stories. The chapter's goals are to offer a glimpse into the process so that mental health professionals can understand it better and to offer a foundation for those who are interested in pursuing further training.

WITNESS

Telling stories, in words, is uniquely powerful because the translation of thought, perception, and memory into language creates a form of shared knowledge that is mirrored and made real through the responses of the listener. However, the role of the mental health professional goes beyond just listening and becomes that of "witness." Aron (1992) calls the survivor's story "testimony" because it recounts injustices suffered accompanied by an understanding of their effects. Child abuse is a crime that typically occurs in isolation—no one except the perpetrator and the child knows what happened. In other instances, adults knew but denied the child's perceptions with statements such as, "You asked for it" or "You're telling lies." Witnesses verify experience by listening, responding, and reflecting back clients' words to ensure complete understanding. When another understands, denial is less possible.

For this very reason, some survivors will back away from the storytelling process. People who have resisted *thinking* the unthinkable may find that *saying* the unthinkable is simply too large a step. Some may have been threatened with dire consequences, even death, if they ever told. Others may have told, only to be disbelieved or punished. And a certain percentage told but saw their families torn apart, their communities scandalized, and possibly themselves ostracized. These sorts of experiences must be taken seriously and other avenues for communication offered. One effective way for some survivors to begin their story is to use drawings or sculptures. Others may find that writing is a suitable first step.

These methods are powerful, but somehow less threatening than the spoken word. Saying out loud that which has been hidden, sometimes even from their own minds, reconnects survivors to volcanic levels of emotion. As a result, clients should never be pushed into telling their stories—regardless of the medium chosen. Seeing understanding reflected in the eyes of an attentive witness is to confront, sometimes for the first time, buried rage and deep sadness as survivors acknowledge the painful truth—their vulnerability and innocence were betrayed, often by the very same person they wanted, and may still want, to love.

LISTENING, HEARING, AND UNDERSTANDING

In this conceptualization of the storytelling process, listening, hearing, and understanding are differentiated to demonstrate three levels of comprehension. We define *listening* as getting the details of the story as the survivor believes them to be. *Hearing* is connecting these facts to the feelings that underlie them. And *understanding* occurs when professional and client together construct a thematic worldview—what the client has come to believe about the way the world works because of his or her experience.

Listening

Getting the Details. Listening to clients' stories means attending closely to the details of their lives. Although it is true that the overall focus is primarily on meaning rather than provable facts, most professionals are responsible for creating some form of written assessment, which generally consists of an outline of clients' developmental, personal, and family histories; the course of their of psychiatric difficulties; and a snapshot of their present situation. This background information precedes a formal summary of the nature of the clients' problems, followed by a treatment plan. Assessments provide the kinds of basic details that help us get to know our clients. These gathered facts represent intimate details (substance abuse, sexual history and orientation, abortion or loss of children to child protection authorities, history of trouble with the law, prostitution, etc.) as well as more prosaic information (names and occupations of parents, names and ages of siblings, whether or not the client has been married, educational level). All are important, because they are essential to understanding the context of clients' lives.

Some survivors may not be able to provide these sorts of details easily. Their stories may be garbled, vague, or chronologically disordered. Some may resist on principle, stating that they have been assessed time and time again and that they resent answering questions all over again. Others may fear that their personal information may be misused or misinterpreted. People with diagnoses that include paranoid symptomatology may be suspicious of the professional's intent and may withhold information based on their individual belief systems. In these instances, we require both patience and excellent listening skills to sort through whatever details we can glean and to place them in some sort of order. It is critical not to rush clients or to question aggressively. They will offer the needed information when comfortable.

Naming. As clients begin to reveal themselves, an important professional role is to assist by "naming" the abuse. Because many survivors feel that what happened was deserved, was brought on by their own actions, or was the natural consequence of being "bad," they tend to minimize events that objective others would think of as horrific. For example, some may say that their parents "got physical" with them. Others may refer to being "tickled" in ways that made them uncomfortable. Mostly, however, there is simply a lack of detail: "My mother and I didn't get on"; "Something bad happened when I was 13." These statements need to be explored thoroughly while at the same time respecting the survivor's right to set the pace. As more and more details emerge, "tickled" may turn out to be molestation, and "getting physical" may translate into beatings so severe that hospitalization was required. The professional role is to point out how others would view these experiences by saying things like, "You think of this as 'tickling,' but what you are describing is what many people call molestation." Survivors also need to know that they can talk about what happened without their professional listeners overreacting. Expressions of shock, anger, or promises of immediate action terrify survivors. Some feel that their own sense of defilement is contagious, and professionals who overreact demonstrate all too clearly that they have, indeed, been harmed. Others may feel that they will once again be abandoned because the professional is showing signs that he or she "can't handle" their story. Still others feel a loss of control as well-meaning professionals rush off to make things better—in ways that have never been discussed or agreed upon. Although we must be prepared to ask survivors for the details of their lives and to "name" certain experiences as abuse, we must do so in ways that are neutral and nonreactive. This relational stance is not to be understood as withholding empathy. Instead, it means adopting a calm demeanor that communicates the message, "I'm able to take care of myself. Don't worry about me. Just tell your story, your way."

Blocks to Telling

Protecting and Minimizing. The pacing of a client's story is rarely mediated through direct requests for the professional to slow down. Instead we must learn to recognize all sorts of indirect messages. One form of message is likely to arise when the perpetrator of the abuse was in an important caregiving role with the client. All children are protective of their parents (or primary caregivers), and as adults, people prefer to remember their childhoods with fondness. Paradoxically, adults who recall being abused as children can be even more protective—to the point of rigidly refusing to acknowledge that their abuser's behavior was in any way hurtful.

Children naturally seek protection when threatened, and if the only available source of comfort is their tormentor, the victim and the abuser can form an especially strong bond, which is sometimes called a "trauma bond." When abuse occurs between parent and child, one set of theories explains the resulting intense connection in terms of insecure attachment (Briere, 1992). Most abusers are not cruel and violent all the time. Often, some form of kindness is interspersed with abuse, leaving children in a chronically anxious state, because they can never predict accurately what the parent will do next. Even when caregivers are almost unremittingly abusive, a brief calm moment or a rare loving act stands out so powerfully that children are left desperately hungering for more. The emotions invoked by these sorts of extreme experiences are themselves extreme. Children's relationships with the perpetrators often remain chaotic and intense, as they cling tenaciously to the belief that, if they pretend it didn't happen, if they wait long enough, if the perpetrator would just change, admit guilt, or apologize—they will be able to recapture those fleeting moments when they felt loved. This bond is so strong that even if the perpetrator has moved away or died, survivors may continue to minimize the hurts they have suffered and infuse the memory of their parent with praise and glowing tributes.

Under these circumstances, as under any other, our role is to respect how clients see their world. If clients have indicated that they are ready to tell their story, yet they continue to protect the abuser and minimize their own suffering, it is possible, within the confines of a carefully constructed and safe relationship, to point out this inconsistency. But it remains the client's choice to continue to speak with inconsistency, just as it remains the professional's role to note when it occurs. Also, if clients clearly recount the details of abuse but fail to recognize it as such, naming these acts as abusive should continue. Pointing out inconsistencies and naming abuse are inherently challenging actions requiring professionals to employ extra tact and gentleness. Although it can be frustrating to listen as clients excuse even the most heinous acts, it must be recognized that for the time being, they need to continue the fantasy that the abuser's actions were in some way for their own good. To think otherwise is to confront profound loss. Time and the stability of physical, relational, and emotional safety will likely allow them to find the courage to talk about what really happened, but clients must never be pushed—nor should those clients who can go no further in the telling of their story be judged or penalized.

The Phantom Listener. For some clients, the shadow of the perpetrator is perceived as hanging over the storytelling process, eavesdropping, criticizing, and threatening retribution for telling. At a certain level of cognitive development, all children credit adults with superhuman powers, because they seem to know what children need even before the children do. In the case of abuse, perpetrators are perceived as always winning, always cutting off escape, and always knowing just how to hurt in the cruelest way. Even survivors who are capable of openly acknowledging that the abuser can't possibly hear them find it hard to shake the feeling that somehow, he or she knows. Sometimes, clients unconsciously feel the phantom presence of the abuser within the professional. At these times, they may react to even the most gentle questioning by accusing us of attempting to make them say things they'd rather not, or of invading their privacy.

It is important for us to respect clients' fears, because these fears represent yet another indirect request for a slower pace in the storytelling process. We need to explore what has led clients to feel that they are being "made" to talk, or why they have begun to feel that their privacy is being invaded. We also need to assure all clients that they can refuse to answer any question that is asked—but we must let them know that there is an obligation to ask at least some questions in service of getting to know what they have experienced. The resulting agreement ("I can ask you what I want and you can refuse to answer—and that's OK") is oddly paradoxical, but nonetheless comforting. Other clients may find this sort of agreement untrustworthy but will respond if they are offered the responsibility of choosing the topic for discussion at subsequent meetings. Setting the sessional agenda and refusing to answer questions are both mechanisms for offering clients control over the pace of storytelling, and professionals should openly label these agreements as such.

Fear of Retaliation. Many survivors fear that not only can abusers hear what they are saying, they are also able to punish them for telling. Retaliation may be defined by clients as anything from rejection (the perpetrator, although no longer abusing, will end the relationship) to assault or even death (the perpetrator is realistically and currently dangerous). In every situation, the client's emotional and physical safety is paramount. In some cases, professionals may have ample knowledge of their clients' histories and know that their fears of retaliation are groundless. It is sensible then to assume that clients are raising these fears in order to ask indirectly that the pace of storytelling be slowed until they are more certain of their general safety. However, if there is a real threat, our role is to help clients decide what they want to do. Some clients may be unable to take any steps at all to ensure their own safety. In fact, they may do the opposite and place themselves repeatedly in harm's way. In these cases, professionals must seek consultation with their supervisors or managers, because there may be laws or organizational rules that require them to intervene—especially in instances when the abuse is of a criminal nature. However, often the abuse, though insidious, cannot be defined criminally—especially when clients are adults. Examples are name-calling, put-downs, broken promises, veiled threats, unwanted but only vaguely sexual touching, slaps, and pushes. At these times, the attainment of personal safety is generally more a matter of education and support than a clear-cut legal matter. Clients must understand that the healing and recovery process *cannot* continue while their safety is threatened. Until they are prepared to take steps to protect themselves from violence, the professional role is to offer support, resources, and information so that when they are ready, they will be able to take action on their own behalf. In the meantime, it is legitimate for professionals to continue to point out the inconsistencies in their behavior. We can also continue to name abusive acts.

In a few cases, sorting out the victims from the victimizers is more complex. Some clients are themselves violent—targeting their more vulnerable family members or preying on other psychiatric patients while in the hospital and on roommates when discharged. In these circumstances, the client must understand that a nonnegotiable condition of a continued client-professional relationship is that the violence stop immediately.

It is normal for professionals to feel both helpless and angry at these times. The urge to rescue will be at its height. Some clients will find the strength to end the violence in their lives. Others will choose to continue old relationships, but with new and firm ground rules that ensure their safety. Some will do neither. Support and professional consultation is critical during this phase because, although it can be heartbreaking to watch as clients allow themselves to continue to be harmed, this may be a necessary phase that they need to go through before they are able to break away and resume the storytelling process.

Shameful Secrets. Survivors of abuse often harbor secrets. Some are ashamed because their body responded during molestation. Others were told that it was their own fault and believe that telling on the perpetrator is equivalent to telling on themselves. Some survivors were made to abuse others under threat of severe consequences. Still others hate themselves for not telling, feeling (and sometimes knowing) that they could have prevented the perpetrator from hurting others. These sorts of secrets are eventually revealed as the story unfolds and as physical, emotional, and relational safety deepens. Other revelations may be reserved for much later in the healing process. However, there are some secrets that may potentially pose complete blocks to telling, and thus to healing and recovery. These are truly shameful acts and usually have something to do with survivors' having abused others, typically their own children. Professionals may only come to know of these events through records or information received from other professionals—or not at all. At other times, clients will refer to these occurrences but admit no responsibility, even when it is patently clear that they took overt actions that were harmful. Openness and honesty are fundamental to the storytelling process, and although healing and recovery cannot continue if clients insist on withholding critical information or fail to take responsibility for their own actions, they nonetheless can be helped to improve other aspects of their lives, such as attaining safe housing, achieving a stable income, or confronting substance abuse.

Collateral Information

Because of our role and work location, many professionals will have access to records and other written information that may augment the storytelling process—especially when it comes to gathering details. Some of us may work in settings where we rely mainly on what the client divulges. Still others prefer to meet with clients and to hear in their own words their view of how life has unfolded for them before turning to formal assessments. Any approach can work if the ultimate focus is on the client and his or her story.

From time to time, however, it will be necessary to obtain documents from other settings or to talk with other professionals involved with clients (e.g., their physician, social assistance worker, or housing support staff). Most jurisdictions have precise laws that call for clients to give voluntary and informed consent in writing before information is exchanged. Also, there are occasions when it may make sense to talk to family members or friends, and legal consent procedures must be followed here as well.

When seeking collateral information, it is important to share the decision with clients so that they are aware of why the information is needed, what it will be used for, whether or not they can see it when it is received, and whether or not they can sit in on meetings with other professionals or with family members and friends. Given that clients are adults, it would be odd indeed if they were not involved in every aspect of the process and invited into all meetings, unless there are specific, agreed-upon reasons as to why not.

When Is the Story Done?

The professional's job is not to track down every single detail of clients' lives and commit it all to paper. We are also not in the business of "opening clients up" or "finding the truth." In the storytelling process, some clients may actually tell very little, whereas others may mine their memories for every single detail. Either approach is valid, if it is what suits the client. The bottom line is that clients will tell just enough to be sure that we understand what has happened to them. In fact, clients are often protective of our feelings—believing that if they shock or frighten us, they will once more be abandoned. Clients hold these beliefs for good reason because, without proper training, many professionals shy away from both the disturbing details of childhood trauma and the strong emotion that accompanies them, unintentionally silencing survivors. On the other side of the coin, listening to harrowing details of sadistic abuse is traumatizing, in and of itself, and seasoned professionals have no desire to know any more than is necessary. Thus, together, clients and professionals tend to naturally limit the storytelling process so that enough is revealed for mutual understanding, and no more. This is not to say that clients won't, over time, continue to offer new details, but these details will be in service of the natural healing process, as opposed to a perceived demand that they have to tell all.

Hearing

Although it is the role of survivors to tell, as best they can, the details of their story, it is the professional's job to connect these details to the feelings that lie behind them. In other words, the professional must listen on a different level and hear what meaning the heart (instead of the head) has made out of all that has happened. Just as before, the focus is not on the literal truth. Instead, professionals are trying to understand the psychological and emotional meaning of events—from the unique perspective of the client. In order to differentiate this type of listening, this conceptualization terms it *hearing*. *Hearing*, in this context, is best defined as reading between the lines of the story.

Listening and hearing are simultaneous tasks for professionals, but how and when clients enter the frightening world of emotions is unique to each. Sometimes, professionals connect the details to the feelings on the spot, reaching for the emotional content of the story as it unfolds. In situations where clients are immensely fragile, the story may unfold twice—once as a set of details and a second time as client and professional move slowly into the emotional content. Some clients will switch back and forth between detail and emotion. It all depends on the client and his or her capacity to name and experience emotion.

The important thing to remember is that although words are frightening, emotions are terrifying. It is often thought that recalling the emotions associated with the abuse will be easier than experiencing the abuse itself. This is untrue. Clients have learned to protect themselves as children by numbing (not feeling) and by splitting off (storing feelings at subconscious levels). Now, they are being asked to confront these hidden emotions without the benefit of their former protective mechanisms. As a result, they are often in real danger of losing control or of entering an emotional state from which they have no ability to escape. Affect dysregulation (McFarlane & Yehuda, 1996)—the inability to find an emotional balance—is one of the hallmarks of life as a survivor of childhood trauma. Thus, hearing demands not only that professionals understand the feelings behind the details of clients' stories, but also that we guide clients carefully through the beginning stages of naming and recognizing their own feeling states.

Emotional Education. Pacing becomes absolutely critical at the hearing stage. A valuable technique for professionals is to deliberately alternate between intellectual and emotional material. Thus, it is not uncommon to discuss emotion with clients—in an intellectualized manner. This approach is sometimes called "psychoeducation," although in this specific application, it simply means teaching clients about the mechanics of emotion.

Our culture is one that values children's intellectual accomplishments over their emotional development. As a result, many adults in the "normal" population lack the necessary emotional skills to competently handle the challenges of life (Goleman, 1995). But survivors of abuse are triply handicapped: They have had to cut themselves off from their emotional lives early in order to survive. In adulthood, they are regularly overwhelmed by emotions they can't control. And they are trying to live in a world where many people are afraid of overt displays of unbridled feeling.

Finding the Words. Given that clients have spent much of their lives fearing or denying their own emotions, they are unlikely to have the necessary vocabulary to begin to describe how they are feeling. An important first step in this education process, and a reasonably nonthreatening one, is to teach clients emotion words. The quintessential question "How did that make you feel?" often leaves abuse survivors staring blankly, quite literally at a loss for words. Some clients will struggle with answers that involve vague descriptors such as *bad, upset, funny,* or *weird.* Others, having spent years in the mental health system, use psychiatric terms such as *depressed, paranoid, suicidal,* or *manic.* Clients have chosen these sorts of words with wisdom, because such words serve to maintain the distance between them and their emotional lives. Teaching new words means acknowledging the role that distancing plays in clients' lives. Also, the suggestion that it is important for clients to learn to speak more directly about emotion should be backed up with reasons: "I need you to describe your emotions to me more clearly so that I can get to know both the thinking and the feeling person—and so that you can get to know yourself." Some clients are able to grope for feeling words, and with the help of the professional, who names hard-to-describe emotions, they can begin to acquire a vocabulary. However, clients often resist our invitations to speak more directly, no matter how gently such requests are phrased. Sometimes, a "cheat sheet" is called for, where all sorts of feelings are listed on a piece of paper for clients to use as a prompt when searching for the right word. Some are so frightened of their own feelings that they simply point to the emotion word while acknowledging (or being helped to acknowledge) that saying the word out loud is a step best left for another day.

The following is an example of a cheat sheet:

ANGRY	DIRTY	LONELY	TRICKED
ENRAGED	FRUSTRATED	OUT OF CONTROL	DEFILED
UNHAPPY	PROUD	ASHAMED	HURT
AFRAID	GUILTY	TRUSTING	OBSESSED
SUSPICIOUS	PITY	HAPPY	STRONG
IN CONTROL	SEXUAL	LOVE	PUT DOWN
FILTHY	BETRAYED	VINDICTIVE	THREATENED

FORCED	MUTE	FOOLED	RESPONSIBLE
OBLIGATED	GRIEVING	TERRIFIED	JOYOUS
ENRAGED	EFFECTIVE	BROKENHEARTED	BAD
COURAGEOUS	STUPID	IGNORED	HUMILIATED
JEALOUS	CRAZY	OUTRAGED	KIND
MAD	SAD	LOVABLE	FRUSTRATED
POWERFUL	DEVASTATED	LOVED	SORRY

Obviously, some of these words don't really describe emotion per se, but they are nonetheless rich descriptors of feeling states. They also represent a range of feelings, from good to bad, and although survivors rarely admit to feeling joyous or courageous, it doesn't hurt to introduce good emotions along with the all-too-familiar bad ones. In addition, there is no order to the list. Clients can use the search for the right word to gain a little time and a little courage, so that when the right word is discovered, they may be more able to say it out loud. Some clients may want to customize their own list, adding new words and crossing out those that they declare they never feel. This tactic allows them a measure of control over the process. Others may belittle the whole thing, calling it silly or infantile, thereby offering another indirect message that the pacing of the storytelling process is too swift and that there is a need to return to a safer topic.

Clients must also learn about how emotion works. This is a complex subject area, but from a clinical perspective, professionals are responsible for having a solid understanding of the nature of emotional reaction under both normal and terrorizing conditions. We also need to know the difference between how children and adults experience emotion.

Clients are generally capable of understanding these sorts of ideas, although each one's abilities and interests will determine the depth and complexity of the material offered. A valuable professional role is the translation of complex research and clinical language into everyday words and the connection of these academic concepts to the individual client's experience. For example, professionals may use the term *alexithymia* among themselves, but they will talk with clients about "searching for words to describe how you feel." *Affect dysregulation* becomes "I notice that you have a difficult time finding middle ground when it comes to your feelings." This translation service is invaluable, because it serves to support the growth of emotional and relational safety (professionals are not seen as distant, cold experts with their own impenetrable language).

It also encourages clients to take control of their own healing and recovery process (they become knowledgeable and informed) and reduces the fear of the unknown (emotions become a little less frightening when they are seen to be subject to some predictable rules).

Professionals can also teach clients about how extreme emotion affects their body and which psychiatric medications may be helpful in alleviating some of their distress. Professionals who are not medically trained will not be able to provide this service directly, but they are nonetheless responsible for referring clients to appropriate psychiatric resources, with the caveat that medication is to be used judiciously and with wisdom, not as yet another tool for numbing and spacing out. Extreme caution is advised when prescribing for clients who struggle with suicidal ideation or who have made past attempts.

In addition to traditional psychiatric services, we can also inform clients of a whole range of services and techniques that are typically outside the formal mental health system such as massage, meditation, naturopathy, herbal remedies, Native healing circles—to name only a few—each of which (depending on individual clients) may have a role to play in dealing with emotional pain.

Often, however, clients have found out through experimentation how to attempt to modulate their feeling-states through the use of street drugs and alcohol or through the misuse of prescribed medication. Some clients are in an ongoing state of overmedication as they and the mental health professionals who serve them search vainly for the magic "cocktail" that will solve their problems. In these instances, clients need to understand that the storytelling process cannot continue until they have had their medication regimen assessed and dosage levels adjusted.

Clients with substance abuse problems must also learn the role that drugs and alcohol play in their lives. Some professional settings will not accept clients for therapy until they are clean and sober. Other settings allow professionals to continue with clients who are actively abusing as long as they do not turn up at appointments high or drunk. Obviously, the level of abuse is a safety issue, and insofar as clients continue to jeopardize their physical safety because of dangerous substance abuse habits, the storytelling process cannot continue until some measure of control is achieved. However, issues around substance abuse and healing and recovery are complex. We are asking clients to experience more, rather than less, disturbing emotion as their journey unfolds. Newly clean and sober clients are unlikely to withstand the onslaught without relapsing. The key seems to be awareness, education, and informed choice.

This kind of learning is multilevel, scoped to the unique needs of the individual client, and ongoing throughout the entire healing journey. However, it begins with the storytelling process. Its goal, aside from providing information, is to assist professionals to access and bond with the competent adult within the client. Education gives clients more power over their own emotional lives. It also offers them the chance to become informed participants in their own healing and recovery journey and better consumers of psychiatric medications and alternative services. It also allows them the best opportunity possible to make aware choices regarding their own substance use.

Allowing Clients to Experience Emotional Pain

During the storytelling process, clients will begin to feel again, but only in exploratory ways, so that they can test the waters of their own and of our reactions. These moments of feeling are a necessary precursor to the raging and mourning stage of healing and recovery. They serve to acquaint clients with their own emotional lives in a safe, slowly paced manner. However, the emotion felt is likely to be intense and painful. No one is comfortable experiencing (or witnessing) extreme emotion. Professionals must learn the skills to allow clients to feel their emotions without cutting them off or shutting them down.

Anger. The emotion that seems to be the most threatening is anger. Most clients have learned that if they express anger, they will be hurt or abandoned. Angry-all-the-time clients prefer the certainty of isolation and aloneness to the terror of risking closeness in a relationship, whereas angry-none-of-the-time clients avoid abandonment at the expense of acknowledging their own feelings. The safety of the client-professional relationship is a place where clients can begin to experience real anger, first at the many people who have hurt them in the past, and second directly at the professional him- or herself. In fact, seasoned professionals will watch for instances when clients become angry with them, because these are opportunities to explore the most frightening situation of all—getting mad at someone who is in a position of authority and who has come to really matter.

Things happen in even the most respectful client-professional relationship—a canceled appointment, something said in haste, a phone call ended too swiftly—and clients can get angry. Clients also get angry at things that have nothing much to do with how professionals have behaved but that are nonetheless believed to be their fault. For example, we may have the same hair color as the abuser, or we may use a turn of phrase that the client doesn't immediately understand. In these situations, clients are likely to express their anger in a variety of ways. Some will rage at everyone but the professional. Others will insist that they didn't notice the problem—but then fail to turn up for the next appointment. If clients can be helped to say, "I was angry at you because . . ." we must respond with a sincere acknowledgment of the anger, without regard for whether or not the incident was our fault. As the incident is talked through, clients will experience, likely for the first time, a relationship that is not only able to survive anger but to grow and develop as a result.

When dealing with clients' anger, however, there are a few words of caution. First, clients who state that they fear they won't be able to control themselves if they become angry are usually correct, and their fears must be respected. This is not to say that they can't talk about anger or learn about emotional mechanisms related to anger, but they will need time before they can actually enter the experience of anger safely. Open discussions about how clients have expressed anger in the past, what happens when they lose control, and how we can work with them to pace the expression of angry feelings are helpful. Some clients use veiled threats such as, "If you make me talk about [whatever topic they fear], I'm not sure how I'll react toward you." At these times, it is wise to confront immediately the issue of safety in the relationship: "Are you saying that you are afraid you might harm me?" This direct question gets the threat out in the open where it can be dealt with in a straightforward manner. Clients need to understand that threats of violence, veiled or otherwise, compromise the safety of the relationship and that no one functions well under such conditions. Typically, when confronted openly, clients will back away from the threat and can then be helped to turn the conversation to more general fears of losing control. Nonetheless, these clients, as well as ones who continue to maintain their aggressive stance, require a clear message—if their behavior places the professional in danger, the relationship will end—it's as simple as that. This kind of stand, however, relates only to client-professional relationships constructed within the voluntary helping frame (as discussed in Chapter 7). It also will require full organizational support with policies that clearly state what action will be taken if clients threaten or engage in violence.

Sadness. Some clients feel angry most of the time. Others will say that they are always sad. The truth is that anger and grief are intimately related. The intertwining of denied sadness along with repressed anger leaves clients feeling almost totally shut down—a state that is often termed *depression.* During the storytelling process, both anger and sadness are expressed in less intense forms than in the later stages of healing and recovery, but preliminary discussions about mourning and grieving lead to valuable opportunities, first, for experiencing sadness in the presence of someone who understands, and second, for beginning to learn the skills of self-comfort.

As clients reacquaint themselves with their emotional lives, old habits can recur. They may begin to self-harm once more (or to increase the frequency of episodes); to repeat revenge fantasies over and over again (out loud or mentally); to berate themselves in a ritualistic way for perceived shortcomings ("I'm stupid, ugly, too fat, too thin, a loser"); or to talk endlessly about suicide and death—all in service of soothing themselves.[2]

Acknowledgment of the value of clients' attempts to control their levels of emotion is important because, even though they are unhealthy, these attempts kept the child alive when an outburst would have led to life-threatening harm. They also served to reduce anxiety, because clients learned early that when bad things happened to them, even worse things were likely to follow. In adulthood, when they are turned down for housing, when a friend hurts their feelings, or when the social assistance check is late, they don't distract themselves with a treat or a pleasant activity. Instead, they actively seek ways to make themselves feel worse so that they won't have to endure waiting for the next blow to land.

Learning healthy self-soothing skills is an ongoing process (as discussed in Chapter 10). At this point in the storytelling, the professional role is to continue to emphasize the value of a repertoire of healthy self-comfort strategies while acknowledging that clients will likely have moments where they regress to earlier tactics. This latitude, however, must be accompanied by organizational support, especially for self-harm and suicidal ideation. Organizations that understand these behaviors as clients' attempts to self-soothe are less inclined to react in alarm. However, there are certain settings (e.g., group living situations) where messy self-harm attempts and suicide threats are so disruptive that clients who need to continue these behaviors should be housed elsewhere.

Understanding

Unlike listening and hearing, understanding is the compilation of the underlying themes that populate clients' stories—their lessons from life, so to speak. Beginning professionals may quail at the thought that they must boil down the many, many details they have gathered, along with the jumble of vaguely expressed feelings that accompanied them, into a set of coherent themes that clients will agree are the way they see things. However, experienced professionals know that these life themes are relatively stable across the myriad of stories that are told in the healing and recovery context. Professionals may expect variations on the following list, but almost all clients will admit to most of these beliefs:

1. The world is an evil place. I don't bother hoping for anything good to happen to me, because it won't. I don't deserve anything good.
2. I'm a bad person. I hate myself, and if anyone gets to know the real me, they will hate me too.
3. Life isn't fair. Whatever happens, I lose out. I am powerless and helpless.
4. I hate my body. I am ugly, too fat, too thin. Too tall, too short. I'm dirty. I resent having to care for my body.
5. I am afraid most of the time. I'm afraid to be with people and I'm afraid to be alone.
6. People always let me down. If I let anyone get close to me, I will get hurt. I am unlovable. I hate men (if the abuser was a man). I hate women (if the abuser was a woman).
7. I am responsible for all the bad things that happen to me. I am defiled. People should stay away from me because I am jinxed.
8. I am so angry, yet so sad. And I can't do anything about it.
9. If I wait long enough, if I wish hard enough, someone or something will come along and take care of me.
10. If I could just die, I would be at peace.

Clients know better than anyone that they are bad people, guilty, defiled, unlovable, and responsible for their own misery. Throughout their stories, they will repeat these assertions endlessly, and the first impulse is to try and convince them that they are wrong. Although it is important to convey the message that what happened is not their fault, it is pointless to argue about whether or not they are bad people. Clients need to talk about their shame, self-blame, guilt, and humiliation without having these sorts of conversations cut off with well-meaning protestations. Professionals need not back away from the "bad" person but should instead listen to the details, hear the feelings, and understand the resulting worldview that is the consequence of childhood trauma.

FINAL CAUTIONS

Throughout this chapter, there have been cautionary statements intended to warn mental health professionals of some of the common pitfalls when helping survivors of childhood trauma. A few are so central that they merit a final emphasis. First, the authors of these stories are the clients themselves, and they have the absolute right to control the content and the pace of the story. They also have the right to say, "No, I won't answer that question, explore that feeling, or tell that secret." Second, professionals are not detectives or lawyers. Their job is not to verify facts and track down proof. Instead, they are capturing perception, feeling, and meaning, rather than absolute truth. Third, it is unethical behavior for professionals to lead or push. Clients must come to their own conclusions and develop their own understandings. Finally, telling one's story in the presence of an attentive witness is enormously powerful. It is healing, in and of itself. Sometimes, for many valid reasons, survivors can go no further. Ending the healing and recovery process at whatever point a survivor wants is also an absolute right.

CONCLUSION

Trained trauma therapists are scarce, and their general availability to the psychiatric population is minimal. However, all mental health professionals can contribute to clients' healing and recovery journeys through the creation of safety and the hearing of stories. To speak one's truth in the presence of an understanding other is a powerful act. In fact, the central message of this chapter is about the power of words and of witness. Listening, hearing, and understanding clients' stories facilitates the reconnection of the past with the present—a crucial step in the process of human growth and development.

NOTES

1. We are referring here to the whole of a survivor's life story, including abuse—not simply to brief disclosure.

2. It is important to note, however, that *talk* about suicide and serious intention are two different things. Clients must be assessed for dangerousness, and specific threats of suicide are to be taken seriously (see Chapter 12).

REFERENCES

Aron, A. (1992). Testimonio, a bridge between psychotherapy and sociotherapy. *Women and Therapy, 13*(3), 173-188.

Briere, J. (1992). *Child abuse trauma: Theory and treatment of the lasting effects.* Newbury Park, CA: Sage.

Goleman, D. (1995). *Emotional intelligence: Why it can matter more than IQ.* New York: Bantam.

McFarlane, A., & Yehuda, R. (1996). Resilience, vulnerability, and the course of posttraumatic reactions. In B. van der Kolk, A. MacFarlane, & L. Weisaeth (Eds.), *Traumatic stress: The effects of overwhelming experience on mind, body and society* (pp. 155-181). New York: Guilford.

van der Kolk, B., McFarlane, A., & van der Hart, O. (1996). A general approach to treatment of posttraumatic stress disorder. In B. van der Kolk, A. McFarlane, & L. Weisaeth (Eds.), *Traumatic stress: The effects of overwhelming experience on mind, body and society* (pp. 417-440). New York: Guilford.

CHAPTER **12**

Crisis Care

Lee Ann Hoff

Personal crisis occurs in social, cultural, and individual historical context. Crisis is intrinsic to life. Broadly speaking, it is as normal and varied as human experience itself. A stressful or traumatic event and the emotional crisis that may follow present both danger and opportunity. Among those injured by physical and sexual abuse during childhood, the danger-opportunity scale often appears tipped in the direction of threats to life, particularly if timely intervention was unavailable or inadequate when the abuse was occurring. Traumatized persons who lack support and an opportunity to heal are more vulnerable than others to repeated crisis episodes across the life span.

This chapter presents the basics for understanding, assessment, intervention, and follow-up care around the crisis situations of those with histories of childhood trauma or who have unresolved issues that can be traced to abuse. Some among this group are in treatment with trauma

AUTHOR'S NOTE: With permission, parts of this chapter are excerpted and adapted from Hoff (1995), Chapters 1-4 and 6-9.

specialists; many, however, have no access to treatment, relying instead on primary- and continuing-care mental health professionals and peer support groups. The chapter assumes that crisis intervention is a necessary but not sufficient ingredient of comprehensive planning and service for this vulnerable population. When skillfully applied, crisis prevention and intervention ranks high among strategies that can enhance opportunities for growth and development despite the pain and damage resulting from abuse during childhood—pain that may linger for years or decades.

RECOGNIZING AND PREVENTING CRISIS STATES

In everyday language, *crisis* is often used to cover a sweeping array of events and conditions. When working with distressed and sometimes desperately ill people, it is important to distinguish between conditions that have some common features but that are essentially different and therefore require distinct responses, for example, stress, emergency, crisis, and emotional or mental breakdown. Stress, predicaments, and upsetting events are endemic to life, but they are not the same as emotional crisis. Emergency situations, often with life-or-death implications, can precipitate an emotional crisis, but these in themselves are not defined as crises. Finally, crisis is distinct from emotional or mental illness, though it tends to occur more often among those already disturbed. *Crisis* is an acute emotional upset arising from situational, developmental, or sociocultural sources and resulting in a temporary inability to cope by means of one's usual problem-solving devices. A full-blown crisis does not occur instantaneously. It is preceded by precrisis phases that are ripe with opportunity for prevention, early intervention, and structured follow-up care. The following sections elaborate on this definition and its ramifications for professionals working with persons suffering and recovering from the trauma of abuse during childhood.

Stress, Crisis, and Illness Interface

Acute stress and unanticipated traumatic events faced without sufficient support hold serious potential for evolving toward a state of full-blown crisis. Although particular crisis episodes are short-lived, they may occur more frequently among those with histories of abuse. Such crisis vulnerability is compounded when professionals lack the understanding and skills necessary for appropriate response. Without such understanding, people with complex histories of trauma who seem to be perpetually in crisis can be discounted as uncooperative, as unmotivated for treatment, or simply as troublemakers in busy service settings. The term *chronic crisis* (referring to such clients) is a contradiction. When the label is examined in context, it often reveals a person with serious emotional or mental problems who lacks the support needed for healing.

Any crisis situation that originates in circumstances beyond the control of the individual holds greater potential for negative outcomes such as substance abuse, violence toward self or others, and psychopathologies. This is because emotional healing from traumatic events requires that people be able to answer the question "Why me?" as they endure these damaging situations. For persons with histories of abuse, the answer to this question is deeply intertwined with the legacy of victim blaming and, frequently, with threats of further injury if the abuse is revealed. For child victims, of course, the burdens of injury; secrecy; and, often, solitary attempts to heal are compounded if the assailant is a parent or other authority figure on whom the child is dependent emotionally, physically, and economically. The result is suppression of anger and emotional pain; this pain is then manifested in physical and psychological symptoms, including increased vulnerability to crisis.

Case Example

Elise was sexually abused by her father from ages 9 through 12. When Elise revealed the abuse to her mother, Corrine, the stormy marriage ended. Custody of Elise and her two siblings, ages 10 and 7, was granted to Corrine. At puberty Elise became sexually active and presented discipline problems at school and at home. After conferring with Corrine, Elise was referred to a child counseling and treatment center. Improvement in Elise's mood and behavior was noted, and termination occurred after 20 sessions, including several that included her mother. Two years later, at age 14, when limits were set on the hours Elise could see her boyfriend, she took an overdose of aspirin and was admitted to a psychiatric inpatient service after emergency treatment. Her 3-week hospital course was difficult, including frequent negative encounters with staff and other patients. Elise's diagnoses included borderline personality disorder.

During hospital visiting hours, Elise met a 22-year-old man with whom she agreed to sexual involvement (technically, statutory rape). This man also introduced her to the drug culture. As the years progressed, Elise gave birth to three children from two different fathers, was severely abused by one of her partners, periodically overdosed on illegal drugs, and also began abusing alcohol. After a 6-week stay in a battered women's shelter, Elise obtained transitional housing assistance and struggled to maintain scheduled appointments for support groups and counseling for substance abuse and job training sessions.

Elise's situation dramatizes the importance of early intervention with abuse survivors. Although many factors contribute to the serious problems Elise still faces, sexual abuse during childhood is pivotal in subsequent adult vulnerability to repeated crisis episodes. Early writings in the crisis field suggested that history has no place in crisis assessment and intervention. We now know that one of the challenges of successful crisis work with people like Elise demands (a) being sensitive to history while keeping it on the back burner; (b) focusing on here-and-now crisis episodes while recognizing their complex origins; and (c) attending to the boundaries of crisis intervention and its interface with other facets of care and treatment. Figure 12.1, the Downward Spiral, illustrates the centrality of prevention as well as the importance of intervening early.

Self-Confidence, Boundary, and Labeling Issues

When confronted with the horrors of childhood sexual abuse and the survivor's shattered trust, lack of self-awareness or inadequate training can leave some persons too ready to act on the human inclination to rescue the survivor from further suffering. On the other hand, because the behavioral aftermath of childhood abuse can be so exasperating and often difficult to treat, some mental health professionals too readily apply psychiatric diagnoses that do not serve well those patients with histories of abuse. Most notable among these is borderline personality disorder (BPD). Self-awareness and knowledge about the connection between a history of childhood trauma and adult behaviors (often disturbed and disruptive) should prompt caution among all providers about the nega-

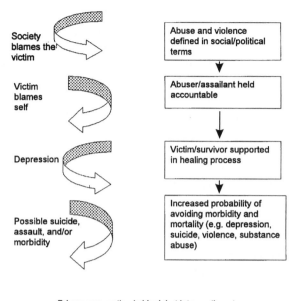

Society blames the victim

Victim blames self

Depression

Possible suicide, assault, and/or morbidity

Abuse and violence defined in social/political terms

Abuser/assailant held accountable

Victim/survivor supported in healing process

Increased probability of avoiding morbidity and mortality (e.g. depression, suicide, violence, substance abuse)

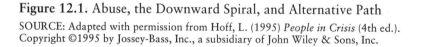

Primary prevention is ideal, but intervention at
Secondary and *Tertiary* levels can also
prevent morbidity and save lives.

Figure 12.1. Abuse, the Downward Spiral, and Alternative Path

SOURCE: Adapted with permission from Hoff, L. (1995) *People in Crisis* (4th ed.).
Copyright ©1995 by Jossey-Bass, Inc., a subsidiary of John Wiley & Sons, Inc.

tive potential of some psychiatric labels. Staff attitudes of hopelessness about a client's capacity for healing and growth are easily read by people whose lives include many shattered dreams. When application of diagnoses is necessary for insurance reimbursement and other purposes, a diagnosis of posttraumatic stress disorder (PTSD) is less damaging than one of BPD when the client's history includes abuse.

Human service providers whose work includes crisis prevention and intervention will find their work made easier by careful attention to the pitfalls of the victim/rescuer/persecutor triangle. Providers are particularly vulnerable to falling into the trap of this interactional maze with clients whose histories include abuse and a diagnosis of BPD. Briefly, the triangle works as follows: Those survivors whose memories of abuse are still like raw unhealed wounds may behave like the classical drowning victim, with cries and behaviors suggesting insatiable needs and demands for rescue (a suicide attempt aptly illustrates this point). Although survivors require support, these unhealed persons do not lose their basic human need for self-mastery and self-determination. It is also critical to remember that violence and abuse, however else defined, are supreme acts of disempowering another human being, stripping the person of self-mastery and control. Therefore, crisis intervention that includes any misuse of power is almost always counterproductive, in that it adds to the injurious experience of feeling disempowered, preventing growth beyond victimhood. Inappropriate power tactics include "rescue" instead of "teaching," doing things *to* rather than *with* the person, and making decisions during an acute crisis episode before ascertaining whether clients are incapable of deciding for themselves. In contrast, an empowering approach during crisis includes recognizing and acknowledging the source of current "cries for help," being there for the person, and searching collaboratively for more effective ways to heal and move beyond seemingly endless crisis episodes.

CRISIS ASSESSMENT: BASIC PRINCIPLES AND TECHNIQUES

Understanding the complex interplay of crisis and a history of childhood abuse is the foundation for this next phase of crisis work: recognizing the distinctive features of crisis assessment, uncovering the components of a crisis (or impending crisis), and distinguishing these from other problems needing attention. Principles include the following:

1. Unlike traditional psychiatric diagnosis, the crisis assessment process is intricately tied to crisis resolution—whether that process lasts 15 min, 1 hr, or 3 hr. This is because an early assessment question such as "What happened?" and an empathic response to the answer in itself send a message of support and hope to the distressed person.

2. Crisis assessment focuses on the immediate, identifiable problem, not on unconscious personality dynamics.

3. It is inappropriate to probe into psychodynamic issues such as unresolved childhood conflicts and repressed emotions. Rather, one must

obtain a person's history of problem solving and success or failure in constructively resolving past crises or dealing with stressful life events by asking, for example, "What have you done in the past that has worked for you when you're upset?" This line of inquiry allows both for an awareness of abuse and its negative impact on successful problem solving and for sensitivity to timely moments for incorporating abuse issues into assessment protocols.

4. Crisis assessment includes collaboration with the distressed person's significant others and his or her primary therapist or case manager, with permission.

5. Evaluating risk to life is integral to crisis assessment.

Distinguishing Levels of Assessment

For any person in an impending or full-blown crisis, two levels of assessment should be completed. The following questions are essential:

Level I: Is there an obvious or potential threat to life? In other words, what are the risks of suicide, assault, or homicide?

Level II: Is there evidence that the person is unable to function in his or her usual life role? Is the person in danger of being extruded from his or her natural social setting? What are the psychological, socioeconomic, or other factors related to the person's coping with life's stressors?

This chapter focuses particularly on Level I assessment because everyone should be able to conduct this type of assessment. This includes people in their natural roles of friend, neighbor, parent, and spouse, as well as various health and human service professionals: physicians, teachers, nurses, counselors and support staff in transitional facilities, home health workers, police, clergy, welfare workers, and prison officials. Level I assessment is critical in terms of life-and-death dimensions, and it forms the basis for mobilizing emergency and comprehensive mental health services on behalf of the person in crisis. Regardless of setting or the person's history, all providers must recognize that no crisis assessment is complete without inquiring directly about victimization and the danger of suicide and of assault or homicide.

When laypersons, professionals, or paraprofessionals are without special crisis training but suspect that someone is a probable risk for abuse, suicide, assault, or homicide, they should always consult an experienced professional crisis worker. Some life-threatening situations should be approached collaboratively with the police or forensic psychiatry specialists.

Briefly, Level II assessment involves consideration of personal and social characteristics of the client by a trained crisis counselor or mental health professional. Level II assessment is comprehensive and corresponds to the elements of the total crisis experience, including

1. Identification of the origins of the crisis.
2. Development of the crisis: Is the client in the initial or acute phase?
3. Individual manifestations of the crisis: How does the client interpret the hazardous events, and what are the corresponding emotional, cognitive, behavioral, and biophysical responses to them?
4. Available resources: What personal, family, interpersonal, and material resources are relevant in this crisis?

Nonspecialists in crisis work should be sufficiently familiar with Level II assessment to be able to (a) focus on effective crisis prevention and intervention in life-threatening situations, (b) set boundaries around the complex issues needing attention once the acute crisis phase is managed, and (c) make necessary linkages to a primary therapist or a specialist for abuse and violence.

Recognizing Phases of Crisis Development: Case Example Continued

The precipitating factor in Elise's crisis was another woman's remark during a group meeting in her transitional housing. The woman stated that she was frightened of Elise. The group leader, Joan, felt insecure and unable to handle the implied threat of violence and had no crisis expert to consult. She terminated the meeting and told Elise that she would probably be expelled from the house. Elise responded by violating house rules, staying out all night, leaving her children with other residents, and getting high on drugs again. As a result, Elise was indeed expelled from the house and was temporarily homeless with her three children. She is now age 28, still trying to come to terms with her tumultuous history.

A full-blown crisis develops in phases, thus offering opportunities for prevention whenever possible (Caplan, 1964; Golan, 1969). Key questions to be asked at each phase address the essentials of Level I assessment and risk to life. A full-blown crisis includes the following components: a hazardous event or situation, a precipitating factor, and acute vulnerability in response to these events. Answers and behavioral responses to questions identifying these components provide the data for immediate intervention, ongoing support, or referral for comprehensive follow-up treatment as needed and available.

Phase 1: A hazardous event or situation results in an initial rise in anxiety level. It sets in motion a series of reactions that may or may not culminate in emotional crisis, depending on psychological and social resources. The helping person should ask directly, "What happened?" (if not already apparent).

Sometimes people are so upset or overwhelmed that they cannot clearly identify the sequence of events. In these instances, it is helpful to ask simple, direct questions about the time and circumstances of the upsetting or dangerous event; for example, in discussing the sequence of events with Elise, one might ask: "What was being discussed during the [transition] house meeting when you started feeling anxious? . . . And then what happened?" Putting events in order has a calming effect. The person experiences a certain sense of self-possession in being able to make some order out of confusion. This is particularly true for the client who is afraid of "losing control" or "going crazy."

In work with those who were abused during childhood, it is crucial to keep in mind two facts: (a) regardless of upsetting events here and now, the *original* trauma of abuse is often the precursor to repeated crisis episodes; and (b) this history and its aftermath affect vulnerability, and therefore coping ability, in response to most, if not all, subsequent upsetting events.

The experience of stressful, hazardous events is not in itself a crisis. The question is: How is *this* particular event unusual in terms of its timing, severity, danger, or the person's ability to handle it successfully? This component of crisis corresponds to Caplan's (1964) "first phase" of crisis development, which may or may not become a full-blown crisis, depending on personal and social circumstances. People who seek and are able to use help at the beginning stage of crisis development may avoid an acute crisis. Those lacking such help usually move to the next phase.

Phase 2: Usual problem-solving ability fails. Persons with histories of abuse often find that attempts to communicate their distress are unsuccessful. Their psychiatric diagnosis, combined with cultural or other factors, can result in low expectations of success in handling stressful events, which, all too often, promotes rapid movement toward full-blown crisis. Elise, for example, erupts with anger at a fellow resident, apparently unable to convey her distress in a constructive manner.

Phase 3: Anxiety level rises even further. Because hazardous events and unsuccessful problem solving alone are insufficient to constitute a crisis state, we need to focus our assessment process further on the immediacy of the person's stress, the precipitating factor. This is the proverbial "straw that broke the camel's back." It is the final stressful event or situation in a series of such events that pushes the person from a state of acute vulnerability into crisis.

Although the precipitating factor is often a minor incident, it can take on crisis proportions in the context of other stressful events or a history of childhood trauma, as Elise's situation illustrates. In a population prone to repeated crises, the precipitating factor in one crisis episode may be the hazardous event in the next. Determining the mutual presence of these two components is useful for distinguishing between chronic stress and an acute crisis state by asking, for example, "What brought you here *today*? [since these problems have been with you for some time now]."

Phase 4: State of Active, Full-Blown Crisis. Social support and internal strength fail; anxiety rises to an unbearable state; and the danger of suicide, assault, or other negative coping activities becomes imminent. Whenever possible, all preventive measures should be taken to intervene before this phase occurs.

Assessing for Individual Crisis Manifestations

Having identified the hazardous situations and the precipitating factor, next we must ascertain the person's subjective reaction to stressful events. This aspect of the assessment reveals the degree of clients' vulnerability to hazardous events, as manifested in their emotional, biophysical, cognitive, and behavioral responses to whatever has happened. For example, crisis professionals might ask Elise, "How do you feel about what Joan said to you at the house meeting?" (emotion); "Can you think of another way to deal with Joan besides cutting yourself again?" (cognitive/behavioral); "Yesterday we talked about a plan for the next time Joan upsets you. . . . What happened that this didn't work for you today?" (cognitive/behavioral).

Information obtained from this line of questioning provides baseline data for recognizing crisis "plumage" or distress signals, such as difficulty in managing feelings; suicidal, assaultive, or homicidal tendencies; danger of alcohol or other drug abuse; trouble with the law; or an inability to effectively use available help. These signals usually indicate ineffective crisis coping and the need for preventive intervention to forestall negative crisis outcomes. For example, in assessing the vulnerability of an assault victim, careful attention must be paid to the circumstances of victimization, not to the character of the victim. To link the assault with attributes of the victim places us very close to victim blaming, which hampers the person's recovery and may contribute to the downward spiral depicted in Figure 12.1.

Level II assessment involves a further understanding of the emotional, biophysical, cognitive, and behavioral responses to hazardous events. These characteristics of crisis plumage—how people in crisis feel, think, and behave—are reviewed below as context for Level I activities and linkage to comprehensive care.

Emotional and Biophysical Responses

People in crisis experience a high degree of anxiety and tension, as well as a sense of loss or emptiness stemming from an actual or threatened loss of self-esteem, material goods, or social relationships or from a failure to meet a particular life challenge. Other feelings frequently experienced are shock, anger, guilt, embarrassment, or shame. Fear is often expressed in terms of losing control or of not understanding why one is responding in a certain way. Anger is directed inward, for not being able to manage one's life, or outward at a significant other for leaving or dying—or in ways that can lead to assault or homicide.

Of all feelings common to the crisis experience, anxiety is probably the most familiar. Anxiety is manifested in a number of ways: a sense of dread; a fear of losing control; inability to focus on one thing; and physical symptoms such as sweating, frequent urination, diarrhea, nausea and vomiting, tachycardia (rapid heartbeat), headache, chest or abdominal pain, rash, menstrual irregularity, and sexual uninterest.

Thoughts, Perceptions, and Interpretations

In crisis, one's attention is focused on the acute shock and anguish being experienced and on the crisis event itself. As a consequence, the person's usual memory and way of perceiving may be altered. The relationship between events may not seem clear, and people in crisis feel caught in a maze of events that they cannot fit together. They often have trouble defining who they are and what skills they have. The state of anguish and resulting confusion can also alter their ability to make decisions and solve problems—the very skills needed during a crisis. This disturbance in perceptual processes and problem-solving ability increases the already heightened state of anxiety, and people in crisis sometimes fear that they are losing control.

This distorted perceptual process should not be confused with mental illness, in which a person's usual pattern of thinking is disturbed or distorted. In a crisis state, the disturbance arises from and is part of the crisis experience, and there is a rapid return to normal perception once the crisis is resolved. For example, Elise interpreted her coresident's remark as part of a plot to have her punished. If the group leader had not panicked and threatened expulsion, Elise's crisis might have been prevented.

Behavior

If people feel anxious and have distorted perceptions of events, they are likely to behave in unusual ways. Survivors of childhood trauma who are from other cultures may face double jeopardy: They are blamed or considered "crazy" for having been victimized, and others may view their cultural norms as "crazy." In order to determine whether behavior is normal or deviant, we need to start with that person's definition of what is usual, not our own. This is particularly important if the human service worker and the client in distress are from different cultural, class, or ethnic groups. If clients are too upset to provide this kind of information, it should be elicited from their family or friends. Failing that, it is desirable to obtain a consultation from the relevant ethnic or cultural group.

Another significant behavioral sign of crisis is the individual's inability to perform normal vocational functions, for example, household chores, study goals, or a paid job. A further sign is a change in social behavior. People may withdraw from usual social contacts, make unusual efforts to avoid being alone, or become "clingy" or "demanding." As social connections break down, clients feel increasingly detached or distant from others. Some people in crisis act on impulse: They may drive a car recklessly, make a suicide attempt, or attack others as a desperate means of solving their problems. And if they have been diagnosed with a mental disorder, and if underlying issues around abuse have not been addressed, they may "act out" in ways that exasperate staff but that are nevertheless understandable in the context of an abuse history.

Sometimes, apparent rejection of assistance or failure to cooperate may arise from a sense of helplessness and embarrassment at not being able to cope in the usual manner. People may also fear that acceptance of help may be misinterpreted as weakness. To allay such fears, it is paramount that we examine the attitudes and biases we, as providers, may bring to the assessment milieu.

In summary, when assessing vulnerability, it is important to find out how this person is reacting here and now. Careful assessment also guides us in deciding when not to intervene—in areas where coping is adequate, or when the person chooses to do without our services. Although acutely upset, people can be helped to realize that they are coping adequately in some aspects of life (e.g., at work but not at home, or vice versa). Finally, simple, direct communication not only elicits data for preventing injury to self and others and for linking the person to comprehensive care, but also conveys empathy and our ability to grasp the depth of another's despair and share the feelings that the crisis has evoked.

SUICIDE, ASSAULT, AND HOMICIDE RISK ASSESSMENT

To be understood is basic to the feeling that someone cares and that life is worth living. Although volumes have been written about suicide, the focus here is on the meaning of self-destructive behavior in crisis situations and the importance of understanding and reaching out to those in pain. Essentially, self-destructive behavior signals that a person is in acute emotional turmoil. Effectiveness in working with suicidal people requires (a) assuming the centrality of communication for eliciting the meaning of self-destructive behavior and for ascertaining where clients are on the ambivalence scale when weighing life and death (understanding), (b) uncovering signs of immediate and long-range risk to life (assessment), and (c) providing support and a link to a caring person and the community (crisis intervention).

Distinguishing Self-Destructive Behaviors

There are four broad groups of self-destructive people:

1. Those who complete suicide—a fatal act that is self-inflicted, consciously intended, and carried out with the knowledge that death is irreversible.[1]

2. Those who threaten or talk about suicide—and whose plans for suicide may be either vague or highly specific.

3. Those who make suicide attempts—any nonfatal act of self-inflicted damage with self-destructive intention, however vague or ambiguous. Sometimes the individual's intention must be inferred from behavior. Technically, the term *suicide attempt* should be reserved for those actions in which one attempts to carry out one's intention to die but in which, for reasons unanticipated (such as lack of knowledge of lethality of the means or unplanned rescue), one fails in that attempt.

4. Those who are chronically self-destructive (self-injurious). This topic is discussed in full in Chapter 4, but we must note that it is critical to ascertain the person's intent in relation to each act of self-injury.

The Messages of Self-Destructive People

Viewed on a continuum, or as a "highway leading to suicide," self-destructive behavior often reveals a process including, for example, alienation, family conflict, abuse, depression, self-doubt, and cynicism about life. Those who relieve their pain by repeated self-injury may be gambling with death. As they move along the suicide highway repeating their cries for help, they are often labeled and written off as manipulative or attention seeking. This usually means that professionals and others regard them as devious and insincere in their "demands" for attention. Some conclude that, if these sorts of clients were serious about suicide, they would try something that "really did the job." Such a judgment implies a gross misunderstanding of the meaning of clients' behavior and ignores their real needs.

Individuals who are thus labeled and ignored will probably continue to injure themselves. These episodes typically become progressively more serious in the medical sense, signaling increasing desperation for someone to hear and understand. Clients may also engage in the "no-lose game" as they plan the next suicide attempt (Baechler, 1979). The "no-lose game" goes something like this: "If they find me, they care enough, and therefore life is worth living" (I win by living); "If they don't find me, life isn't worth living" (I win by dying). The suicide method chosen is usually fatal, but with the possibility of rescue, such as swallowing pills. No-lose reasoning is ineffective in instances when one could not reasonably expect rescue (e.g., a family member rarely checks a person at 2:00 a.m.). It is nevertheless an indication of the person's extreme distress and illustrates the logic of the no-lose game.

Among those with histories of abuse, the first suicide attempt is often the most powerful in a series of behavioral messages given over a period of time. We should all be familiar with suicidal clues such as, "You won't be seeing me around much anymore" and "I'm angry at my mother. . . . She'll really be sorry when I'm dead." Studies reveal that a majority of persons who commit suicide have made previous attempts (Brown & Sheran, 1972). In the absence of attempts, 80% have given other significant clues of their suicidal intent. Overall, behavioral, verbal, and affective clues can be interpreted in two general ways: (a) "I want to die," or (b) "I don't want to die, but I want something to change in order to go on living."

It is up to the helping person to determine the meaning of suicidal behavior and to identify clues from words and attitudes. We are not to infer the person's meaning, but rather, to ask directly. For example, we might ask, "What do you mean when you say you can't take your problems anymore? Are you thinking of suicide?" or "What did you hope would happen when you took the pills (or cut your wrists)? Did you intend to die?"

There is no substitute for simple direct communication by a person who cares. Besides providing needed assessment information, it tells the person that we are interested and concerned about their motives. Often self-destructive people have lacked the advantages of direct communication all their lives. They are relieved when someone is sensitive enough to surmise and respond to their despair and thus to help protect them from themselves. As self-destructive people weigh the odds between life and death, we must remember that suicide is not inevitable. People can change their minds if they can find realistic alternatives to dying.

Applying Suicide Risk Assessment Criteria

It is important to recognize the signs that distinguish (a) those who are in immediate high risk of killing themselves, (b) those who are chronically self-destructive—not in immediate but rather long-range risk, and (c) the general population. For example, of those who commit suicide, about 66% have signs of clinical depression. A vast majority of those in the general population who injure themselves repeatedly by low-lethal means are depressed. Depression is one of the most common mental and emotional phenomena, ranging from postpartum "blues" to normal grief responses to bipolar affective disorder (Brown & Harris, 1978). Therefore, when assessing immediate suicide risk, depression is a significant factor in providing an opening for further direct questioning about the following signs, which, in combination, signal high risk:

1. Client has a specific high-lethal plan with available means. No matter how depressed the client, without a plan with lethal means, no suicide will occur. The oft-cited point that very depressed people are at low risk because they lack the energy to act can result in misguided complacency, because regardless of energy level, a specific plan and available lethal means signal high risk. It is also necessary to frequently reassess for suicide risk. Sample assessment questions include these: "You seem very down.... Are you so depressed that you've thought of hurting yourself? What have you thought about doing? Do you have a gun (or

pills)? What kind of pills do you have? How would you get the pills (or gun)?"

2. Client has a history of suicide attempts. About two thirds of those who kill themselves have a history of suicide attempts. On the other hand, for every 10 persons making suicide attempts, a majority has found an alternative to suicide; that is, something has changed to move them toward the desire-to-live end of the ambivalence scale. If the history shows a pattern of increasingly lethal attempts or of only accidental rescue, the immediate risk increases. Sample questions include these: "Have you ever hurt yourself before? What did you do? What happened after your last suicide attempt? Did you plan any possibility of rescue?"

3. Client has problems with resources and with communication with others. Those with a specific suicide plan and a history of attempts who also lack psychological resources (self-esteem and the ability to reach out for help) and social support (feeling bonded with and cared for by significant others) are at immediate and long-range risk of suicide, regardless of all other factors. Sample questions include these: "Is there anyone you feel sincerely cares about you? So you have a very close friend, but don't feel free to call her when you're feeling really down? Have you ever called a suicide prevention hotline when you've been tempted to hurt yourself?"

Assessing for Assault and Homicide Risk

The issue of victimization during childhood as a predictor of assaultive behavior as adults is highly controversial (Egeland, 1993; Kaufman & Zibler, 1993). Gender differences in socialization and learned behavior account in part for higher rates of aggression and violence by men, including those who were abused as children. Learned behavior and cultural messages of violence and physical force as acceptable conflict and crisis resolution tactics have also resulted in increasing rates of violence by girls and women—often in response to their own victimization. All human service workers must therefore be familiar with the following criteria and communication tactics for assessing assault potential as an integral facet of crisis assessment:

1. Current homicidal threats and plan: "Are you so upset or angry that you've considered hurting your abuser or anyone else?"

2. History of homicidal threats and assault: "Have you ever threatened to hurt or kill people when you feel angry? Have you ever been violent with anyone?"

3. Possession of lethal weapons: "When you feel like you're losing control, what do you think about doing? Do you have a knife or a gun? Where would you get a gun? Have you ever used a gun?"

4. Use or abuse of alcohol or other drugs: "So you started drinking in order to get up the courage to strike back? You mean you lose control when you start drinking (or shooting up) with him?"

5. Conflict in significant social relationships, such as infidelity or threat of divorce or labor/management disputes: "How do you usually settle arguments when you're upset or hurt by someone?"

6. Threats of suicide following homicide. "Have you thought about what would happen to you if you killed him?" Answer: "Yes, they'd want to put me in prison, but I'd kill myself first." For example, Elise's mother Corrine was so furious with her husband after learning about the incest that she fantasized about killing him. With the help of a crisis counselor, she finally decided that spending the rest of her life in jail was not worth it.

PLANNING AND IMPLEMENTING CRISIS CARE

Answers to assessment questions provide the essential data for an intervention plan. A plan involves (a) a thinking process; (b) an ability to draw relationships between events and the way the person is feeling, thinking, and behaving; and (c) an ability to respond empathetically, implement safety measures, offer continued support, and establish linkages and referral for comprehensive care. Because the plan may suggest hospitalization for safety, psychiatric treatment, or both, all providers must have current information on referral sources and admission criteria, which may vary across locales.

Empowerment and Contracting in Crisis Intervention

Effective crisis work assumes the importance of self-mastery and empowerment, but with those who have been disempowered by abuse, it takes center stage. Crisis prevention and intervention occur within the context of the comprehensive service plan that the provider and the client arrive at mutually. This plan should be formalized in a service contract that (a) is problem oriented and appropriate to the person's functional level, dependency needs, culture, and lifestyle; (b) spells out realistic treatment goals, target dates, and the expectations of the client and provider; and (c) includes significant others identified by the survivor as supportive. Implicit in the contract are these principles: (a) the person is essentially in charge of his or her own life and able to make decisions in most situations; (b) a complementary relationship between client and provider fosters empowerment, whereas a superior-subordinate one rarely does; and (c) the very idea of a contract means that both the client and provider have rights and responsibilities.

A well-structured service contract helps to achieve order amidst the chaos of crisis. It reassures the client that something definite will happen in a clear time frame to change the present state of discomfort, and that negotiation and care will continue until there is satisfactory crisis resolution. For the person who fears he or she is "going crazy," who is threatened with or is threatening violence, or who finds it difficult to depend on others, it is reassuring to anticipate that within a certain period of time events will probably be under control again.

Specific Crisis Care Strategies

Having assessed the person's coping ability in each of the functional areas (feeling, thinking, and behaving), the provider assists the person to avoid unhealthy or destructive outcomes and to move toward growth and development while resolving the crisis. Depending on the overall service plan and level of training, all providers can implement the following strategies:

1. Respond to loss or threat of loss, a common theme observed in most crisis situations.

2. Listen actively and with concern.

3. Encourage the open expression of feelings.

4. Help the person gain an understanding of the crisis.

5. Help the individual gradually accept reality. Abused persons *feel* and *are* victimized, but they are also survivors (Hoff, 1990). Although trauma accounts in part for their increased crisis vulnerability, they can be encouraged to persevere with the longer-term treatment that is usually needed for healing and with finding substitute supports for the losses suffered.

6. Help the person explore new ways of coping with problems. Instead of responding to crises as helpless victims, or with self-injury or hurting others, people can learn new responses.

7. Link the person to a social network. For survivors of abuse, peer support groups are especially helpful.

8. Engage the use of chemical restraint with caution, keeping empowerment principles in mind. With chemical tranquilization, clients lose the advantages of their increased energy during a crisis state. The opportunity for psychosocial growth is often lost because of the temporary tranquility of a drugged psyche, and the danger is increased. Although the traditional psychiatric management of behavioral emergencies has some aspects in common with crisis care, it should not be equated with the crisis model if a strictly medical approach is used. The nonmedical provider doing crisis work needs to remember that requesting a consultation from medical personnel may result in a drug prescription, when what is actually needed is the experience of highly skilled crisis or trauma specialists. Ideally, psychiatric stabilization programs, such as in emergency departments with "holding" beds, should also have access to the services of skilled crisis counselors.

9. Reinforce the newly learned coping skills and follow up after resolution of the crisis, as specified in the service plan. When carefully designed, follow-up work can often be the occasion for reaching people who are unable to initiate help for themselves *before* an acute crisis occurs. This is especially true for suicidal and very depressed people, those threatened with violence, and those with severe psychiatric illness.

Crisis Intervention With Suicidal Persons

Three kinds of service should be available for suicidal and self-destructive people: (a) emergency medical treatment, (b) crisis intervention, and (c) follow-up counseling or therapy.

Mobilizing emergency medical services requires a knowledge of local resources in cases of life-threatening self-injury, such as poison control and rescue services. Also, every provider should know that a lethal dose of powerful drugs is ten times the normal dose, and that if combined with alcohol, only half that amount is necessary to cause death.

Crisis intervention techniques for a suicidal person include the following:

1. Relieve isolation. If there is no friend or supportive relative with whom the person can stay temporarily, and if the person is highly suicidal, he or she should probably be hospitalized until the active crisis is over. However, in hospital or residential settings, the suicidal person should *not* be placed in isolation.

2. Remove lethal means. Lethal weapons and pills should be removed by a provider, relative, or friend, keeping in mind the need for active collaboration with the suicidal person. If caring and concern are expressed, the misuse of power is avoided, and clients' sense of self-mastery and control are respected, clients will usually dispose of pills or surrender a weapon voluntarily.

3. Encourage alternate expressions of anger. Actively explore other ways of expressing anger short of the price of suicide. For example, "I can see that you're very angry with him for leaving you. Can you think of a way to express your anger that would not cost you your life?" Or, "Yes, of course he'll probably feel bad if you kill yourself after the divorce. . . . But he most likely would talk with someone about it and go on with his life. Meanwhile, you've had your revenge, but you can't get your life back."

4. Avoid the final decision of suicide during crisis. We should assure clients that seeing suicide as the only option is a temporary state. Also, we should try to persuade them to avoid a decision about suicide until they have considered all other alternatives during a noncrisis state of

mind, just as other serious decisions should be postponed until the crisis is over.

A cautionary note about "no-suicide contracts" is in order here. This is a technique employed by some therapists and crisis workers in which clients promise not to harm themselves between sessions and to contact the therapist if contemplating harm. Such contracts offer no special protection against suicide, nor do they offer legal protection for the therapist or other provider (Clark & Kerkhof, 1993). Any value the contract may have flows from the quality of the therapeutic relationship in which one conveys caring and concern. In no way should a contract serve as a convenient substitute for the time spent in empathic listening or in planning nonlethal alternatives with a suicidal person. Also, if these sorts of contracts are used, they should be situated within the context of the overall service plan as discussed above.

5. Regenerate social ties. We should make every effort to help clients reestablish social bonds. This task can be accomplished through referrals for family crisis counseling sessions or through finding satisfying substitutes for lost relationships, such as peer support groups.

6. Relieve extreme anxiety and sleep loss. To a suicidal person, the world looks bleaker and death seems more desirable at 4:00 a.m. after endless nights of sleeplessness. A good night's sleep can temporarily reduce suicide risk and put the person in a better frame of mind to consider other ways of solving life's problems. It is appropriate to consider medication on an emergency basis (Bongar, Maris, Berman, & Litman, 1992), but *always* in conjunction with daily crisis counseling sessions for those who are highly suicidal. Without effective counseling, the extremely suicidal person may interpret such an approach as an invitation to commit the suicidal act. A tranquilizer will usually take care of both the anxiety and the sleeping problem, since anxiety is the major cause of sleeplessness. If medication is needed, the person should be given a 1- to 3-day supply at most, always with a specific return appointment for crisis counseling. Nonchemical means of inducing sleep should be encouraged. This requires a thorough assessment and attempts to apply various psychosocial strategies of intervention before prescribing drugs. We must never forget that many suicide deaths in North America are by prescribed drugs.

Besides these crisis intervention measures, comprehensive service for suicidal persons always includes counseling or psychotherapy, and frequently group or family therapy should be considered as well—particularly for those who have been abused and who are also psychiatrically disturbed.

Crisis Intervention With Assaultive or Homicidal Persons

The principles of crisis intervention that apply to the violent person are summarized as follows:

1. Keep communication lines open. As long as a person is communicating, violence is usually not occurring.
2. Facilitate communication and problem solving between a disgruntled employee, for example, and the person against whom he or she is threatening violence.
3. Develop with the dangerous person specific plans for the nonviolent expression of anger, such as "time out," jogging, punching a pillow, or calling a hotline.
4. When dealing with armed persons, especially until rapport is established and the person's anxiety subsides, whenever possible communicate only by telephone or from behind closed doors.
5. If dangerous weapons are involved, collaborate with police for their removal; implement emergency procedures for appropriate application of force, such as calling security or police, mobilizing a team effort, and warning fellow workers. Failure to work in teams in these circumstances can be life threatening.
6. Insist on administrative support and emergency backup help.
7. Make hotline numbers and emergency call buttons readily available for all staff.
8. Examine social and institutional sources of violent behavior, for example, failure to assist disturbed persons in seeking professional help as an alternative to violence, rigid structures and rules, or harsh authoritarian attitudes toward psychiatric clients.
9. Warn potential victims of homicide, based on risk assessment and principles of the Tarasoff case (see VandeCreek & Knapp, 1993).
10. Remember that a violent person also threatening suicide is at greater risk of homicide.

CONCLUSION

These crisis care strategies can be mastered by any helping person who chooses to learn them. However, as noted above, in highly charged and potentially violent crisis situations (both individual and group) additional techniques and training are indicated. Health and human service workers, teachers, police, clergy, and others increasingly incorporate crisis work as a part of their training (Hoff & Adamowski, 1998). Whether in offices, institutions, homes, or mobile outreach situations, effective helping techniques save time and effort spent on problems that can develop from ineffectively resolved crises. For survivors of childhood trauma, crisis prevention is much less costly in both human and economic terms than hospitalization or jail.

NOTE

1. Formal death classification criteria include four causes of death: natural, accidental, suicide, and homicide. A death may appear to have been by suicide, but if investigation reveals a plan for rescue that did not materialize and an absence of intent to die, it is classified as "accidental." Although self-destructive behavior is part of the picture, technically, it is not suicide, just as many self-injurious behaviors cannot be classified as suicide. The suicide/accident distinction may be difficult to ascertain in instances of the "no-lose game" discussed later in the chapter.

REFERENCES

Baechler, J. (1979). *Suicide.* New York: Basic Books.
Bongar, B., Maris, R. W., Berman, A. L., & Litman, R. E. (1992). Outpatient standards of care and the suicidal patient. *Suicide & Life-Threatening Behavior, 22,* 453-478.
Brown, G., & Harris, T. (1978). *The social origins of depression.* London: Tavistock Press.
Brown, T. R., & Sheran, T. J. (1972). Suicide prediction: A review. *Suicide & Life-Threatening Behavior, 2,* 67-97.
Caplan, G. (1964). *Principles of preventive psychiatry.* New York: Basic Books.
Clark, D. C., & Kerkhof, A. J. F. M. (1993). No-suicide decisions and suicide contracts in therapy. *Crisis, 14*(3), 98-99.
Egeland, B. (1993). A history of abuse is a major risk factor for abusing the next generation. In R. J. Gelles & D. R. Loseke (Eds.), *Current controversies on family violence* (pp. 197-208). Newbury Park, CA: Sage.
Golan, N. (1969). When is a client in crisis? *Social Casework, 50,* 389-394.

Hoff, L. A. (1990). *Battered women as survivors.* London: Routledge.

Hoff, L. A. (1995). *People in crisis: Understanding and helping* (4th ed.). San Francisco: Jossey-Bass.

Hoff, L. A., & Adamowski, K. (1998). *Creating excellence in crisis care: A guide to effective training and program designs.* San Francisco: Jossey-Bass.

Kaufman, J., & Zibler, E. (1993). The intergenerational transmission of abuse is overstated. In R. J. Gelles & D. R. Loseke (Eds.), *Current controversies on family violence* (pp. 209-221). Newbury Park, CA: Sage.

VandeCreek, L., & Knapp, S. (1993). *Tarasoff and beyond: Legal and clinical considerations in the treatment of life-endangering patients* (Rev. ed.). Sarasota, FL: Professional Resource Press.

CHAPTER **13**

The Invisibility
of Men's Pain

John McManiman

Men commit suicide at significantly higher rates than women. Between the ages of 18 and 29, men suffer alcohol dependency at three times the rate of same-aged women. More than two thirds of all alcoholics are men, and men are twice as likely to be regular users of illicit drugs. Over 80% of America's homeless are men (Kimbrell, 1991). In 1920, a man's life expectancy was, on average, 1 year less than a woman's. Today, men live fully 10% shorter lives than women (Farrell, 1993). With these figures in mind, the obvious question is: Are men really doing all that well?

Much of the information in other parts of this text, including why we miss histories of childhood trauma, the multidimensional model, and the many practice issues discussed, are as relevant to men as they are to women. For this reason, I have chosen as the unique focus of this chapter the issues of gender socialization and stereotyping that male survivors often confront. Specifically, I examine the gender socialization patterns that render men's pain invisible both to themselves and to the rest of the world. Men are assigned the role of aggressor, whereas women occupy the role of victim—and neither stereotype supports human health or well-being. In order to challenge these harmful stereotypes, I will begin with a review of the increased prevalence rates of the sexual victimization of male children. I will also challenge the assumption that adult male survivors automatically complete the cycle of violence by becoming sex offenders or perpetrators of interpersonal violence. Finally, using case examples from my own group practice in a community mental health setting,[1] I will explore the impact of physical and sexual traumatization on adult men. I will pay particular attention to the multiplicity of roles (i.e., abuser, victim, protector) they may take on to try to compensate for the pain they feel. I will also examine the utility of a less rigid male gender identity as one of the keys to healing and recovery.

PREVALENCE RATES

Counseling agencies throughout North America are experiencing an upsurge in the number of men presenting with issues related to childhood sexual abuse (Hunter, 1990; Lew, 1988). It also appears that the gap in prevalence rates between men and women who have been sexually abused as children is narrowing (Watkins & Bentovim, 1992). From 1979 to 1998, the rates of child sexual abuse reported by men in some studies rose from 4% to as high as 28%. In 1979, David Finkelhor surveyed over 900 college students and found that 19% of the women and 4.1% of the men reported child sexual abuse. Fritz, Stoll, and Wagner (1981) confirmed these findings, reporting a 4.8% prevalence rate among male students.

Finkelhor (1984) and Briere, Evans, Runtz, and Wall (1988) found anywhere from 3% to 9% of males reporting that they had been sexually victimized as children, but the rate for women was still considered to be two to three times higher (Lew, 1988). By 1990, however, research findings had begun to shift. Herschel, Briere, Magallanes, and Smiljanich (1990) found that male sexual abuse rates had reached as high as 20% in some nonclinical populations. In 1996, Lisak, Hopper, and Song (1996) studied 595 male college students and found that fully 250 subjects reported sexual and physical abuse before the age of 16. When sexual abuse alone was studied, 28% reported contact and noncontact forms of sexual abuse. (When only contact forms of sexual abuse were considered, the percentage dropped to 18%.) Almost two thirds of the sexually abused subjects (61%) were abused by a male perpetrator, and 28% were abused by a female. Eleven percent were abused by both male and female perpetrators.

As these studies demonstrate, the prevalence of abuse in the general population is high, but abuse among the psychiatric population (both sexes) is even higher. In a recent study of psychiatric patients, 39% of the men and 52% of the women reported a history of childhood sexual abuse, but only 14% of the subjects had previously revealed their experiences (Wurr & Partridge, 1996). These figures would suggest that a high proportion of psychiatric inpatients have not disclosed their sexual abuse histories to the mental health professionals serving them.

UNDERREPORTING

The rise in prevalence rates for male childhood sexual abuse is attributed not to an actual increase in the incidence of abuse, but to an increased number of men revealing their experiences. In her article entitled "Suffering in Silence," Nasjleti (1980) was among the first to explore the issue of underreporting among men. She examined how strongly adolescent males resisted describing incidents of molestation. In general, researchers have speculated that there are a number of possible reasons why both boys and men have found it difficult to talk about their abusive pasts. First, Lew (1988) states that "our culture provides no room for men as victims" (p. 41). Real men are able to protect themselves under all circumstances, and the concept of man-as-victim is an oxymoron. Men must be warriors with the capacity to endure pain without complaint. Warriors also deny vulnerable feelings, creating a barrier both to the disclosure of victimization and to the healing process. Second, when boys are sexually abused by men, it creates confusion around their sexual identity, resulting in a secret but strong fear of being gay (for heterosexual men) or of having been "made" gay (for gay men). The associated shame, often expressed as homophobia, can prevent male survivors from revealing their abuse (Lew, 1988).

A third reason for underreporting may relate to a central symptom that is a known result of an abusive background. Sexual compulsivity tends to go unremarked in men because it is deemed an admirable demonstration of virility (Dimock, 1988). In fact, Finkelhor (1984) discovered that males don't report as many negative effects of their sexual abuse as women do. Although this finding could be interpreted literally—that men don't experience themselves as having been particularly harmed—a valid alternative explanation relates to the reality that our culture supports male sexual hyperactivity, whereas it condemns women as "promiscuous."

A fourth reason why men may underreport sexual abuse relates to instances of abuse by women. Although it is true that the majority of boys are abused by men, it is now well documented that women abuse as well. Boys who are sexually abused by women fear disbelief and ridicule—and rightly so. The corollary of the stereotype that holds that men can't be victims also dictates that women can't be perpetrators. Men who reveal that they were abused as children by a woman are often told that they are "lucky," denying completely the harmful aftereffects. The stereotype of female-as-victim-only leads men to sexualize their abusive experiences and may also result in an underreporting of incidents of abuse by female sex offenders.

Abuse by women, especially mothers, is hard for our culture to contemplate and therefore especially difficult for sons to report. However, Michele Elliott's (1993) book *Female Sexual Abuse of Children* challenges the assumption that women don't perpetrate by studying female abusers exclusively. Men, too, are beginning to speak out. For example, Berendzen (1993), a professor at a prominent Washington, D.C., university, broke his silence in his book *Come Here,* in which he describes his own experiences of mother-son incest. Research has also shown that the rate of abuse by women, either alone or jointly in polyincestuous activities, accounts for from 5% to 15% of male cases coming to professional notice (Watkins & Bentovim, 1992). Finkelhor and Russell's (1984) review of the clinical literature showed that approximately 24% of all male victims and 13% of female victims had been abused by women. Dimock (1988) found that, out of a sample of 25 abused men, 28% reported female perpetrators. McCarty (1986) studied sexual-abusing mothers and found that sons are victims 43% of the time. Fehrenbach and Monastersky (1988) reported that 40% of the children abused by female adolescent perpetrators are male, and in a study that focused exclusively on female perpetrators, boys were found to be victims at a ratio of 2-to-1 over girls (Johnson, 1989). Finally, two studies of male college students reported a higher percentage of female versus male perpetrators. Fromuth and Burkhart (1989) found that, of those male participants reporting abuse, 70% were abused by women. Fritz and colleagues (1981) reported that 60% of perpetrators were female.

Matthews, Matthews, and Speltz (1990) have developed a typology of female offenders. The *predisposed/severe history* type is often a single parent or a relative of the victim. She is likely to have been sexually abused as a child, and it is thought that her behavior is a reenactment of her own abuse. The *experimenter/exploiter* type is typically an adolescent 16 years or younger who usually abuses a young male (under 6) whom she is baby-sitting. This offender tends to lack social confidence and feels safer with a young male over whom she has authority and whom she can control. The *teacher/lover* type is an older woman who abuses young men from 11 to 16 years of age. She is dissatisfied with relationships in her own age group, and her victim can be her own son, a stepson, a teenaged friend of her children, or perhaps a student or resident with whom she works in a professional capacity. She usually rationalizes the abuse as a love affair. The *male accomplice* type is usually coerced into abusing her own children or others by her male partner. Her partner also abuses her. Although she is forced to abuse initially, the abuse can later become self-initiated. These women are extremely dependent and feel completely inadequate if they are not in a relationship with a man.

To expose the prevalence of sexual abuse perpetrated by women is to challenge the stereotype of women exclusively as victims. Feminist Charlotte Kasl (1990) believes that female sex offenders express the pain and rage that most women are conditioned to deny. When women become accountable for their own violence, they also confront their hidden feelings regarding their parenting roles and their own sexuality. The open exploration of feminine rage can heal as well as empower women.

Research on the female sex offender is in an embryonic stage. As knowledge increases, male victims may silence themselves less often, because they will be more likely to be believed when they tell. It is important that mental health professionals critically examine their own role in the underreporting of men's sexual abuse. Chapter 6 sets out the many issues related to asking clients about their abusive pasts, but overwhelmingly, accurate prevalence rates depend on whether or not professionals bother to inquire about abusive pasts (van der Kolk, 1987). In addition, in figures related to only one of the mental health professions, it has been demonstrated that one third of male psychologists and over two thirds of female psychologists report some form of abuse during their own childhood, adolescence, or adulthood (Pope, 1996). Lew (1988) believes that there is a large number of men and women incest survivors in the helping professions. These backgrounds, if not wisely handled, can seriously affect relationships with clients. For example, how will the fact that a female mental health professional has been sexually abused by a man affect how she deals with male clients? In a recent study of female nurses with a history of sexual abuse, 40% believed their abuse had affected their comfort level when working with male patients. Some described avoiding men, being extra cautious about boundaries, and having difficulty dealing with male professional authority figures (Gallop, McKeever, Toner, Lancee, & Lueck, 1995). This work raises a number of questions: Are women mental health professionals able to recognize the power inherent in their professional status? Are they at risk of taking a defensive relational stance with male clients based on perceptions of threat? Although male professionals abused by men can have the same issues, they are statistically likely to be in the minority, first as victims, and second as caregivers. The reality is that the majority of direct service roles in psychiatric hospitals, community mental health, and social service agencies are filled by women, and as responsible professionals, they must challenge themselves to acquire the skills to be vigilant against gender bias in their relationships with male clients, regardless of their backgrounds. They may also need to confront realistically the types of clients they cannot serve.

In order to fully understand the issues involved in underreporting, it is important to acknowledge the role of the feminist movement, which first brought the issue of child abuse to public awareness. As men listened to women's accounts of sexual abuse, they increasingly saw their own experiences mirrored. Slowly, they have started to come forward. Recently, the Canadian media have also begun to play a role. In 1989, it was revealed that, for years, Christian brothers who ran the Mount Cashel orphanage in Newfoundland had been sexually abusing the boys in their care. In 1992, the sexual abuse of boys at St. John's and St. Joseph's training schools in Ontario came to light. More recently, a professional hockey player, Sheldon Kennedy, disclosed to the world his sexual abuse as a youth at the hands of his coach. In addition, the courts have convicted a number of male staff at Toronto's Maple Leaf Gardens for preying upon young boys, bribing them with promises of free tickets to professional hockey games and then luring them to parties afterward where they were sexually abused. Martin Cruze, one of the first victims to come forward in the scandal, jumped to his death from one of the city's bridges in 1997, highlighting further the toll that sexual abuse takes. Although it is true that the sexual victimization of boys is becoming more visible, there is no doubt that there is a long journey ahead. In a recent survey of sexually and physically abused adolescent boys conducted by the Commonwealth Fund in New York (1998), nearly half (48%) said they had not revealed the abuse to anyone.[2]

MYTHS ABOUT MALE SURVIVORS

Although it has become more common for professionals to acknowledge men's experiences of sexual abuse, survivors are finding that they must struggle with yet another stereotype—that they already have or will sometime soon complete the "cycle of violence" and abuse others. For example, a number of my own clients have told me that, when they finally found the courage to ask for help with their past sexual abuse, professionals automatically referred them to sex offender groups. In a further example, I recently counseled two men whose partners broke off the relationship when they disclosed their sexual victimization. The reason given in both instances was that the women feared that their children would not be safe if they continued to live with a man who had a sexual abuse history.

These stereotypical views require challenge. In an estimate based on clinical experience, Lew (1993) believes that approximately 5% of the sexually abused men that he has counseled have sexually abused others—a figure that concurs with my own experience as a counselor. From a research perspective, Bagley, Wood, and Young (1994) anonymously surveyed a random sample of 750 men, aged 18 to 27 years. Respondents were asked about unwanted sexual acts imposed on them before the age of 17 and were asked if they had perpetrated as adults. Of the 750 men, 117 reported experiencing sexual abuse; of these 117 men, 7.7% acknowledged that they themselves had abused a girl under age 13. Another 7.7% acknowledged that they had abused a boy under the age of 13. Although these figures are disturbing and, like those on sexual abuse in general, may be underreported, they clearly indicate that the vast majority of abused men do not abuse as adults.

There is also evidence that the majority of sex offenders were never sexually abused as children. Hanson (1991) reviewed 18 different studies of child molesters, totaling 1,717 subjects. Hanson (1991) found that overall, an average of only 28% of the sample reported having been sexually abused as children, with figures ranging from 0% to 60%. Although underreporting may apply in this instance as well, the figures are lower than stereotypical views would dictate.

Thus, from both a research and a clinical perspective, there are three distinct groups that must be considered: men who were sexually abused as children who go on to offend; men who were not sexually abused as children yet have offended; and the largest group, men who were sexually abused as children but do not offend. It is critical that professionals be aware of these facts, because many male clients themselves believe the prevailing stereotype and fear that they will one day harm others as a result of their past experiences. It is a great relief to them when they learn that, even though they have been sexually abused, the statistics show that most abused men don't become sex offenders.

THE ROLE OF GENDER SOCIALIZATION

Stereotypical forms of male gender socialization are characterized by control, independence, aggression, competitiveness, and strength. Vulnerability is a man's enemy, and crying is for the weak. Anger is the only emotion that a real man can express. How rigidly a traumatized man clings to these "rules" of masculinity can affect how he deals with the impact of his abuse. Lisak and colleagues (1996) examined the question of why some men who are abused as children complete the cycle of violence and become abusers. In their sample group of 595 men, 257 (45%) reported being either sexually or physically abused. Of the abused subjects, 38% exhibited some form of interpersonal violence as adults (defined as the sexual or physical abuse of another man, woman, or child). But 62% of the sample did not engage in any form of interpersonal violence. Although these results confirm some form of link between experiences of childhood trauma and violence in adulthood, the question the research-ers sought to answer was, which factors interrupted what had heretofore been assumed to be the inevitability of the cycle of violence?

Lew (1988) suggests that childhood trauma results in three roles for men: abuser, victim, and protector. Roles, however, have something of a static quality, implying that men have only three outcomes available to them as they cope with the aftermath of abuse. Lisak and colleagues (1996) expanded this thinking by proposing the idea of pathways rather than roles. The first pathway is characterized by gender rigidity. Men who take this path unquestioningly embrace the male gender role and ex-tend its central dictates to the point that they are emotionally constricted, nonempathetic, homophobic, misogynistic, and chronically angry. In their attempt to resolve the conflict between the overwhelming emotion they experienced as abused children (along with a shameful sense of weakness, powerlessness, and vulnerability) and the demands of the male gender role (strength, power, invincibility), they lash out at others who display the very characteristics they despise within themselves. They are deeply at risk of becoming abusers and completing the cycle of violence.

The second and more common pathway is to achieve some sort of rec-onciliation between the experiences of abuse and the adult male gender role. In Lisak and colleagues' (1996) research, men who had experienced abuse as children were compared to their nonabused counterparts. It was found that the abused men, particularly those who had been sexually abused, actually scored lower on measures of gender rigidity, emotional constriction, empathy deficits, misogyny, and homophobia. As a result, they displayed less gender stress, held fewer stereotypical views of the male gender, and were better able to express themselves emotionally. Somehow, they had found their way to the second pathway and resolved the inherent conflict between boy-as-victim and man-as-invincible.

CASE STUDIES

In my work with abused men who also have psychiatric histories, I was interested in using both Lew's (1988) idea of roles (abuser, victim, protec-tor) and Lisak and colleagues' (1996) concept of pathways to examine how men deal with the aftermath of trauma. I asked the question, is there case evidence that these concepts are clinically helpful in assisting men to heal and recover from their experiences?

In 1997, I had the opportunity to co-lead a men's trauma group for psychiatric clients. The group consisted of 12 men ranging in age from 25 to 50 years. Among them, they had the following psychiatric diagnoses: depression, schizophrenia, dissociative identity disorder, borderline personality disorder, antisocial personality disorder, and posttraumatic stress disorder. One man struggled with an eating disorder.[3] In assessing the men's level of trauma symptomatology, the Trauma Symptom Checklist (40) (Briere et al., 1988) was employed. Only six of the men were able to complete the questionnaire, but the average score of 66.5 was indicative of the high levels of distress all members were experiencing. It should be noted for comparison that Briere and colleagues (1988) used a somewhat shorter version of the same questionnaire with 20 therapy clients who were also survivors, resulting in an average score of 46.2. Briere and colleagues' comparison group of 20 nonabused men scored 30.05. We also employed a second measure of impact, the Dissociative Experience Scale (Carlson & Putnam, 1993). Again, the six members who took the test produced an average score of 38.55, ranging from 24.10 to 58.60. Note that a score over 30 can result in a diagnosis of dissociative identity disorder (Carlson & Putnam, 1993). Although I acknowledge that these results are not scientific, they nonetheless serve to provide at least some benchmarks against which to view the group's level of active symptomatology.

Let me now place a human face on the suffering of these men by introducing three members, chosen because of their close approximation to Lew's (1988) roles (abuser, victim, and protector). All names have been changed and identifying information disguised.

Frank (Abuser Role)

Frank was large, tense, and intimidating. Although group safety guidelines stipulated no abusive or threatening behaviors, on occasion, he verbally attacked other members; although he never physically threatened anyone, the possibility was present in everyone's mind.

Frank's early life was as tough as he was. When he was an infant, his mother had what he believed to be a nervous breakdown, and on two separate occasions she tried to kill him. Frank had requested his medical files from that period in his life and had discovered that, as a result of the abuse, he had undergone a series of brain operations. Frank's father was also physically abusive but not nearly as bad as his mother. However, his father, along with an uncle and two aunts, sexually abused him.

After his mother's breakdown, his parents had four more children. Frank remembers his father telling him to protect the younger ones from his mother. On one occasion, when she was attacking his younger brother, he ran to place himself between his mother and his brother. His enraged mother grabbed him by the throat, dragged him to the basement door, and threw him down the stairs. His brothers and sisters told him later that his mother was terrified that, this time, she'd gone too far. Even though she rushed him to the hospital, Frank believes that it was for her sake, not his own.

Frank's hospital stay brought him to the attention of the child welfare authorities, and they took him away from his family. As is typical of the reasoning of a 4-year-old, Frank felt that he had been removed because he was being punished, and he longed to return to the only family he had known. There were attempts to place him in other homes, but he thought that if he showed prospective foster parents how really "bad" he was, the authorities would have no recourse but to send him home.

Eventually, his behavior was so completely out of control that he was sent to a facility for emotionally disturbed children. There, he attempted suicide, believing death was better than never going home. He managed to obtain a box of pills and swallowed them, but he only got sick and didn't die.

At the age of 8 he was transferred to a second institution. He recalls that as soon as his social worker left, a male staff member hit him across the back of the head with a wooden brush. Crying while wiping the blood away, he asked what he had done wrong. The staff member informed him that he had done nothing wrong—yet—but that little boys always got into trouble and he needed to know what would happen to him when he did. Three days later Frank was raped in the washroom by an older inmate. When he told a staff member, he was advised to "get used to it." As time went on, Frank, like the other children, was submitted to special tortures perpetrated by the staff. He remembers having the bottoms of his feet hit until they bled. Even small infractions resulted in forced cold showers or being tied to the bed. Sexual assault was common, with other inmates preying on the more vulnerable boys. When Frank was 13, staff members began to teach him how to fight in preparation for regular matches with the other boys, which were held for the amusement of the watching workers. As Frank grew up, he became tougher and stronger, threatening some staff and abusing other inmates. In his environment, he believed that the "law of the jungle" held and that only the strong could survive.

When Frank was released from the institution at the age of 16, he began a long history of involvement with the law, amassing a lengthy record of convictions—mostly for assault. For example, when youths harassed an elderly lady, he "smashed the crap out of them." When he witnessed an 11-year-old attacking a younger boy, he roughed up the bully. When his first wife went "berserk"—as he called it—he felt he had to defend himself and was once more charged. He felt that he was not unlike the heroes in action movies who perpetrate violence in the name of justice.

Daniel (Victim Role)

When Daniel was very small, his mother broke his shoulder by hitting him with a two-by-four. As he grew older, the beatings became so regular that Daniel tried to take some measure of control by arriving home from school and fetching the broom with which his mother hit him. He reasoned that sooner or later she was going to attack him, so he might as well get it over with as quickly as possible. She often hit him so hard that the broom broke. Daniel's father did not interfere, although he did not participate in the beatings.

Daniel felt that that his mother favored his sister. He remembers having to wait on her and clean up after her and her friends. His sister, who was 2 years older than he, also beat him. He recalls, as well, that his sister sexually abused him when he was 5 years old. He also suspects that when he was 3 years old he was sexually abused by a female baby-sitter. He can clearly remember this woman lying nude on the bed. He remembers vividly the blue-and-pink-flowered wallpaper in the bedroom and he felt quite certain that something had happened, but he just couldn't remember.

When he was 5 years old, his sister, his cousin, and he were sexually abused by a man while on a visit to a historical location in Toronto. He recalls the man taking them down into a room, and he remembers being told by his parents later that the man had been criminally charged.

The incidents of abuse that occurred outside the home had an impact, but Daniel felt most betrayed by the abuse he suffered at the hands of his mother and sister. In his adult life, he still feels powerless, especially in the presence of women he views as being aggressive and dominating. In relationships, he finds that his partners simply take over his life. He often feels stalked by women and used sexually, but he is unable to take effective action to protect himself. He explains that he just can't say "no."

Daniel joined our men's group when he was 50 years of age. As he recounted his story, he experienced overwhelming feelings of sadness and felt that he simply could not manage his suicidal feelings without admission to the hospital. When I accompanied him to the emergency department, I observed how Daniel was able to draw women to him. Although he had described himself as totally lost in his own suicidal thoughts before we arrived at the hospital, I watched him tend to the needs of a woman whom he met in emergency. He acted as though his own crisis was nonexistent.

Indeed, while in the hospital, Daniel soon figured in the affections of one of the women patients, who followed him constantly, to the point that he felt terrorized. Unfortunately, in this case, matters got out of hand. The woman entered Daniel's room late at night and crawled into his bed. Although Daniel's body responded against his will, he felt raped. The ensuing commotion brought the staff. Daniel's account of the incident was ignored and he was reprimanded for his behavior, whereas the female patient was comforted. Later, Daniel's psychiatrist, taking a man-to-man approach, asked him to please keep his sexual activities more discreet. The next day, staff insisted that Daniel attend a group for sexual abuse survivors. He was the only man present.

During Daniel's hospitalization, he was permitted to attend our men's group concurrently. As he recounted the story of his hospital experience, he lamented, "This always happens to me."

Ray (Protector Role)

Ray was referred to our men's trauma group by his probation officer. He had been charged and convicted of assaulting his female partner. Previously, he had attended a court-mandated group for batterers. However, he had not adjusted well because he did not see himself as a "woman hater" or as a batterer—the assault was the first and only time Ray had ever hit anyone.

In group, Ray was quick to step in when other members were struggling with problems. He had already figured out the solution, and he moved quickly to share his ideas to spare the member further pain. He had substantial knowledge in the areas of massage, nutrition, and new-age spirituality. In fact, Ray's helpfulness took on a competitive edge as he jockeyed for position with my co-leader and me. He even reported that he was solving his probation officer's personal problems.

When Ray was 2 years old, he was adopted. His new parents told him stories of severe neglect by his biological mother and father, but his memories of that time are vague, and he often wonders what really happened to him during the first 2 years of his life. The only thing he remembers, and he is unsure even of this, is the sense that he is looking through bars, perhaps of a crib, and outside the bars is absolute chaos. He associates a feeling of profound aloneness with this image.

Ray's adoptive father was a police officer. He recalls him repeating over and over again to Ray: "You're useless. You'll never amount to anything." His adoptive mother never interfered when his father got into one of his "moods." His grandmother, however, was warm and caring. He felt safe with her, but she died when he was 5 years old. He felt her loss deeply and sensed that now he was all alone. By the time he was 16 years old, he felt so troubled that he tried to commit suicide. At the time, he was admitted to a psychiatric hospital, but he had no further association with the mental health system until he entered our group.

THE WORK OF THE GROUP

As the men began to tell their stories, it was obvious that Lisak and colleagues' (1996) research on the relationship between gender rigidity and violence was confirmed by at least some of the men's experiences. Frank's adopted role had a strong contextual component, because his environment left him few options. It would hardly have been safe in the terrorizing conditions of his childhood to be emotionally vulnerable or empathetic. In the kinds of institutions where he was held, "might is right," and one survives by becoming a warrior. Out of necessity, he chose the pathway of gender rigidity and completed the cycle of violence. Daniel lacked a male presence in his life and, perhaps as a result, took on the victim role, a role more closely associated with the female stereotype. Certainly, in my overall clinical practice, I have worked with hundreds of men like Daniel, who repeat the patterns of victimization in their adult lives. Ray, as the protector, rejected the only male role in his life—that of his cruel adoptive father. He defied the continual insult "you're useless" and made himself extremely useful, to everyone but himself. Both Daniel and Ray chose the pathway of nonviolence.

As the group entered fully into its work, I found that many of the men began to speak about how different they had always felt because they had been abused. Each, in his own way, had attempted to blaze new trails. Frank wrote poetry and stories. Daniel had at one time been what he called a "hippie" and had found that the ideals of that cultural role suited him. Ray was a bartender off and on, putting his protector skills to good use by listening to his customers' stories and giving them advice.

The artistic temperament became highly valued among group members. Three (including Frank) were amateur writers, one member was an amateur actor, and another acted professionally. One member dreamed of becoming an artist, and three others played musical instruments. Some of the gay group members also offered different ways of being male and talked of the support they received as members of the gay community.

With the help of the group, Frank began to acknowledge his behavior, and eventually he was able to take off his macho mask and show his grief and pain by crying in front of the other men. It was a hugely symbolic moment for all of us, because Frank's letting go encouraged others to venture into their vulnerability. Since the group, Frank has not reoffended, and he has stayed out of jail.

Daniel identified the revictimizing patterns in his life. With group support he was able to describe his feelings of powerlessness. Slowly, he came to rely on his own perceptions, and he eventually confronted the staff at the hospital regarding their stereotypical views of him. As he became stronger, he organized an arts and crafts group in the housing project where he lived that eventually became a political forum for ousting a drug dealer from the building. He said, "I've finally learned to say 'no.'"

Over time, Ray was able to speak about his anger toward his adoptive father and hear from the other group members that his feelings were valid. As he expressed his anger in group, he became more peaceful and less compelled to help others. As he turned from solving other people's problems to solving his own, he told the group how ashamed he felt about the assault charge, and he hastened to explain his actions. He recalled feeling trapped by his partner, who had her hands around his throat, fingernails digging in. He knows that he responded by slapping her, but he doesn't recall doing so. Ray regretted his actions deeply and did not see himself as a violent man. He associated the feelings with his early memories of bars and the accompanying sense that he was trapped. However, he was adamant that it was his responsibility to heal the part within him that was capable of such acts.

CONCLUSION

In our group, it was *not* common for men to take the pathway of male gender rigidity. In fact, the experience of abuse seemed to leave the men with the feeling that they had been set apart. Although the resulting isolation was painful, it released them from the narrow gender expectations of the male role and allowed them to adopt a broader view of manhood and maleness. Artistic pursuits were extremely valued and allowed group members to express their vulnerabilities in ways that they saw as compatible with being a man. In some senses, the larger issue was how to break free not from the male stereotype—but from the female stereotype of victim or protector. Lew's (1988) idea of roles, though holding true, appeared to be just another form of stereotype, with the real healing beginning when the men allowed themselves to adopt the best of both male and female qualities, expressing vulnerability and strength at one and the same time.

In this chapter, I have challenged the stereotypical views that few men are sexually abused and that those who are automatically become sex offenders or perpetrators of interpersonal violence. Although Lisak and colleagues' (1996) findings of a link between rigid male gender roles and violence were confirmed, my work also verified the most commonly neglected fact about abused men—most don't go on to abuse anyone.

Pigeonholing people is never helpful. Human nature is far more complex. If women are always seen as victims, how can they become accountable for their own behavior and take responsibility for their lives? Likewise, assigning the abuser role exclusively to men renders their pain invisible and their healing impossible. It is critical that professionals, both men and women, uncover their gender biases and modify their helping approaches so that they speak to the whole person. Clients, both men and women, can only benefit.

NOTES

1. I wish to thank Grant Fair, M.S.W., my colleague and co-leader for the men's group that forms the central case examples in this chapter. His experience and knowledge in the area of men's trauma is extensive and has been a support and an inspiration in my work.

2. In the same study, 29% of abused girls had not talked to anyone about their abuse.

3. Although eating disorders are often thought of as occurring exclusively among women, men also struggle with this problem. In a study of adolescent boys who had been sexually and physically abused as children, 23% said they binged and purged, with most doing so daily. Also, abused boys were found to be four times more likely to have eating disorders than nonabused boys (Commonwealth Fund, 1998).

REFERENCES

Bagley, C., Wood, M., & Young, L. (1994). Victim to abuser: Mental health and behavioral sequels of child sexual abuse in a community survey of young adult males. *Child Abuse & Neglect, 19,* 683-697.

Berendzen, R. (1993). *Come here.* New York: Villard Books.

Briere, J., Evans, D., Runtz, M., & Wall, T. (1988). Symptomatology in men who were abused as children: A comparison study. *American Journal of Orthopsychiatry, 58,* 457-461.

Carlson, E., & Putnam, F. (1993). An update on the dissociative experiences scale. *Dissociation, 6,* 16-27.

The Commonwealth Fund. (1998). *The health of adolescent boys: Commonwealth Fund survey finding.* New York: Author.

Dimock, P. (1988). Adult males sexually abused as children. *Journal of Interpersonal Violence, 3,* 203-231.

Elliott, M. (1993). *Female sexual abuse of children.* New York: Guilford.

Farrell, W. (1993). *The myth of male power.* New York: Berkley.

Fehrenbach, P. H., & Monastersky, C. (1988). Characteristics of female adolescent sexual offenders. *American Journal of Orthopsychiatry, 58,* 148-151.

Finkelhor, D. (1979). *Sexually victimized children.* New York: Free Press.

Finkelhor, D. (1984). Boys as victims: Review of the evidence. In D. Finkelhor (Ed.), *Child sexual abuse: New theory and research* (pp. 152-171). New York: Free Press.

Finkelhor, D., & Russell, D. (1984). Women as perpetrators: Review of the evidence. In D. Finkelhor (Ed.), *Child sexual abuse: New theory and research* (pp. 171-187). New York: Free Press.

Fritz, G. S., Stoll, K., & Wagner, N. N. (1981). A comparison of males and females who were sexually molested as children. *Journal of Sex and Marital Therapy, 7,* 54-59.

Fromuth, M. E., & Burkhart, B. R. (1989). Long term psychological correlates of childhood sexual abuse in two samples of college men. *Child Abuse & Neglect, 143,* 533-542.

Gallop, R., McKeever, P., Toner, B., Lancee, W., & Lueck, M. (1995). The impact of childhood sexual abuse on the psychological well-being and practice of nursing. *Archives of Psychiatric Nursing, 9,* 137-145.

Hanson, K. (1991). Characteristics of sex offenders who were sexually abused as children. In R. Langevin (Ed.), *Sex offenders and their victims: New research findings* (pp. 77-85). Toronto, Canada: Juniper Press.

Herschel, D., Briere, J., Magallanes, M., & Smiljanich, K. (1990, April). *Sexual abuse related attributions: Probing the role of "traumagenic factors."* Paper presented at the annual meeting of the Western Psychological Association, Los Angeles.

Hunter, M. (1990). *The sexually abused male.* Washington, DC: National Institute of Health.

Johnson, T. C. (1989). Female child perpetrators: Children who molest other children. *Child Abuse & Neglect, 13,* 571-585.

Kasl, C. D. (1990). Female perpetrators of sexual abuse: A feminist view. In M. Hunter (Ed.), *The sexually abused male* (pp. 259-274). Lexington, MA: Lexington Books.

Kimbrell, A. (1991, May/June). A time for men to pull together. *Utne Reader, 45,* 66.

Lew, M. (1988). *Victims no longer: Men recovering from incest and other sexual child abuse.* New York: Nevraumont.

Lew, M. (1993, September/October). *Working with men: Identifying and treating sexual child abuse.* Workshop presentation, Toronto, Canada.

Lisak, D., Hopper, J., & Song, P. (1996). Factors in the cycle of violence: Gender rigidity and emotional constriction. *Journal of Traumatic Stress, 9,* 721-743.

Matthews, R., Matthews, J., & Speltz, K. (1990). Female sexual offenders. In M. Hunter (Ed.), *The sexually abused male* (pp. 275-293). Lexington, MA: Lexington Books.

McCarty, L. M. (1986). Mother-child incest: Characteristics of the offender. *Child Welfare, 65,* 447-458.

Nasjleti, M. (1980). Suffering in silence: The male incest victim. *Child Welfare, 59,* 269-275.

Pope, K. (1996). Scientific research, recovered memory, and context: Seven surprising findings. *Women & Therapy, 19,* 123-140.

van der Kolk, B. (1987). *Psychological trauma.* Washington, DC: American Psychiatric Press.

Watkins, B., & Bentovim, A. (1992). The sexual abuse of male children and adolescents: A review of current research. *Journal of Child Psychology and Psychiatry, 33*(1) 197-248.

Wurr, C. T., & Partridge, I. M. (1996). The prevalence of a history of childhood sexual abuse in an acute adult inpatient population. *Child Abuse & Neglect, 20,* 867-872.

CHAPTER 14

Racism, Oppression, and Childhood Trauma

Kathy J. Lawrence

I would say I am neurotic, but at different levels, usually triggered by neurosis itself. But more on a mental level because of past abuse . . . Yet [my] mental and physical [faculties] couldn't co-exist then to recognise what was happening. But now I do. I see for the first time in my life, to understand I am not crazy. . . . now I can put a name to it, to attempt to explain it now. It is not incurable. I can cure myself. Since I have a reason that caused it. So if I deal with the reason, then I can work to make the problem go away.

—*Wiebe and Johnson*, Stolen Life, *1998, pp. 175-176*

A "stolen life," to describe Yvonne Johnson's journey, is at best an understatement. The great-great-granddaughter of Big Bear and the second youngest of six children born to a Cree mother and a white father, Johnson's life is permeated by a background of vicious racism, injustice, and poverty. Neither glamorizing nor valorizing her experience, Johnson shares with her readers countless stories of family violence, incest, sexual assault, gang rape, and spousal abuse. But her suffering did not end with these painful experiences. As with many survivors of abuse, daily life was complicated: Alcohol dulled her pain, cutting interrupted her numbness, and suicide was always but a moment away. Her message is clear: Oppression and the betrayal of family and culture alienate and separate all people.

Johnson's story encompasses more. Tragically, unable to quell her own deep fear and rage, Johnson, her husband, and their companions killed a man whom they suspected of sexually abusing children. Johnson was subsequently convicted of murder, served time in the Kingston Federal Prison for Women, and is currently completing her life sentence in the Okimaw Ohci Healing Lodge for Native Women in Saskatchewan.

An uncommon story? Perhaps. Perhaps not. The story of Yvonne Johnson has captured the hearts and minds of the Canadian public and has received literary honors, including two nonfiction prizes and a nomination for the Governor General's Award for Literature. Johnson eloquently shares her personal life story and heritage as a woman of Cree descent. Her mother's own story of being robbed of her culture and childhood upon placement in the Canadian residential school system is foundational[1] and marks the turning point in her family's story.[1] Racism, poverty, violence, and injustice marred her mother's life and left Johnson with a legacy that mirrors the stories of many oppressed peoples. It could be argued that women are more likely to be the victims rather than the perpetrators of lethal violence, leading to a conclusion that Johnson's story has little to offer. Yet such a conclusion is perhaps even more dangerous than the rage that overtook Johnson that one day. Unable to find solace in the community and health care systems, Yvonne Johnson became another statistic in the North American criminal justice system, which disproportionately convicts and incarcerates indigenous peoples, people of color, and people who have suffered childhood abuse. Her story cannot be avoided, as it repeatedly highlights the racism, sexism, and injustice of North American society, coupled with the gaps and failures of the community and health care systems. It calls out for a response.

Yvonne Johnson's experience is not limited to the life of one Cree woman; it is the story of many who have suffered from direct forms of violence through physical and sexual abuse and who have encountered the broad range of social, economic, and political oppression that is deeply rooted in North American society and history. Although it is not possible to fully document the profound influence of such oppression in one chapter, it is my hope that the reader will engage in two processes. First, I hope that the following pages will encourage critical thinking regarding epidemiological and mental health research relative to ethnoracial and ethnocultural perspectives,[2] to child abuse, and to traumatization in general.[3] Particular attention will be given to posttraumatic stress disorder (PTSD) research and the influence of medical-model conceptualizations. And second, I would like readers to use this chapter to begin to examine their own clinical conceptualizations, manner of practice, and style of service delivery. This examination will facilitate more sensitive, respectful practices in the promotion of mental health. It will also encourage the incorporation into practice of the richness of all ethnocultural and ethnoracial backgrounds, coupled with a human rights perspective that acknowledges and works to eradicate injustice, racism, and oppression.

Before proceeding further, I would like to add a personal note. When initially asked about my interest in contributing this chapter, I had some hesitation. I am a white, middle-class woman. I have done my best to engage in the processes I have named as important, and I bear witness to many stories of tragedy and hope: the stories of friends and clients; my memories of the children and the riots in Los Angeles in the early 1990s; and the raw despair and courage of those I met in Guatemala, El Salvador, and Brazil. I continue to reflect upon, honor, and hold sacred all of the stories I have heard. Yet I am frequently reminded of the limits of my own experience, and I fear that the contents of this chapter may appear to be nothing more than an academic exercise. Without a doubt, I value scholarship and empirical research that highlights important issues, and I have seen how research can influence the development of social policy and change. But I hope that this chapter does not end as a review of scholarship integrated with a few ideas for the workplace. What I do hope is that readers will take a journey into a sacred space shared by the presence of the many women, men, and children who, like Yvonne Johnson, have honored us with their stories of despair and courage and who have dared to hope that telling us about their lives would change the world.

EPIDEMIOLOGY AND DEFINITIONS OF CHILD ABUSE

Understanding the limits, difficulties, and possibilities of the research about ethnoracial and ethnocultural aspects of child abuse and traumatization is an important task because it sets the stage for understanding current clinical practice and defining what needs to change. I will start this task by providing a brief survey of some of the current studies that have attempted to answer questions about the actual frequency or epidemiology of child abuse, and I will intertwine this with the complicated issues of how one defines abuse.

National and Community Studies. To begin with, studies regarding the frequency of child abuse in Canada and the United States have yielded different results because of differences in definitions of child abuse used, in the ages of the children studied, in the groups of people studied, and in what questions were asked. Current research emphasizes physical contact between child as victim and adult (or older individual) as perpetrator, with ethnoracial or ethnocultural background (if queried) considered a demographic variable. Perhaps the most commonly cited American study was conducted by Finkelhor, Hotaling, Lewis, and Smith (1990); it found that approximately 27% of women and 16% of men reported experiences of childhood sexual abuse. This study found that ethnocultural background was not a significant component in the rates of abuse reported by women, though men from English and Scandinavian backgrounds were more likely to report childhood sexual abuse.

Another American study (Finkelhor & Dziuba-Leatherman, 1994) surveyed 2,000 children between the ages of 10 and 16 regarding the occurrence of physical and sexual victimization within the previous year. Of these children, approximately 25% reported at least one "completed victimization" experience. Sexual abuse was reported by 3.2% of the girls and 0.6% of the boys, and 2.2% of the children reported an attempted kidnapping. Considered "fairly well matched" to U.S. Census statistics for race within this particular age group, risk factors for abuse included ethnicity, family income, region of residence, and type of urban area. The study found that black and Hispanic children, children from Mountain and Pacific states, and children from large cities were more likely to be victimized. Black youth had the highest rates for sexual assault and kidnapping, and children from poor families also had high rates of assault and genital violence (Finkelhor & Dziuba-Leatherman, 1994).

A small number of community-based studies have explored ethnoracial differences among adult women reporting child abuse. For example, community studies by Russell (1986) and Wyatt (1985) found that approximately 20% of the women interviewed had at least one unwanted sexual experience with a relative before the age of 18. This figure rose to 40% when sexual experiences with non-family members were included. Rates of abuse between black and white respondents were not significantly different, though Russell (1986) found a lower reporting rate among Asian Americans.

An important, but missing, ingredient in these studies is information regarding the survivor's relationship to the abuser and the ethnoracial or ethnocultural background of the abuser. It may quite validly be argued that the focus was on the survivor and that therefore the information collected was to be specific to the survivor only. Yet, as professionals, we need to question the impacts both of our own ethnocultural or ethnoracial background and of the abuser when we work with survivors. Does speaking about abuse by one's own people bring shame? Are we asking survivors to inadvertently support the proliferation of societal stereotypes about their people as violent? If the abuse was by someone of another ethnocultural or ethnoracial background, how does the survivor make sense of the event relative to racism,[4] and how do these crimes manifest themselves in the legal system or in the media? Furthermore, does the survivor define his or her experience as abuse or as a form of discipline?[5] These and other questions must continually shape the professional's approach to understanding clients' experiences of abuse.

Canadian perspectives and social policies have been significantly influenced by the 1984 report of the Committee on Sexual Offences

Against Children and Youths, which found that 42.1% of respondents reported victimization by at least one type of sexual offense. The more recent Ontario Health Supplement (MacMillan et al., 1997) included questions about childhood abuse and found that child physical abuse was reported by 31.2% of the men and 21.1% of the women, whereas 4.3% of the men and 12.8% of the women reported sexual abuse. Each of these studies has been hailed as significant because of their impact on the development of social policy and service related to child abuse, but neither study included analyses of ethnoracial backgrounds or of other factors related to ethnocultural variables.

Although research regarding child abuse as it intersects with ethnoracial or ethnocultural background is markedly absent in Canada, there is a growing acknowledgment of childhood trauma within First Nations communities. More specifically, the final closing of government- and church-sponsored residential school systems in the 1960s and 1970s not only revealed severe social and cultural disruption of First Nations communities, but also yielded horrific stories of physical, sexual, and emotional abuse at the hands of school authorities. The consequence of this assault on the First Nations communities has, in part, manifested itself through family violence. A study by the Ontario Native Women's Association (1989) found that 8 out of 10 aboriginal women had personally experienced violence. Of these women, 87% reported physical injury, and 57% reported sexual abuse. A 1987 report by the Child Protection Centre of Winnipeg stated that there is "an apparent epidemic of child sexual abuse on reserves" (LaRocque, 1995, p. 105). Stressing the scope of the problem in a 1993 report regarding aboriginal health and social issues, LaRocque wrote, "There is growing documentation that Aboriginal female adults, adolescents and children are experiencing abuse, battering and or sexual assault to a staggering degree" (LaRocque, 1995, p. 105). Understanding these disproportionate prevalence rates in terms of the historical context of First Nations communities is essential. Colonization, racism, and sexism (LaRocque, 1995), particularly as expressed through the residential school system and the criminalization of various aspects of aboriginal cultural and societal structure, are core to the breakdown of the family unit in many communities and are perhaps most aptly interpreted as cultural genocide (Union of Ontario Indians, 1995). The First Nations experience, therefore, highlights our need to contextualize child abuse within a social, political, and historical framework.

BROADENING THE DEFINITION OF CHILD ABUSE: COMMUNITY VIOLENCE, WAR, AND TORTURE

Children traumatized by community-based violence pose an additional difficulty for research regarding child abuse. The few available studies indicate that community violence occurs in combination with poverty and with severe social-cultural disruption (Finkelhor & Dziuba-Leatherman, 1994; Garbarino, Dubrow, Kostelny, & Pardo, 1992), two social factors that affect persons of color disproportionately (Root, 1996). The enormity of the problem is highlighted by Bell (1991), whose survey of elementary school children in one high-risk area indicated that 26% had observed a shooting and 29% had witnessed a stabbing. Another Chicago study of middle and high school students indicated that 35% had witnessed a stabbing, 39% had seen a shooting, and 24% had observed a killing (Garbarino et al., 1992). In their summary of studies regarding community-based research, these authors also found that 46% of the students interviewed reported being the subject of at least one violent crime, ranging from armed robbery to rape, shooting, or stabbing. Although acknowledging that neither ethnoracial nor ethnocultural background was reported, these studies strongly suggest that child abuse, as defined by exposure to community-based violence, is particularly problematic for children of color, having tremendous impact on their psychosocial development and, most tragically, on their mortality rates.

The paucity of research available regarding children suffering from the effects of war or of state-sponsored torture and the impact on their development is also of concern. Prevalence rates pertaining to children with these experiences who have immigrated to Canada and the United States are basically absent, though occasional articles are written regarding their clinical assessment and care (e.g., Beattie, 1995; Friere, 1995).

EPIDEMIOLOGY AND DEFINITIONS RECONSIDERED

Although comparison across countries regarding the epidemiology of child sexual abuse has yielded rates similar to those found in Canadian and American research (Finkelhor, 1994), ethnoracial or ethnocultural factors within Canada and the United States have yet to be fully explored. I would suggest that there are seven basic reasons for these limitations:

Generalized Barriers. Epidemiological study of child abuse and neglect is still in its infancy, with barely two decades' worth of study and data available. Current research provides broad perspectives focused on contact forms of abuse and on the nuclear family unit, but research has yet to integrate specific ethnoracial, ethnocultural, social, political, historical, or community variations that may affect risk factors, subsequent psychosocial difficulties related to trauma, or resilience. Furthermore, child abuse remains an uncomfortable, if not taboo, subject across most cultural groups and is not an issue readily acknowledged or studied.

Epistemology. Epidemiological research is grounded in an empirical framework that may be considered an affront to many ethnoracial and ethnocultural traditions that have strong oral roots. More specifically, this kind of research relies heavily on the quantification of numerical data as *the* method of understanding reality and conveying information. It does not allow people's stories to define truth and experience. *Epistemology* (defined as methods of knowing and expressing truth and reality) often plays a pivotal role in understanding and expressing information, and it influences subjects' willingness to participate in research.

Methodology. Methodological issues, such as English-only research and restricted access to specific populations (using only those with a telephone), have been cited as problems in current research regarding violence (Rodgers, 1994). Such limitations can easily exclude individuals living in poverty and those who may be isolated because of language barriers.

Political Resistance. Leadership within these groups may resist research endeavors as they are thought to divert needed funding from the pressing problems of racism, oppression, and poverty. The needs are obvious, it is argued, and require real action—not further study and quantification.

Access to Research Results. With a few notable exceptions (e.g., femicide research by Crawford & Gartner, 1992), research tends to be written by academics for academics, with seemingly little effort made to convey results in a usable form to the community that was studied.

Misuse and Abuse of Research Data. Because a substantial amount of research is affiliated with governments and universities, some ethnoracial and ethnocultural groups may be hesitant to disclose personal information because of concerns regarding inappropriate use by authorities (Root, 1996) or the perpetuation of stereotypes. References to research regarding intelligence are frequently cited,[6] with examples of its misuses believed to foster stereotypes and hinder access to educational opportunities. Related concerns, such as the history of different clinical disciplines and their association with racist practices or oppressive regimes,[7] also serve to create apprehension regarding participation in research, especially research related to mental health or trauma.

Violent Repercussions. Some research related to trauma has resulted in violence. Perhaps most notable was the April 1998 assassination of Bishop Juan Gerardi of Guatemala within 48 hr of his presentation of the Interdiocesan Recovery of Historic Memory Project.[8] This project, which recovered stories of violence and human rights violations from more than 6,000 survivors of Guatemala's civil war, was designed to be part of a political narrative. The stories were collected in a manner to protect people's identities, written to ensure that the community narrative would not be suppressed, and presented publicly as a political statement. The violent murder of Bishop Gerardi is a graphic reminder of ongoing repression and contributes to refugee concerns regarding the use and application of information.

MENTAL HEALTH

Diagnostic and Statistical Manual of Mental Disorders and Post-traumatic Stress Disorder. The biopsychosocial impact of trauma and violence across the life span has come under increased attention from researchers, clinicians, and frontline workers. This increased emphasis within North America may be best understood as the interaction of the health care system with several significant historical events and social movements during the 1960s and 1970s (Foy, 1992; Saigh, 1992). Prior to that point in time, war veterans and accident victims yielded the majority of clinical study and dialogue regarding trauma. Problems and difficulties in functioning were often minimized, pathologized, or considered evidence of moral cowardice (Saigh, 1992).

The social landscape of the 1960s and 1970s, however, was intense: the return of Vietnam veterans from a horrendous wartime experience to a country that was in deep debate regarding their military involvement; the rise of the feminist movement, which clearly spoke against violence against women and children as one of its primary themes; the civil rights movement, which graphically illustrated the depth of racism in North America; and increasing evidence of severe trauma suffered by surviving civilians during times of great political repression, such as the Jewish Holocaust in Europe and the Pol Pot regime of Cambodia. Each of these events and movements challenged traditional, medical-model conceptualizations and facilitated a more serious examination of the impact of trauma on mental health within the context of health care and the wider sociopolitical landscape. Especially relevant to mental health professionals was the emergence of a medical-model description of traumatic stress, which was formally named posttraumatic stress disorder (PTSD) in the 1980 edition of the *Diagnostic and Statistical Manual of Mental Disorders (DSM-III)* of the American Psychiatric Association.

Research regarding PTSD has found that, across different forms of trauma, such as natural disasters, military assault, or domestic violence, and across different ethnoracial and ethnocultural groups, the core experiences of intrusion, avoidance, and physiological arousal remain the same (de Girolamo & McFarlane, 1996; Marsella, Friedman, & Spain, 1996). Aspects that have yielded differences include the expression of these experiences, the risk and protective factors associated with PTSD, and the social implications of experiencing a traumatic event.

1. Regarding the expression of traumatic experiences, Kirmayer's (1996) work strongly suggests that we should be mindful of the numerous ways that different language and cultural groups convey body experiences and memory. Interpretation of bodily sensations, metaphors, memory, and representations of self and others are often foundational in trauma-related therapy, yet these may vary radically across different groups. In my own practice, for example, a client from West Africa referred to some of her physiological experiences of PTSD as "spiders

dancing all over my arms and body." Her manner was so intense that I briefly wondered if she was experiencing some form of hallucination. I quickly realized, however, that this was a rich and powerful way of using metaphor to describe her experience. Yvonne Johnson's story also provides a striking example of a body metaphor. Describing a dream, she says that a visiting spirit woman "split me open from the back of my skull to the bottom tip of my spine. It seemed she was scraping me clean inside . . . shaking whatever she scraped off onto a hide lying on the ground. I was opened, cleaned out, circled by love and ceremony" (Wiebe & Johnson, 1998, p. 434).

2. Risk factors, which refer to influences that may increase the possibility that a person will experience PTSD, have become a major focus of PTSD research. Examining this issue relative to ethnoracial background, Marsella and colleagues (1996) found that PTSD rates were higher for American Indian and Asian American Vietnam War veterans and noted that "minority-status stress, racial prejudice, and identification with Vietnamese people and culture may have increased the risk of PTSD" (p. 111). Although this study is not specific to child abuse, it highlights the negative impact of racism on one's psyche, which subsequently makes one even more vulnerable to psychosocial distress following trauma.

3. In regard to the social implications of child abuse, it must be acknowledged that disclosure of trauma may differ depending on different definitions of what constitutes abuse; the impact of social service interventions on the individual, family, and community; perception and actual experience of police investigations; and expectation or actual experience of justice. Furthermore, when abuse, subsequent interventions, or investigations are interracial, the social stigma may be more severe (Root, 1996).

PTSD and Clinical Conceptualizations. The clinical conceptualization of posttraumatic stress has been strongly influenced by cognitive-behavioral theory, which proposes that the interaction of individual belief systems about self, others, and the world at large is especially important. Studies of victims of political torture, sexual assault, and domestic violence, for example, have indicated that belief systems play an important role in the expression or nonexpression of PTSD (Creamer, 1995; Pakar et al., 1997; Resick & Schnicke, 1992). Pakar et al. (1997) found that the a priori beliefs of political activists who were tortured served to protect them from more severe mental health problems. These activists were able to predict that suffering was a likely outcome of their political involvement and were able to make meaning of the event, compared to individuals who were randomly pulled from their homes and tortured for no obvious reason. In addition, the clinical research of Resick and Schnicke (1992) found that adult women who had been sexually assaulted responded to specific cognitive-behavioral interventions that addressed trauma-related beliefs regarding power, control, and safety[9] and yielded a significant reduction in PTSD symptoms.

The work of Ronnie Janoff-Bulman (1992) has stressed that trauma "shatters assumptions" regarding the self as worthy and the world as benevolent and meaningful. The therapeutic task, therefore, is to integrate the memory of the trauma by developing a new understanding of oneself, others, and the world. An understanding of one's vulnerability, of the unpredictability of events, and of the encounter with evil are important components of this new belief system. Application of Janoff-Bulman's (1992) model in working with survivors of state-sponsored torture is illustrated in the work of Yaya de Andrade (1995), who writes:

> For victims of torture and violent repression, their traumatic experiences can shatter basic beliefs about life, themselves and the world around them, affecting their ability to function and adjust to a new culture . . . stress caused by such trauma can lead to a disruption of self which affects bio-psycho functioning; suddenly the survivor is unable to concentrate, to sleep, experiences extreme anxiety, and so on. Traumatic experiences can also cause survivors to be extremely distrustful of other people, which in turn, leads to difficulties adjusting both socially and culturally to the community in which they have resettled. . . Perpetuating factors also play an important role. Living in a community in which there are threats of violence, racism, polarized politics, intolerance, indifference, and lack of sensitivity or empathy will serve to perpetuate the trauma. (p. 38)

PROBLEMS, CRITIQUES, AND NEW FRAMEWORKS

Although the inclusion of PTSD and subsequent acknowledgment of certain social variables as foundational to particular psychiatric disorders have certainly marked a positive shift in medical-model-based health care approaches, problems and critiques abound. First and foremost, the *DSM-IV* (1994) remains reductionistic in its labeling of posttraumatic distress as a "disorder," inadvertently perpetuating a limited, if not oppressive, perspective on human suffering. One particular challenge to reductionistic thinking that I have found integral to my own understanding of trauma is the work of Ignacio Martin-Baro, a psychologist assassinated in El Salvador in 1989 for his work in developing what has become known as a "liberation psychology." Foundational to Martin-Baro's framework of what constitutes mental health and illness is the sociopolitical contextualization and interpersonal history of the people, the idea that "[w]e cannot separate mental health from the social order" (Martin-Baro, 1994, p. 121). Commenting on the medical model of human functioning that focuses on the individual psyche, Martin-Baro wrote,

> The problem is rooted in a limited conception of human beings that reduces them to individual organisms whose functioning can be understood in terms of their individual characteristics and features. Such a conception denies their existence as historical beings whose life is developed and fulfilled in a complex web of social relations. (Martin-Baro, 1994, p. 109)

Martin-Baro's perspective is shared by others, including Derek Summerfield of the Medical Foundation for the Care of Victims of Torture, who stated the issue bluntly: "Medical models are limited because they do not embody a socialized view of mental health" (Summerfield, 1995, p. 19).

Critiques regarding the *DSM* definition of PTSD have followed the aforementioned theme of an overemphasis on the individual at the expense of the historical, community, or cultural experience. Maria P. Root (1996), for example, has highlighted the fact that the *DSM* definition of a traumatic event includes only physical, life-threatening forms of trauma specific to an individual and ignores sociocultural and transgenerational experiences. Root subsequently proposes the term *insidious trauma* as a more relevant conceptualization, particularly for people of color. According to Root (1996),

> Insidious trauma is characterized by repetitive and cumulative experiences. It is perpetrated by persons who have power over one's access to resources and one's destiny and directed towards persons who have a lower status on some important social variable. The types of experiences that form insidious traumas are repeated oppression, violence, genocide, or femicide—

both historical and contemporary. The effects of insidious trauma can be passed down transgenerationally through stories of atrocities about what has been done to those who have come before to prepare or protect the next generation from an unrealistically naive view of the world. (p. 374)

Root (1996) also challenges psychological conceptualizations that assume benevolence and justice as the norm and view injustice as a traumatic aberration. She is particularly critical of Janoff-Bulman's (1992) assertion that traumatic events universally shatter assumptions about the world as fair and benevolent. Indeed, Root (1996) asserts that, for oppressed groups, insidious trauma means that they expect poor treatment and injustice: Insidious trauma "shapes reality and reinforces the subsequent construction of reality" (p. 374) and subsequently "reinforces assumptions that the world and life is unfair" (p. 375).

Medical-model conceptualizations such as PTSD have yielded a much-needed framework for North American mental health professionals because of their inclusion of an external, social event as a necessary antecedent to psychological distress. Yet the remaining problems inherent in the medical model should not be underestimated. The need to incorporate themes related to history, culture, gender, and social status within a community and intergenerational framework remains. This broader perspective needs to be considered as a central task for our work as mental health professionals.

IMPLICATIONS FOR PRACTICE

However, thoughts I couldn't control often made me hate myself more than ever. There were times when I could not haul myself out of despair, no matter how bright the day or how cheerful and happy the children. Who would care for them if I were gone? I felt only I could save them from suffering as I had—as I did—and yet I despaired of myself so much that once I actually thought of killing them and myself—but that was too horrible. Impossible. So I tried to find help: woman's shelters, mental health, even church; nothing helped basically. (Wiebe & Johnson, 1998, p. 214)

"Nothing helped" can be a common theme for oppressed peoples who interact with mental health services that are unable to understand or intervene in the myriad issues that may be present. The despair expressed in the writings of Yvonne Johnson, intricately woven with her family and community's experience of oppression and alienation, eloquently points to the depth of suffering of insidious trauma. Johnson's daily struggle to survive in a world that minimized and denied her suffering, and that devalued if not actively destroyed her community, was devastating. Her despair and the health care response were aptly described by Johnson as she recounted an exchange between ambulance and emergency room staff overheard as she was about to receive treatment for an overdose: "Another Indian trying to kill herself. Too drunk to do it right . . . So what do we do with her? Our civic duty, I guess" (Wiebe & Johnson, 1998, p. 185).

The question of how we, as mental health professionals, should respond is a challenging one. In her work regarding the development of culturally sensitive services, Vijay Agnew (1998) strongly urges institutions to carefully examine their own perspectives and practices regarding race, class, and gender as starting points in the change process. An examination of values, particularly regarding how organizational power structures interact with race and gender, is intrinsic to the development of culturally sensitive services.

Therefore, as professionals, it is incumbent upon us that we review our own conceptualizations, practices, and structures to ensure empowering mental health care. Practical implications of this kind of examination include the assessment of services relative to the ethnoracial and ethnocultural background of clients and staff, language, economic access, and sensitive models and processes that can accommodate diversity. Questions that I have found essential include the following.

Organizational:

- Does my organization recognize the impact of racism, discrimination, sexism, social injustice, oppression, and poverty on the mental health of individuals? Does it integrate these factors into its assessments and treatment plans?
- Does my organization actively seek ways to integrate mental health knowledge with ethnoracial and ethnocultural knowledge so that a balanced approach to client services can be reached?
- Are there antiracist and equal opportunity policies and hiring practices within my organization? Does the staff composition resemble the racial, cultural, and ethnic diversity of the community it serves?
- Are there policies in place that define formal sanctions for racist remarks or for denial of care based on race?
- Does my organization recognize barriers to service based on disadvantage and discrimination? Does it have strategies in place to lower these barriers?

- Does my organization involve itself in advocacy activities and the production of public policy centered on fighting poverty, racism, and social injustice?
- Are there formal mechanisms of communication with housing agencies, police, and children's services so that clients' needs are met and their race, ethnicity, and culture are understood and respected?

Community relations:

- Has my organization developed collaborative relationships with the various ethnocultural communities for whom it provides services?
- Do we have active outreach programs that are compatible with the language and culture of the surrounding community?
- Have we published our service brochures in the languages of the surrounding communities?

Educational:

- What stereotypes currently exist among staff, and are they addressed in training and education in a way that is nonthreatening but effective in achieving change?
- What training and educational programs are available for staff regarding antiracism, as well as ethnocultural sensitivity?
- What nontraditional educational resources exist in my organization's community that could be accessed for a better understanding of race, ethnicity, and culture?
- Are there opportunities to learn about indigenous healing practices and alternative health remedies (such as Chinese herbs)? Do staff understand how these practices can be integrated with traditional helping models and psychiatric treatment? Are they aware of potential drug/herb/dietary interactions?
- Is research on ethnocultural and ethnoracial issues in mental health and illness part of available educational opportunities?

Practice approaches:

- What languages are currently spoken in the organization?
- What process is currently available for accessing trained language and cultural interpreters? Are family members or friends of clients being utilized as interpreters? If so, is there an understanding regarding the potential problems and boundary confusion that is likely to occur with such a practice?

Note that the question of who interprets is especially important for trauma survivors.

- Do assessment processes recognize the influence of poverty, racial discrimination, sexism, and class structure in clients' lives? How are these and other social factors integrated into treatment plans?
- Do clinical models and therapeutic practices incorporate diverse modalities that reflect healing and spiritual traditions specific to the ethnoracial and ethnocultural backgrounds of the clients being served?
- Do services accommodate different religious practices and dietary laws?
- Do we understand how different cultures define and deal with mental illness?
- Do we have practices in place to communicate Western norms around child rearing and the role for women? Can we discuss our laws regarding female circumcision, wife battering, and child abuse?
- Are we aware of the role of extended family and the community in some cultures, and do we treat those interested in our client's care with respect?

Personal:

- Have I explored my own culture, race, history, gender, and ethnicity? What have I discovered about myself in this process, and how will this help or hinder my relationships with my clients?

When these questions are asked, many mental health organizations, services, and individual professionals may find that they fall short. However, an important aspect of the change process is awareness. The first step is to ask questions, as questions are a necessary precursor to developing effective organizational mechanisms that will produce new policies and more sensitive helping strategies.

CONCLUSION

I guess when I talk I express myself like I listened, story form. It's actually an easy way to understand if you yourself can listen. But not many people are good listeners and that doesn't matter to me. I tell little stories so you can see, live, feel what I am trying to explain to you. . . . But the Elders say that storytelling is a gift too. If a person with a story can go deep, where people are angry, sad, when they're hiding thought and emotions, raise the past they've maybe forgotten and can't really recognize any more, push them to spirit-walk into themselves—to do that with a story is a gift. (Wiebe & Johnson, 1998, pp. 11-12)

Yvonne Johnson's story does not end in prison; it continues into a journey of recovery. Many aspects of her journey powerfully illustrate how essential the expression of personal and community story is to the healing process. Johnson's story is one of many gifts offered to the professionals, agencies, and systems involved with the mental health care of those suffering violence and oppression. Listening to and joining with such stories can be painful and can demand time and effort. Yet the journey and experience of this "spirit-walk" is profound and life changing. Yvonne Johnson dared to hope that her story would make a difference. Are we listening?

NOTES

1. About 1900, the Canadian government instituted a policy that removed First Nations children from their parents at the age of 5 and placed them in schools, sometimes as far as 1,000 miles away from their homes. Parents who resisted were jailed. Some children never saw their families again (Hodgeson & "Phyllis," 1990).

2. The term *ethnoracial* is used to refer to people of color, whereas *ethnocultural* refers to nondominant groups whose origins are European (Ali, Khatim Ali, & Gutbi, 1996).

3. As mentioned later in this text, there is very little information available regarding the impact of personal, familial, or community state-sponsored torture on children. Subsequently, to acknowledge the importance of such issues, reference to research on adults will be included.

4. That is, if survivors are from an oppressed background, do they incorporate the abuse into their sense of self as a form of internalized racism?

5. One of my African American clients reported that the Children's Aid had defined his corporal discipline of his children as abuse, yet he and his family considered it an appropriate form of discipline to ensure that their children would not engage in any acting-out behaviors that would put them at risk of coming into contact with the police, contact that they assumed would include brutality.

6. Arthur Jensen's (1972) work has been particularly controversial in the assertion that genetic factors are strongly implicated in the development of intelligence and often favor Caucasians. For a more thorough overview of this issue from a cognitive assessment perspective, see J. M. Sattler's (1988) *Assessment of Children,* 3rd ed.

7. For example, psychiatry as a profession contributed to the eugenics movement, which supposedly "scientifically" demonstrated genetic defects in immigrants. See Ali, Khatim Ali, and Gutbi (1996) for a more thorough discussion on this and related problems associated with psychiatry and racism.

8. The most recent war began in 1960, and the Peace Accords were signed in 1996. More than 200,000 people were killed, a majority of whom were Mayan. With land and

economic reform central to the conflict, the United States has been severely criticized, by groups ranging from grassroots groups to the United Nations Historical Clarification Commission, for their role in the funding and training of death squads, police, and Guatemalan military (Ogle, 1999).

9. For example, cognitive processing therapy works with beliefs such as "It was my own fault. If I had just fought back . . ." and works to transform them to beliefs such as "I did not deserve to be raped, and I did the best I could to defend myself."

REFERENCES

Agnew, V. (1998). *In search of a safe place: Abused women and culturally sensitive services.* Toronto, Canada: University of Toronto Press.

Ali, S., Khatim Ali, S., & Gutbi, O. (1996). *The healing journey: A review of relevant information.* Toronto, Canada: Across Boundaries. (Available from Across Boundaries: An Ethnoracial Mental Health Centre, 51 Clarkson Avenue, Toronto, Ontario, Canada M6E 2T5)

American Psychiatric Association. (1980). *Diagnostic and statistical manual of mental disorders* (3rd ed.). Washington, DC: Author.

American Psychiatric Association. (1994). *Diagnostic and statistical manual of mental disorders* (4th ed.). Washington, DC: Author.

Beattie, S. (1995). Lifeline: The education of young survivors of war and violent oppression. In K. Price (Ed.), *Community support for survivors of torture: A manual* (pp. 99-105). Toronto, Canada: Canadian Centre for Victims of Torture.

Bell, C. (1991). Traumatic stress and children in danger. *Journal of Health Care for the Poor and Underserved, 2*(1), 175-188.

Committee on Sexual Offenses Against Children and Youths (Canada). (1984). *Sexual offenses against children.* Ottawa, Ontario, Canada: Ministry of Supply and Services.

Crawford, M., & Gartner, R. (1992). *Woman killing: Intimate femicide in Ontario, 1974-1990* (Report prepared for the Women We Honour Action Committee). Toronto, Canada: Education Wife Assault.

Creamer, M. (1995). Cognitive processing formulation of posttrauma reactions. In R. J. Kleber, C. R. Figley, & B. P. R. Gersons (Eds.), *Beyond trauma: Cultural and societal dynamics* (pp. 55-74). New York: Plenum Press.

de Andrade, Y. (1995). Breaking the silence and circles of support: Assisting survivors of psychosocial trauma. In K. Price (Ed.), *Community support for survivors of torture: A manual* (pp. 37-43). Toronto, Canada: Canadian Centre for Victims of Torture.

de Girolamo, G., & McFarlane, A. C. (1996). The epidemiology of PTSD: A comprehensive review of the international literature. In A. J. Marsella, M. J. Friedman, E. T. Gerrity, & R. M. Scurfield (Eds.), *Ethnocultural aspects of posttraumatic stress disorder: Issues, research, and clinical applications* (pp. 33-85). Washington, DC: American Psychological Association.

Finkelhor, D. (1994). The international epidemiology of child sexual abuse. *Child Abuse & Neglect, 18,* 409-417.

Finkelhor, D., & Dziuba-Leatherman, J. (1994). Children as victims of violence: A national survey. *Pediatrics, 94,* 413-420.

Finkelhor, D., Hotaling, G., Lewis, I. A., & Smith, C. (1990). Sexual abuse in a national survey of adult men and women: Prevalence, characteristics, and risk factors. *Child Abuse & Neglect, 14*, 19-28.

Foy, D. W. (1992). *Treating PTSD: Cognitive-behavioral strategies.* New York: Guilford.

Friere, M. (1995). Children and repression: Issues for child care workers and school personnel. In K. Price (Ed.), *Community support for survivors of torture: A manual* (pp. 88-98). Toronto, Canada: Canadian Centre for Victims of Torture.

Garbarino, J., Dubrow, D., Kostelny, K., & Pardo, C. (1992). *Children in danger: Coping with the consequence of community violence.* San Francisco: Jossey-Bass.

Hodgeson, M., & "Phyllis." (1990). Shattering the silence: Working with violence in Native communities. In T. Laidlow (Ed.), *Healing voices: Feminist approaches to therapy with women* (pp. 33-44). San Francisco: Jossey-Bass.

Janoff-Bulman, R. (1992). *Shattered assumptions: Towards a new psychology of trauma.* New York: Free Press.

Jensen, A. R. (1972). *Genetics and education.* New York: Harper & Row.

Kirmayer, L. J. (1996). Confusion of the senses: Implications of ethnocultural variations in somatoform and dissociative disorders for PTSD. In A. J. Marsella, M. J. Friedman, E. T. Gerrity, & R. M. Scurfield (Eds.), *Ethnocultural aspects of posttraumatic stress disorder: Issues, research, and clinical applications* (pp. 131-163). Washington, DC: American Psychological Association.

LaRocque, L. D. (1995). Violence in the aboriginal communities. In M. Valverde, L. MacLeod, & K. Johnson (Eds.), *Wife assault and the Canadian criminal justice system: Issues and policies* (pp. 104-122). Toronto, Canada: Centre of Criminology, University of Toronto.

MacMillan, H. L., Fleming, J. E., Trocme, N., Boyle, M. H., Wong, M., Racine, Y. A., Beardsle, W. R., & Offord, D. R. (1997). Prevalence of child physical and sexual abuse in the community. *Journal of the American Medical Association, 278*, 131-135.

Marsella, A. J., Friedman, M. J., & Spain, E. H. (1996). Ethnocultural aspects of PTSD: An overview of issues and research directions. In A. J. Marsella, M. J. Friedman, E. T. Gerrity, & R. M. Scurfield (Eds.), *Ethnocultural aspects of posttraumatic stress disorder: Issues, research, and clinical applications* (pp. 105-129). Washington, DC: American Psychological Association.

Martin-Baro, I. (1994). War and mental health. In A. Aron & S. Corne (Eds.), *Writings for a liberation psychology* (pp. 108-121). Cambridge, MA: Harvard University Press.

Ogle, K. (1999). Guatemala: Never again—Touching the wounds of a violent past. *Challenge: Faith and Action in the Americas, 9*(1), 3-7, 15.

Ontario Native Woman's Association. (1989). *Breaking free: A proposal for change to aboriginal family violence.* Thunder Bay, Ontario: Author.

Pakar, M., Sahin, D., Aker, T., Gok, S., Taybilli, B., Cakir, U., Ozmen, E., Demir, T., Demir, D., & Geyran, P. (1997). *Impact of torture and political activism on posttorture psychological response.* Poster session presented at the meeting of the International Society for Traumatic Stress Studies, Montreal, Quebec, Canada.

Resick, P., & Schnicke, M. (1992). Cognitive processing therapy for sexual assault victims. *Journal of Consulting and Clinical Psychology, 60*, 748-756.

Rodgers, K. (1994). Wife assault: The findings of a national survey. *Juristat Service Bulletin.* Canadian Centre for Justice Statistics. Statistics Canada Cat: 14(9), 85-002.

Root, M. P. (1996). Women of color and traumatic stress in "domestic captivity": Gender and race as disempowering statuses. In A. J. Marsella, M. J. Friedman, E. T. Gerrity, & R. M. Scurfield (Eds.), *Ethnocultural aspects of posttraumatic stress disorder: Is-*

sues, research, and clinical applications (pp. 363-387). Washington, DC: American Psychological Association.

Russell, D. E. (1986). *The secret trauma: Incest in the lives of girls and women.* New York: Basic Books.

Saigh, S. (Ed.). (1992). *Posttraumatic stress disorder: A behavioral approach to assessment and treatment.* New York: Allyn & Bacon.

Sattler, J. M. (1988). *Assessment of children.* San Diego, CA: Author.

Summerfield, D. (1995). Addressing human response to war and atrocity: Major challenges in research and practices and the limitations of Western psychiatric models. In R. J. Kleber, C. R. Figley, & B. P. R. Gersons (Eds.), *Beyond trauma: Cultural and societal dynamics* (pp. 17-29). New York: Plenum Press.

Union of Ontario Indians. (1995). *Family Healing: Stopping the violence! Caring for our future!* Nipissing First Nation, Thunder Bay, Ontario, Canada: Anishinabek Nation.

Wiebe, R., & Johnson, Y. (1998). *Stolen life: The journey of a Cree woman.* Toronto, Canada: Knopf Canada.

Wyatt, G. (1985). The sexual abuse of Afro-American and white women in childhood. *Child Abuse & Neglect, 9,* 507-519.

CHAPTER 15

Personal and Professional Self-Care

As mental health professionals, we have chosen our work because we care about people, but we often don't give our own well-being anywhere near the same attention, energy, and commitment that we give our patients and clients. Mental health is one area of health service that depends significantly on the healing power of human-to-human interaction. The locus for our success as practitioners is the small, intimate relational space that we create between ourselves and our clients.

Professionals walk a fine line when they establish helping relationships with survivors of childhood trauma. We must care, but not so much that we are drained. We must get close, but not so close that we become enmeshed. We must empathize while protecting our own boundaries. One of the critical components in our ability to develop healthy client-professional relationships is our capacity to care for ourselves. However, when we attempt to build these relationships with survivors of childhood trauma, we add an urgent dimension to the issue of personal and professional self-care that elevates it to an ethical responsibility.

This chapter will examine topics such as personal balance, professional effectiveness, and the quality of the work environment. These areas of self-care are important no matter what aspect of mental health care we deliver, but they are crucial for professionals who work with trauma survivors. In addition to the basics of self-care, trauma professionals are also exposed to specific dangers such as secondary trauma and vicarious traumatization. The chapter concludes with a discussion of personal and professional self-care for professionals who are themselves survivors of trauma.

PERSONAL BALANCE

The primary tools with which mental health professionals do their work are their "selves." Although it seems all too obvious to begin a discussion of self-care with such basics as exercise, nutrition, and a good night's sleep, the simple lessons we learned in grade school regarding the essential building blocks of physical health remain true. So, too, do those many things that make up a balanced life—having a full life outside of work, maintaining supportive relationships with family and friends, pursuing personal hobbies and interests, participating in our communities, and enjoying holidays and vacations. We also need to feed our souls with spiritual pursuits, which may include the enjoyment of music, nature, and art or membership in an organized religion of our choice. Again, it is easy to list these self-care items, and it is a rare professional who couldn't recite them by heart—but how many of us follow through with action? Our own self-care seems to be the first thing we neglect when life begins to overwhelm us, but if we don't take care of ourselves—daily—we will suffer, and sooner or later, our clients will suffer, too.

In addition to the basics, we must recognize that professionals, too, can experience their own emotional and mental health problems. When these arise, we may choose to take medication, enter therapy, or attend marriage or partner counseling, as our situation dictates. However, it can happen that some of us look with disfavor upon the very services we offer our own clients. We may secretly be ashamed of our own vulnerability and strive to propound the fiction that we are invincible. If we are wise, we will use moments of personal pain to acknowledge the level of courage it takes to ask for help and to expose our secret fears to another. Being on the client side of the helping equation is valuable experience that not only assists us with the maintenance of our own mental health but also teaches us a particular kind of compassion and self-awareness, as well as, perhaps, a needed level of humility in our professional role.

Sometimes, professionals resist taking full advantage of the rewards that may exist in our private lives because we see them as guilty evidence of an undeserved bounty that extends far beyond anything our clients may ever have. Clients, too, will often say things such as, "How can you ever understand what life is like for me? You have a family, a nice house, and a car. I will never have those things." The key here is not to neglect our own well-being in a misguided attempt at solidarity, but to recognize the disguised message. To do so, it is helpful to recall that clients also say, "You can't understand me because—you were never abused, don't have children, didn't come from a foreign country, have never been to war, are too young, too old, a man, a woman, white, black, straight, gay." When clients make these sorts of statements, they are really asking, "Can I trust you to treat me with respect and not judge me unfairly because I am different from you and because I have problems?" Obviously, we *are* different from our clients, and there is no need to attempt to persuade them otherwise. Our job, as professional helpers, is to apply our knowledge and skills so that we can understand, as best we can, each client's unique situation and assist him or her to make changes.

PROFESSIONAL EFFECTIVENESS

There is no greater support for our professional well-being than the feeling that we are effective—that we know what to do, we do it well, and it works. But professional effectiveness is not doing "well" (competing with our peers on the basis of technical prowess), nor is it doing "good" (dispensing sage advice to those who are less fortunate) (Kennedy & Charles, 1990). Instead, effectiveness is both a daily and a career-long pursuit that challenges us to be the best we can be.

Self-Awareness. In order to be professionally effective, we must dedicate ourselves to our own internal journey, because *we* are our primary practice instrument. An openness to interior reflection and personal discovery is a subtle attitudinal stance that survivors find comforting. Obviously, professionals are entitled to privacy, and there is no demand that we share personal discoveries with clients, but a general willingness to answer questions honestly and to respond to challenges nondefensively signals a level of personal confidence and self-acceptance that contributes greatly to professional effectiveness. In addition, professionals who present themselves consistently as learners rather than as distant experts are more likely to gain clients' confidence. Survivors challenge us on many levels, but the most important challenge is to know ourselves emotionally. But knowledge is not enough. We must also develop a sophisticated awareness of our own reactions as well as a refined skill base for managing these reactions in ways that serve the health of the client-professional relationship. These are huge demands on a professional's internal resources. An active journey of self-discovery is often begun through our own personal therapy, and therapy is one of the primary methods by which these resources can be refreshed and renewed so that our own mental health is not jeopardized in the pursuit of another's well-being.

Knowledge and Skill. Knowledge and skill are key components in professional effectiveness. Mental health professionals must commit to a lifetime of learning, often in formally accredited venues. Our basic training is typically at a postsecondary level, with most of us achieving degrees at the diploma, bachelor's, master's, or doctoral level. When we enter our first professional jobs, we have spent most of our lives in the classroom, and in the course of our careers, we will spend many more hours taking advanced training and attending seminars, workshops, and conferences. Eventually some of us will become presenters and teachers ourselves, as we pass on our knowledge to others. In addition, many of us will invest in our own personal stock of books filled with the latest reading material in our particular area, and we will utilize library facilities for our work—if we are lucky enough to have them. Throughout this process, we will learn to read research and theory with a critical eye, evaluating the utility of any given finding or approach in light of its potential to increase our ability to help our clients.

Although these forms of formally produced and usually academic sources of knowledge are invaluable, they do not substitute for skill. Providing effective help for survivors of trauma is complex and, as a result, demands extensive knowledge and a particularly high level of skill. Professionals have to learn how to apply all that they have learned, with clients and within the context of their particular practice mandate and setting. When we do, we begin to access another level of knowledge—that which is acquired through experience, often referred to as "the things the textbooks don't cover." Of course, textbooks and many other resources *do* cover a host of experiential learning topics, but nothing brings these lessons alive better that seeing for ourselves exactly how things work in real life.

Establishing and Managing the Helping Frame. A helping frame is essential in our work with trauma survivors, both because it helps us keep our bearings and because it aids survivors, who have lived a boundaryless existence, to find theirs. Together, professional and client define where they are going and how they are going to get there. Sources of confusion are anticipated and averted (insofar as they can be), and expectations are laid out and negotiated. This is a fairly straightforward task, but it requires a considerable amount of up-front thinking on the part of professionals, who must understand their organizations' policies, know the relevant laws, and decide on their own professional working styles. It also seems to be the most forgotten task, until professionals acquire the painful experiences of having relationships go off the rails because of issues that could have been negotiated right at the outset, or of having problems grow out of all proportion because of an undiscussed misunderstanding.

Professional Boundaries. The sheer weight of our clients' problems can overwhelm. The reality is that we can only do so much to be helpful, and sometimes our efforts seem appallingly inadequate. In the face of the extent of human misery we witness, one of our most important self-care skills, and one intimately related to the concept of the helping frame, is the maintenance of professional boundaries. Boundaries honor the professional's own needs and limitations while at the same time managing the client's needs in a healthful manner (Pearlman & Saakvitne, 1995). Boundaries are particularly important for survivors of childhood trauma, because these are people who have experienced profound boundary violations as children. In the pursuit of their need for love and attention, they will regularly attempt to transgress normal relational boundaries by demanding more—more appointments, more phone calls, and more time.

We cannot fill the real void these demands represent, and if we try and fail—as we ultimately will—our good intentions only serve to confirm what the clients know all too well: Sooner or later, everyone abandons them. Clear, consistent, flexible, emotionally neutral, and nonpunitive boundaries allow space and time for growth so that clients can begin to develop their own internal and external resources.

A sure sign that we have failed to establish our professional boundaries occurs when we find ourselves adopting one of the following roles: all-giving saint, all-knowing expert, or world-weary cynic. All-giving saints set no boundaries. They believe (in the beginning) that if they care enough, they can rescue their clients, and they often fall into the additional trap of believing that they, and only they, can make things better. These professionals give clients the impression that they are bottomless pits of caring, forever available and completely without needs of their own. In doing so, they inadvertently deny clients the experience of their authentic humanity. The other side of the equation is that sooner or later they stagger under the burden of the impossible task they have set for themselves and begin to suffer physically or mentally. Some leave the profession, never to return. Others become angry at clients for not getting better despite repeated rescue, or for not being grateful for all they are doing. The telltale signs of this sort of boundary loss are extending appointments, calling clients frequently, coming in on days off, making excuses for clients' behaviors, and becoming angry with other professionals who don't understand clients' needs in the same way.

All-knowing experts relate to their clients from behind a barrier of cool, objective, "professional" distance. They structure most interactions around advice giving. This is a particularly seductive role for us, because we obtain our credentials through the acquisition of knowledge. Having learned the solutions to our clients' problems in the classroom, we are anxious to dispense this information. As we do so, we give clients the message that they have little expertise of their own. The trap here is that credit for success tends to go to the professionals alone—but the burden for failure is ours, too. The entanglement of boundaries inherent in this role means that professionals work harder and harder at ensuring that clients are complying and conforming, rather than growing and developing. This stance leads to an anxious roller-coaster ride, as our sense of professional worth rises and falls with the fortunes of our clients. Work becomes increasingly frustrating, and these professionals, too, may pay with their own physical or mental health. They may also become more distant and certainly angry as they struggle, but fail, to solve the puzzle of why so many clients won't just do as they are told. When things go wrong, the all-knowing expert tends to blame, calling clients resistant to treatment, hard to serve, and noncompliant.

World-weary cynics protect themselves by pretending to no longer care. Clients come and clients go, and after a while, they all sound pretty much the same—the same problems and the same dismal outcomes. Like their clients, these professionals have acquired feelings of powerlessness, helplessness, and hopelessness. They erect an attitudinal barrier around themselves that says, "I've seen it all before," and they consider their work an exercise in going through the motions. But they continue onward because they secretly believe that one day, they might get lucky and achieve some measure of success—it's not likely, but they retain a faint memory of what it was like to be hopeful and optimistic, and it holds them in place. However, they are angry—at their clients for being so messed up, at themselves for being so powerless, and at the world for being so predictably cruel and heartless.

These sorts of roles are indicative of the place that boundaries have in the healthful management of transference and countertransference. Clients will project their understanding of the world onto their helpers—seeing them as desirable all-giving parental figures on one hand, and as abandoning, neglectful abusers on the other. Mental health professionals can be buffeted by their own responses to these unrealistic views. Boundaries provide a neutral framework that protects us from taking our clients' transference issues personally, thereby liberating us to react in healthful ways with clients' well-being in mind. In short, boundaries define the helping pathway—for both clients and professionals—and as such are integral to professional effectiveness.

Finally, sexual contact of any kind with clients, including former clients, represents a serious boundary violation. Avery and Disch (1998) have shown that clients with a history of sexual abuse are at high risk for violation by professionals. Sexual abuse by professionals represents a profound reenactment of powerlessness, exploitation, and body violation that so many experienced as children. Many professional organizations have set prohibitions regarding sexual contact between professionals and current or former clients—with serious consequences for violations (Gallop, 1998).

Limitations of the Professional Role. Professional effectiveness means understanding what we *can't* do in our professional role. For example, we can't make our clients change, do better, or choose the wisest course of action. In order to fully understand this point, it is important to make a distinction between *process* and *content*. Process refers to how clients go about making decisions, and content refers to what they actually decide to do. Our job is to serve the decision-making process, not to try and control the outcome. Knowing this fact allows a great weight to slip from our shoulders. As we learn to devote our attention to *how* clients choose, we are freed from the temptation of getting into a tug-of-war over *what* they choose. It also places the responsibility for the consequences of that choice fully with the client—where it belongs.

Just as professionals can't ensure that clients make the "right" choice, we also can't fight their battles for them. There are exceptions, of course. For example, certain mental health programs and services only accept professional-to-professional referrals, and thus the ups and downs of this often-intricate process must be negotiated on behalf of the client. In addition, confronting big bureaucracies (social assistance, the court system) often requires the combined efforts of both professional and client in order to make any headway at all. However, survivors of trauma, given their relationship difficulties, tend to engage in a myriad of personal battles (with their families, friends, spouses, neighbors, roommates), as well as battles related to their involvement in the mental health system (with psychiatrists, landlords, police, lawyers); finally, they may also be fighting systemic battles (political action, formal complaints, general advocacy). It is not uncommon for people fighting battles to try and pull in a third party to be on "their side," and clients are no exception. However, survivors also have the added burden of feeling helpless and hopeless. They will ask, or more likely demand (as their anxiety rises), that professionals confront their "enemies" on their behalf.

> Can you tell my psychiatrist that I want my medication reduced?
> Take me to the emergency department and make them admit me.
> Talk to my Mom and tell her she can't treat me like a child anymore.

If we respond uncritically to these requests, we can inadvertently invite a number of unhappy consequences. First, it is the professional, rather than the client, who ends up in conflict—often with the very colleagues with whom we need to build and maintain working relationships. Second, this form of advocacy is weak because, without the client present to confirm his or her wishes, the point remains open for unproductive debate: "The client never told me that"; "He was just here and we got along fine"; "You are not qualified to comment on my prescribing practices." It is also not uncommon for clients who are terrified of confrontation to deny that they ever said anything at all when tracked down and questioned by an outraged colleague or family member, effectively sabotaging the credibility of the advocating professional. Some situations may deteriorate even further when clients, fearful of retaliation, join with their former adversary and denounce the advocating professional as the "bad guy." This form of triangulation (two against one, with the players forever shifting sides) is often called "splitting," particularly when discussing clients who have been diagnosed with borderline personality disorder. It is thought that professionals reenact different sides of the client's internal conflict, such as the wish to be taken care of versus the fear of being close.

Attempting to fight clients' battles is a no-win situation. Professionals increase their own stress load by alienating their own colleagues—the very people with whom they need high-quality working relationships. They also begin to feel ineffective because their clients don't learn the necessary skills to advocate on their own behalf, and even if the advocating professional appears to be successful, he or she only robs clients of the joy of savoring their own victories.

The pull to intercede is a strong one because professionals are trained to protect clients from hurt. But professional effectiveness demands that we focus on growth and positive change. In order for clients to realize their potential as independent adults, they have to learn how to deal with authority and with authority figures. Effective professionals may empathize, encourage, provide information, coach, and teach skills, but they recognize that most battles are the clients' own and that they must be won or lost by the clients themselves.

THE WORK ENVIRONMENT

Awareness of childhood trauma typically arises from women's services, and trauma-focused work is often found in feminist organizations and community services that are notoriously underfunded. When money is scarce, employee supports critical to professional self-care, such as benefits and supervision, may be scarce or nonexistent. Although mental health professionals have an individual responsibility to care for themselves personally and professionally, their employers also have a role to play by creating and maintaining safe, humane, and accountable work environments.

Congruence. The first question professionals should ask is: Is this the right workplace for me? There is no greater source of career dissatisfaction than working in environments where practice values collide with our own. Working with survivors of childhood trauma is intensely personal and value-laden. Sometimes, collisions are a matter of poor fit—a therapist who prefers close teamwork finds herself in a setting where independent practice is valued, or a case manager used to creating close, supportive relationships is assigned to a housing program where he must enforce eviction notices. In other instances, conflicts can be systemic. For example, the mental health system as a whole suffers from an inherent split in philosophies (medical model versus social causation). The services and treatments that each side has developed don't easily accommodate professionals from the "wrong" side of the issue. Typically, although not always, hospital and institutional services are more disease focused, and community services are more concerned with social factors. Knowing this fact can help professionals choose a compatible practice environment.

The most difficult situations, however, arise when environments *appear* compatible but turn out not to be. Usually when this happens, there is a clash of values at the level of basic beliefs—beliefs that are fervently but perhaps unconsciously held. For example, most professionals would agree that clients have the right to make their own choices. However, some professionals take this declaration to mean that clients have the right to choose—even to choose unwisely—as long as their choice is informed and does not violate the rule of law. Other professionals believe that clients must be prevented from making wrong choices for their own protection and that they have the right to choose only as long as their choices are judged to be wise. Others take the position that clients can choose as long as they are "well" but become incapable of choosing when they are "sick." Certainly, mental health laws take this view. Still others see it as their job to help clients choose wisely and take it as a professional failure when their clients—despite excellent advice—choose the wrong course of action.

Obviously, professionals will never agree on all things, but it is our responsibility to examine our own personal belief system and find ways to articulate them clearly and respectfully in our work environment. Practice truisms also need to be interrogated regularly, ensuring that the many ways they can be interpreted are exposed so that professionals make informed practice choices. Obviously, there needs to be room for compromise and for tolerance for how others see the world, and professionals must decide for themselves what's important and what's not—and select their battles wisely.

Organizational Policies. Human service employers should endeavor to develop policies that acknowledge the rigors inherent in the helping professions in general and in trauma work in particular. Some examples would be policies that balance workloads and client-professional ratios. Other policies should describe provisions for supervision and consultation, and codes of conduct and ethics should be in place (this is discussed more fully later in the chapter). The employer should also make available ongoing professional development opportunities as well as specific forms of training. Although not as common, some enlightened employers make provisions for critical incident debriefings[1] and counseling, acknowledging the hazardous side of working with the seriously mentally ill. At the very least, employees should have access to an insurance package that offers health benefits and disability coverage. Although these sorts of provisions may seem obvious, some employers believe that personal and professional self-care is a luxury item, easily dispensed with when time is tight and money is scarce.

Supervision and Consultation. The point of supervision and consultation is to help professionals develop a practice stance that is self-reflective. In other words, as others question us about what we are doing and why, we learn the habit of questioning ourselves: Why am I doing it this way? What outcome do I expect? Would I get a better outcome if I tried something else? If it worked, why did it work? If it didn't work, what went wrong? How can I use this knowledge in other situations? What have I observed that has led me to this conclusion? When and where have I allowed my own issues or biases to cloud my judgment? This kind of self-questioning teaches us to adopt the necessary habit of backing up our opinions and actions with solid, logical thinking as well as references to observable evidence. We need this evidence to produce credible assessments and treatment plans that we can, in turn, explain coherently to our colleagues and our clients.

Beginning professionals often find the idea of supervision difficult to grasp and anticipate an intimidating and stress-inducing process. These feelings are natural because the uninitiated think of "supervision" in terms of the somewhat adversarial process by which employers monitor their employees' work—searching for instances of poor performance and doling out disciplinary action. In professional environments, supervision is much more like coaching. A more experienced professional meets regularly with each of his or her supervisees and, through the medium of case presentations (or less formal forms of discussion), imparts academic and experiential knowledge, teaches new skills, provides information, makes suggestions, points toward resources, helps solve problems, and gives feedback.

In an ideal world, supervision should be provided by someone who is not in a position of direct authority, because it is hard to discuss difficulties and uncertainties when we know that we are talking to someone who can make decisions about our job or promotion. However, in most work settings, supervision is provided by a manager or clinical supervisor who focuses on performance as well as professional development—introducing what is clearly an accountability factor. Supervision is one method by which agencies or hospitals ensure themselves that they are delivering the kind and quality of service that they should.

Some work environments support peer supervision, where colleagues meet to present cases and advise each other on how to proceed. In these groups, it is important that professionals treat one another with respect, provide feedback in a sensitive manner, and avoid blaming or criticizing. Of course, mangers and clinical supervisors must also follow these rules.

The need for safety cannot be stressed strongly enough when providing feedback in the supervisory encounter. The professional who is presenting a case or asking for advice is taking a risk by exposing his or her work. The point of supervision is to foster professional growth by linking learning to an immediate work-related need. However, if an environment evolves that overtly or covertly promotes competition or one-upmanship, professionals will begin to protect themselves, and learning will stop. Another pitfall is that participants (either managers or peers) may lose their job-related focus and begin to transgress personal boundaries. Occasional self-disclosure within the context of a case presentation can be appropriate, but repeated, ongoing personal discussions or feedback that includes remarks about, for example, an employee's family background, relationships, or sexual orientation are inappropriate and even unethical, depending on the specifics. Professional supervision is not therapy. The personal lives of the participants are not grist for the mill, and if employees report that personal problems are interfering with their performance, they should be referred to an employee assistance program (if available) or asked to seek their own therapy outside the work situation.

Sometimes, mental health professionals, particularly those in private practice, choose to purchase their supervision. They contract with a more experienced professional whose skills they admire and establish an hourly fee. In this context, there may well be a component of personal as well as professional growth in the supervisory encounter. The key is permission. Professionals can develop whatever service contract they believe will suit their needs. This is a form of supervision that occurs outside the employment context and does not include issues of performance. It is, however, related to accountability, because private mental health practitioners are often required to demonstrate that they are receiving supervision as a prerequisite for membership in accredited associations.

Another way professionals receive needed advice is through consultation with experts who specialize in certain practice areas. Consultation is distinct from supervision, because it is sought only when a need is identified—when a particular client's situation is especially complex or unique and the employer or individual professionals feel they would benefit from advice from an objective and qualified third party. Whereas supervision is an integral part of the workplace environment, consultation typically has an extra cost associated with it, often as a one-time fee. Consultants may advise on a case basis or they may conduct in-house workshops or seminars when staff members have identified a common need.

Codes of Conduct and Ethical Behavior. One of the greatest sources of support can come from colleagues who are in the unique position of knowing how stressful our work can be, as well as where the many pitfalls lie. However, it is also true that peers can be critical; intrude on personal boundaries; offer hurtful judgments; and, in rare instances, engage in accusations, insults, and even screaming matches. Formally written codes of conduct can define the basics of good collegial behavior, but they must be supported by sanctions that are fairly applied. All too often, the workplace culture is left to evolve spontaneously, with the assumption that professionals are inherently "professional" and will naturally treat one another with respect. Indeed, many, if not most, professionals behave responsibly, but a code of conduct ensures against the contamination of unprofessional behavior in the workplace.

Codes of ethics are developed, adopted, and enforced through professional colleges and associations. A breach of ethics is a serious matter that can threaten a professional's career. They include behavior such as fraudulent billing, sexual relationships with current patients or clients, negligence, breach of confidentiality, or incompetence. Sanctions are severe and may include fines, letters of censure, suspensions, or loss of license. Some professional groups publish a list of members who have been disciplined, adding the further weight of public humiliation to the process. Codes of ethics that govern therapists include these gross breaches but have also sought to tackle the grayer areas of unprofessional behavior, such as engaging in dual relationships (providing therapy and hiring a client to clean your house or do your tax return), dating former clients, or talking about clients at social gatherings—even when they are not named and no identifying material is disclosed.

VICARIOUS TRAUMATIZATION

There are a number of fates that can befall mental health professionals who care for survivors of childhood trauma: burnout, secondary posttraumatic stress, and vicarious traumatization. *Burnout* is defined as accumulated dissatisfaction with one's work and work environment. Burnout can occur in any job situation and is usually solved by a vacation or finding a new employer. The main culprit with burnout is stress—too much work, work of the wrong sort, uncooperative colleagues, a poor work environment, and authoritarian or rigid management.

However, mental health professionals who work with trauma survivors have other sorts of problems to guard against—in addition to burnout. We hear horrendous stories of cruelty, far beyond anything we could have imagined prior to entering the field. No one can hear survivor stories and remain unchanged, and we must actively learn techniques to protect our own mental health. The symptoms of secondary posttraumatic stress or compassion fatigue, as well as vicarious traumatization, are by-products of the kind of work we do, and they can creep up on us. One basic protective measure we can take is to recognize them early on.

Secondary posttraumatic stress occurs when professionals feel themselves developing some of the same symptoms as their clients—intrusive memories of some of the stories we have heard, a generalized state of anxiety, an overall sense of impending danger, numbing in response to our own emotions, and a need to avoid certain situations that are reminiscent of the types of traumatic experiences our clients have told us about. Compassion fatigue is the result if these sorts of symptoms go unaddressed. Observable consequences are a drop in morale and performance on the job and a deterioration in the professionals' personal relationships and home life (American Continuing Education, 1999).

Vicarious traumatization is "soul sadness" (Chessick, as quoted in Pearlman & Saakvitne, 1995, p. 282). Professionals become deeply pessimistic and are prone to bouts of grief and despair. They lose their sense of professional effectiveness, and success at helping one client only means that there will be another and another, all with the same horrific tales of human cruelty. These professionals recast their former energy and optimism as naïveté as they conclude that they have been utterly foolish to think that one person could make a difference in the face of all this madness. Sometimes these feelings are fleeting, and the professional is able to shake them off and return to work with the old sense of vigor. Sometimes they are permanent, and there is no choice but to leave the field. Pearlman and Saakvitne (1995) have found that some form of vicarious traumatization is inevitable and can affect anyone who "engages empathetically with trauma survivors" (p. 281)—researchers, journalists, police, clergy, lawyers, emergency room staff, as well as mental health professionals. Our perception of humanity has been permanently altered by what we have seen and heard. We don't just think or suspect that the world is unjust. We *know* it.

The essence of vicarious traumatization is a loss of faith in happy endings. Fairness and justice do not always prevail; good guys can lose, and bad guys go free. This realization shatters our basic beliefs on a number of fundamental levels: in God, in family, and in humanity. We are left adrift. Protection against the extremes of vicarious traumatization are inherent in the professional and personal self-care strategies that are the basis of this chapter. These strategies retain our human connections—to colleagues, friends, family, and community. These connections also help us to avoid the kind of black-and-white thinking that is at the base of vicarious traumatization and allow us to hold two realities in consciousness: Humans are capable of great kindness, courage, and justice *and* the extremes of sadism, violence, and cruelty.

PROFESSIONALS WHO ARE SURVIVORS OF CHILDHOOD TRAUMA

Professionals who have their own experiences of childhood trauma are often loath to reveal this fact in their workplace for fear of being judged. Indeed, the idea that survivors can become effective trauma counselors or therapists has been viewed with skepticism, and those who attempt to do so have occasionally found themselves open to a higher level of scrutiny than their nonsurvivor colleagues. However, given the prevalence of sexual and physical abuse in general, there is no doubt that many mental health professionals have these experiences in their backgrounds, whether or not it is revealed. The key to their effectiveness is to have embarked upon their own journey of healing and recovery and to have come to some level of resolution. In doing so, they have, in fact, become models of self-care for both their clients and their colleagues, because they know that the ability to continue in their work depends on an ongoing dedication to their own health needs. Some survivor professionals may choose to work in nontrauma areas because the threat to their own well-being is too great if they are required to respond to clients whose experiences are close to their own. Others particularly choose work with trauma survivors because they feel they have something special to give that comes from having "been there." They also offer their clients incontrovertible proof that healing and recovery can occur and that, above all, there is hope.

But Dolan (1991) warns that there are also disadvantages to be considered. Survivor professionals may become trapped by the belief that they have to demonstrate at all times and to everyone that they are "over it." They may begin to hide recurring symptoms that are the natural aftermath of their experiences but that may grow worse if denied. Flashbacks are not always controllable, and bad days can happen. No one is helped if the professional becomes guilt-ridden because he or she is not an unassailable paragon of strength. In addition, survivor professionals must early on make a clear decision about self-disclosure—who am I going to tell and why? Some decide that their background is a private matter and choose never to reveal it or discuss it in a professional context even though they may apply the lessons they have learned in their helping relationships. Others may feel comfortable utilizing their firsthand knowledge more openly. However, it is rare for survivor professionals to reveal their pasts to clients, because the focus of the helping relationship is exclusively on client needs. Self-disclosure must always be carefully thought through with both the professional's and the client's well-being in mind.

CONCLUSION

One of our most important professional assets is our own well-being. Although our work is rewarding, it can also be emotionally, physically, and even spiritually dangerous. We have an ethical responsibility both to ourselves and to our clients to take care of the "self" that is our principal practice tool.

As the authors of this text, we are not unaware of the irony of placing the topic of personal and professional self-care last. We are mental health professionals ourselves, and we recognize how often we and our colleagues neglect our own well-being even as we exhort our clients to consider theirs first and foremost. Throughout the writing of this entire text, we have tried to impart the theoretical and practical knowledge that we have gained as trauma researchers and clinicians—knowledge that is hard-won because it is based on tough realities and painful experiences. As we pondered upon what note to end, we decided to offer the most valuable lesson we have learned, and it is this: The work is hard. The road is long. Look after yourselves.

NOTE

1. Assaults can occur in certain mental health workplaces, such as shelters, hostels, emergency departments, and hospital wards. Professionals who visit clients in their homes can also encounter threatening situations. Employers have a responsibility to provide training in de-escalation techniques and nonviolent restraint. They should also provide critical-incident debriefings in the event that an assault or other traumatic event occurs. Critical-incident debriefings (or other sorts of supportive techniques) are designed to help employees talk through their feelings about the traumatic event and begin a recovery process.

REFERENCES

American Continuing Education. (1999). *Current hot topic: Compassion fatigue, the stress of caring too much* [On-line]. Available: www.ace-network.com/cfspotlight.htm

Avery, N., & Disch, E. (1998, October). *Effects on clients of sexual abuse by clergy, mental health practitioners and medical practitioners.* Paper presented at the Fourth International Conference on Sexual Misconduct by Psychotherapists, Other Health Professionals and Clergy, Boston.

Dolan, Y. (1991). *Resolving sexual abuse: Solution-focused therapy and Ericksonian hypnosis for adult survivors.* New York: Norton.

Gallop, R. (1998). Abuse of power in the nurse-client relationship. *Nursing Standards, 12,*(37), 43-47.

Kennedy, E., & Charles, S. (1990). *On becoming a counselor.* New York: Continuum.

Pearlman, L. A., & Saakvitne, K. (1995). *Trauma and the therapist: Countertransference and vicarious traumatization in psychotherapy with incest survivors.* New York: Norton.

Index

Gender stereotypes:
  as disclosure barrier, 7, 24
  male clients, 253-254, 260-261
    abuse pathways, 261
    abuse roles, 261
    gender rigidity, 261
    underreporting and, 255, 256
  violence and, 7, 24
Genetic influences:
  environment and, 25, 26
  multidimensional model, 21-22, 25-26, 31, 32
  nature-nurture debate, 26
  resilience, 25-26
  temperament, 26
  vulnerability, 25-26
Gerardi, Juan, 279
Glucocorticoid excretion, 27, 86
Grounding, 194
Group homes, 197
Group therapy, 173-174

Helping frame:
  client safety, 182-183
  power and
    involuntary commitment, 123-124, 136-137
    legislation, 122, 123, 136-137
    liberation tactics, 130
    power with relationships, 123-124, 125
    therapeutic frame similarity, 137n.2
    transformative power, 124
  professional self-care, 297
  traumatic memory, 94, 96
Hippocampal function, 27, 86
Homicide:
  assessment for, 243-244
  intervention for, 249
Homophobia, 255
Hopelessness, 73-74
Hospitalization:
  research literature on, 49-51
  revictimization and, 50-51
  See also Involuntary commitment
Housing, 203n.1

apartments, 197
economics and, 196-197
female-only, 197
group homes, 197
guidelines for, 197-198
Hyperarousal, 27-28
Hypnosis, 83

Imagery rescripting/reprocessing therapy, 164-165
Impulse regulation, 27-28
Individual responsibility, 6-7
Inner-child work, 175
Insidious trauma, 283-284
Insight-oriented therapy, 84
Institutional abuse, 25
Internalized representations, 29
Interpersonal relationships:
  abuse consequences, 28-29, 74-75
  dissociation and, 63-64
  intergenerational impact, 75
  professional response and, 75
  revictimization and, 75, 189-190
  safety and
    family, 189, 203n.1
    friends, 189-190
    guidelines for, 190-191
    revictimization, 189-190
    violence, 200, 203n.1
  self-fulfilling prophecy, 74
  self-isolation, 72, 74
  sexuality, 28, 74-75
    client safety, 198
  trust, 28
    authoritative, 5
    worldview development, 30
Involuntary commitment:
  client safety, 201-202
    revictimization, 202
  helping frame, 123-124, 136-137
  legislation, 122-123, 135-137
  liberation tactics, 135-136
  questionnaire contract, 139-141
Isolation, 72, 74

Johnson, Yvonne, 272-274, 284-285, 287-288

false memory syndrome, 93-94
guidelines for, 94-96
helping frame, 94, 96
hypnosis, 83
insight-oriented therapy, 84
knowledge development, 94-95
legal process, 84-85, 97n.1
psychodynamic therapy, 84
realistic expectations, 95
recall process, 84-85, 97n.1
See also Crisis care; Disclosure
guidelines; Power; Storytelling;
Treatment models
Professional self-care:
disclosure guidelines and, 113-114
overview, 293-294, 309
personal abuse and
advantages of, 308
as disclosure barrier, 12-13, 103,
104
disadvantages of, 309
self-disclosure, 309
personal balance
elements of, 294
guilt, 295
mental health, 294-295
vulnerability, 294-295
professional effectiveness
all-giving saint, 298
all-knowing expert, 298-299
boundary maintenance, 297-299
helping frame and, 297
knowledge development, 296-297
limitation acceptance, 300-301
self-awareness, 295-296
sexual contact, 299
world-weary cynic, 299
vicarious traumatization, 306-308
burnout, 306
compassion fatigue, 307
secondary posttraumatic stress,
307
soul sadness, 307
work environment, 301-306
congruence, 302-303
consultation, 303-305
ethics, 305-306

organizational policy, 303
supervision, 303-305
Pseudo-seizures, 69, 70
Psychodynamic therapy, 84
Psychoeducation, 216-217, 220
Psychological abuse defined, 38
Psychotic disorders, 176-177

Racism:
abuse rates and
African Americans, 275
Asian Americans, 275
females, 274-276
males, 274-276
Native Canadians, 275-276,
288n.1
perpetrator ethnicity, 275
perpetrator relationship, 275
African Americans, 275
Asian Americans
abuse rates, 275
posttraumatic stress disorder, 281
epidemiological limitations, 277-279
epistemology influences, 278
generalized barriers, 278
methodology, 278
politics, 278
research accessibility, 278-279
research misuse, 279, 288n.7
violent repercussions, 279, 288n.8
Johnson, Yvonne, 272-274, 284-285,
287-288
mental health and
posttraumatic stress disorder, 280-
282
social movement impact, 279-280
Native Americans, 281
Native Canadians, 275-276, 288n.1
posttraumatic stress disorder
Asian Americans, 281
belief systems and, 281-282,
289n.9
classification, 279-280
classification limitations, 282-284
cognitive-behavioral therapy, 281-
282, 289n.9
cultural experience of, 280-281

About the Authors

Barbara Everett, M.S.W., Ph.D., has worked in both hospital and community mental health services in a variety of professional roles, from social worker to senior manager. Her clinical focus has been the provision of psychotherapy for people suffering from complex posttraumatic stress disorder. She presently works as a consultant providing services such as clinical skills development workshops, clinical consultation and supervision, and program development and evaluation. She is also the author of *A Fragile Revolution: Consumers and Psychiatric Survivors Confront the Power of the Mental Health System* and has published a number of journal articles.

Ruth Gallop, R.N., Ph.D., is Professor and Associate Dean of Research in the Faculty of Nursing, University of Toronto. She is cross-appointed to the Department of Psychiatry and the Women's Mental Health Program at the Centre for Addiction and Mental Health. She writes, researches, and consults extensively on issues related to the treatment and care of women in the mental health system who receive the diagnosis of borderline personality disorder and of women in the mental health system who have experienced childhood sexual abuse.

Lee Ann Hoff, Ph.D., author of *People in Crisis* and (with K. Adamowski) *Creating Excellence in Crisis Care,* is an internationally renowned educator, crisis practitioner, nurse-anthropologist, and consultant. She is the first recipient of the National Services Award for her work in developing crisis service standards.

Kathy J. Lawrence, Ph.D., C. Psych., is a clinical psychologist who is currently working with young offenders and their families at Lutherwood Community Opportunities Development Association (CODA) in Waterloo, Ontario, Canada. Her primary clinical and research interests are in the areas of psychosocial impact of sexual violence against adolescents and adults, sexual offending behavior, and the development of clinical and community-based interventions. She has worked extensively with women and men who have been traumatized by family violence, and she has also worked with those who have been traumatized by community-based violence and civil war. Dr. Lawrence has provided workshops for health care professionals regarding the identification and assessment of and interventions related to woman abuse, and she has published in the area of posttraumatic stress disorder.

John McManiman, M.Ed., M.Div., Th.M., in 1988 co-led one of the first Toronto groups for male survivors of sexual assault, and he has continued to work extensively with traumatized men throughout his career. He added to his knowledge by becoming an addictions counselor and a co-leader of numerous groups for violent men. Presently, he works for a family-counseling agency, and in his spare time, he writes.